Police and Society in Brazil

Advances in Police Theory and Practice Series

Series Editor: Dilip K. Das

Police and Society in Brazil
Edited by Vicente Riccio and Wesley G. Skogan

Ethics for Police Translators and Interpreters
Sedat Mulayim and Miranda Lai

Delivering Police Services Effectively
Garth den Heyer

Civilian Oversight of Police: Advancing Accountability in Law Enforcement
Tim Prenzler and Garth den Heyer

Corruption, Fraud, Organized Crime, and the Shadow Economy
Maximilian Edelbacher, Peter C. Kratcoski, and Bojan Dobovsek

Collaborative Policing: Police, Academics, Professionals, and Communities Working Together for Education, Training, and Program Implementation
Peter C. Kratcoski and Maximilian Edelbacher

Policing in Israel: Studying Crime Control, Community, and Counterterrorism
Tal Jonathan-Zamir, David Weisburd, and Badi Hasisi

Policing Terrorism: Research Studies into Police Counterterrorism Investigations
David Lowe

Policing in Hong Kong: History and Reform
Kam C. Wong

Cold Cases: Evaluation Models with Follow-Up Strategies for Investigators, Second Edition
James M. Adcock and Sarah L. Stein

Crime Linkage: Theory, Research, and Practice
Jessica Woodhams and Craig Bennell

Police Investigative Interviews and Interpreting: Context, Challenges, and Strategies
Sedat Mulayim, Miranda Lai, and Caroline Norma

Policing White-Collar Crime: Characteristics of White-Collar Criminals
Petter Gottschalk

Honor-Based Violence: Policing and Prevention
Karl Anton Roberts, Gerry Campbell, and Glen Lloyd

Policing and the Mentally Ill: International Perspectives
Duncan Chappell

Security Governance, Policing, and Local Capacity
Jan Froestad and Clifford Shearing

Police Performance Appraisals: A Comparative Perspective
Serdar Kenan Gul and Paul O'Connell

Police and Society in Brazil

Edited by
Vicente Riccio
Graduate Program on Law and Innovation
Federal University of Juiz de Fora
Juiz de Fora, Brazil

Wesley G. Skogan
Institute for Policy Research
Northwestern University
Evanston, IL, USA

Routledge
Taylor & Francis Group

NEW YORK AND LONDON

First published 2018
by Routledge
711 Third Avenue, New York, NY 10017

and by Routledge
2 Park Square, Milton Park, Abingdon, Oxon, OX14 4RN

Routledge is an imprint of the Taylor & Francis Group, an informa business

Library of Congress Cataloging-in-Publication Data
Names: Riccio, Vicente, editor. | Skogan, Wesley G., editor.
Title: Police and society in Brazil / edited by Vicente Riccio, Graduate
    Program on Law and Innovation, Federal University of Juiz de Fora, Juiz de
    Fora, Brazil; Wesley G. Skogan, Institute for Policy Research,
    Northwestern University, Evanston IL USA.
Description: New York, NY : Routledge, 2018. | Series: Advances in police
    theory and practice series
Identifiers: LCCN 2017019050 | ISBN 9781498769037 (hardback)
Subjects: LCSH: Police—Brazil. | Police corruption—Brazil. |
    Police-community relations—Bazil.
Classification: LCC HV8183 .P64 2018 | DDC 363.20981—dc23
LC record available at https://lccn.loc.gov/2017019050

ISBN: 978-1-4987-6903-7 (hbk)
ISBN: 978-1-315-15411-4 (ebk)

Typeset in Minion Pro
by Apex CoVantage, LLC

MIX
Paper from
responsible sources
FSC
www.fsc.org   FSC® C013985

Printed in the United Kingdom
by Henry Ling Limited

Contents

Series Editor's Preface

While the literature on police and allied subjects is growing exponentially, its impact upon day-to-day policing remains small. The two worlds of research and practice of policing remain disconnected even though cooperation between the two is growing. A major reason is that the two groups speak in different languages. The research work is published in hard-to-access journals and presented in a manner that is difficult to comprehend for a layperson. On the other hand, the police practitioners tend not to mix with researchers and remain secretive about their work. Consequently, there is little dialogue between the two and almost no attempt to learn from one another. Dialogue across the globe, among researchers and practitioners situated in different continents, are of course even more limited.

I attempted to address this problem by starting the IPES (International Police Executive Symposium), www.ipes.info, where a common platform has brought the two together. IPES is now in its 17th year. The annual meetings, which are the major events of the organization, have been hosted in all parts of the world. Several publications have come out of these deliberations, and a new collaborative community of scholars and police officers has been created whose membership runs into the several hundreds.

Another attempt was to begin a new journal, aptly called *Police Practice and Research: An International Journal, PPR*, that has opened the gate to practitioners to share their work and experiences. The journal focuses on issues that help give scholars and police officers a single platform. *PPR* is completing its 18th year in 2017. It is certainly evidence of growing collaboration between police research and practice, given that *PPR* began with four issues a year, expanded into five issues in its fourth year and is now issued six times a year.

Clearly, these attempts, despite their success, remain limited. Conferences and journal publications do help create a body of knowledge and an association of police activists but cannot address substantial issues in depth. The limitations of time and space preclude larger discussions and more authoritative expositions that can provide stronger and broader linkages between the two worlds.

It is this realization of the increasing dialogue between police research and practice that has encouraged many of us—my close colleagues and I connected closely with IPES and *PPR* across the world—to conceive and implement a new attempt in this direction. This led to the idea of a book series, *Advances in Police Theory and Practice*, that seeks to attract writers from all parts of the world. Further, the attempt is to find practitioner contributors. The objective is to make the series a serious contribution to our knowledge of the police as well as to improve police practices. The focus is not only on work that describes the best and most successful police practices but also challenges current paradigms and breaks new ground to prepare the police for the 21st century. The series seeks comparative analysis that highlights achievements in distant parts of the world as well as one that encourages an in-depth examination of specific problems confronting a particular police force.

The chapters in this volume, *Police and Society in Brazil*, examine the relationship between policing and Brazilian society. There are tight linkages between many of the most important features of Brazilian life and the police and their problems. These include poverty, inequality, racial divisions, debilitating levels of violence and a state that cannot protect large segments of its population. Individually, each of these issues presents a daunting challenge to reformers; collectively, addressing them will require heroic levels of policy effort, coordination and investment. Although most of the chapters focus on the problems facing Brazil, along the way each addresses avenues toward reform. The editors of this book are experienced observers of the Brazilian scene, and much of what they report is presented here in English for the first time. A few of the chapters originally appeared in a special issue of *Police Practice and Research*, and they have been updated for this book.

It is hoped that through this series it will be possible to accelerate the process of building knowledge about policing and help bridge the gap between the two worlds—the world of police research and the world of police practice. This is an invitation to police scholars and practitioners across the world to come and join in this venture.

Dilip K. Das, Ph.D.
Founding President,
International Police Executive Symposium, IPES, www.ipes.info

Founding Editor-in-Chief, Police Practice and Research:
An International Journal,
PPR, www.tandf.co.uk/journals

Preface

The post-authoritarian Brazil is a complex society marked by many challenges and a lot of potential. The democratic institutions have passed through challenges in this period, and the return to an authoritarian model is improbable. The consolidation of a network of social policies has allowed the reduction of misery and poverty in the last few years. Additionally, the Brazilian society is watching more critically the role of its rulers independently of their partisan background. Despite the conjuncture of crisis, this tendency will not change in the future.

However, the Brazilian post-authoritarian agenda has an open issue that is hard to solve: public security. The problem of public security is well known by Brazilians on a daily basis and most affects the population in need. This problem not only affects a specific group in society, but also brings suffering to different social segments, regardless of social class, gender, ethnicity or way of life. Thus, the need for action to reduce the levels of violence in the country is urgent.

Despite public security being considered one of the top issues on the Brazilian agenda, the political leaders of all parties still persist on policies based on old models and keep acting only after the eventual crisis. The success of innovative public security policies in Brazil depends on a cultural change to a more responsive model of policing based on the integration of police and society. There is need for a long-term perspective instead of the prevailing short-term logic.

To implement this paradigm change, it is necessary to rethink the role of police officers in Brazilian society. The prevailing model places them in conflict situations when interacting with communities. This logic raises the risks inherent to the police work and does not promote a real integration with the communities, especially the poorer ones. As a consequence, police legitimacy has been low in Brazil.

The institutional structure of the police in Brazil does not allow a different role for a police officer. To sustain the principles erected in the Brazilian Constitution proclaimed in 1988—the respect for human rights and the promotion of social justice—public security's traditional practices and police action must change. Thus, the police officer must be seen not only as a law enforcer, but also as a promoter of human rights and social change.

This is relevant because public security is a fundamental asset for the impoverished communities in the country that suffer mainly the effects of violence. In some cases, the action of armed groups does not allow people to exercise their right to come and go. The control of territories by criminal gangs prevents the right to work freely for the poorest population. In many popular communities in Brazil, it is possible to find an entrepreneurial population running small businesses to fulfill the neighborhoods' demands and to have a source of income. Crime directly affects these businesses. Those problems can also be observed at the associative level, because the population does not have freedom to organize their fight for citizenship rights.

For these reasons, the search for innovative solutions in the public security field needs to place the police work in another perspective. The police officer can be a leading figure on deep social changes. The enforcement of basic civil rights in poor communities is true democratic revolution in Brazil. It will never be achieved without legitimate policing. There is still a huge gap between the daily reality and the desired change, but the search for a new model cannot be abandoned.

Finally, it was a great pleasure to receive this work that aims to highlight the dilemmas of Brazilian police forces in their interactions with society. The multidimensional look adopted by the book depicts the police problems in all their complexities and avoids reductionisms and one-sided perspectives. The publication of this book in English will provide the international public with a deeper understanding of the context and the challenges faced by Brazilian police forces. I hope that this work will promote an exchange among researchers and public security professionals in Brazil and abroad. I also expect that this book will stimulate the needed cultural change to adopt a new paradigm of policing in Brazil.

Ricardo Balestreri
Former Brazilian National Public Security Secretary 2008–2010

Editors

Vicente Riccio is a Professor in the graduate program of Law and Innovation at Federal University of Juiz de Fora, Brazil. He also has worked as a consultant for many public institutions in Brazil, such as the Ministry of Justice, Public Security Secretary of Rio de Janeiro, and the Civil Police of Amazonas, among others. He has coordinated many educational programs for police officers and criminal justice professionals in different states of Brazil. His research interests cover diverse topics such as police reform, police cultures, legal systems in developing democracies, media and justice, and video evidence.

Wesley G. Skogan is Professor of Political Science and a Faculty Fellow of the Institute for Policy Research at Northwestern University. His research focuses on policing, community responses to crime, victimization, and fear of crime. He is a Fellow of the American Society of Criminology, and was a Senior Fellow of the Center for Crime, Communities, and Culture of the Open Societies Institute. He organized the Committee on Police Policies and Practices for the National Research Council and served as its chair. He is the co-author (with Kathleen Frydl) of the committee report *Fairness and Effectiveness in Policing: The Evidence*. Earlier, he spent two years at the National Institute of Justice as a Visiting Fellow. In 2015, he received the Distinguished Achievement Award in Evidence-Based Crime Policy from the Center for Evidence-Based Crime Policy.

Contributors

Mario Aufiero
Civil Police of Amazonas
Manaus, Brazil

Ricardo Balestreri
Former Brazilian National Public Security Secretary
Independent Consultant
Natal, Brazil

Eduardo Cerqueira Batitucci
Graduate Program on Public Administration
Fundação João Pinheiro
Belo Horizonte, Brazil

Marcus Vinícius Gonçalves da Cruz
Graduate Program on Public Administration
Fundação João Pinheiro
Belo Horizonte, Brazil

Amanda Matar de Figueiredo
Researcher
Fundação João Pinheiro
Belo Horizonte, Brazil

Paulo Fraga
Graduate Program on Social Sciences
Federal University of Juiz de Fora
Juiz de Fora, Brazil

Janaína Lawall
Habitation Studies Center
Federal University of Juiz de Fora
Juiz de Fora, Brazil

Renato Sérgio de Lima
Business Management School
Getulio Vargas Foundation (University)
São Paulo, Brazil

Marcio Rys Meirelles de Miranda
Amazonas Society for Cultural Development
Law School (Uninorte)
Manaus, Brazil

Angélica Müller
History Department
Fluminense Federal University
Niterói, Brazil

Ludmila Mendonça Lopes Ribeiro
Center for Crime and Public Safety Studies
Federal University of Minas Gerais
Belo Horizonte, Brazil

Vicente Riccio
Graduate Program on Law and Innovation
Federal University of Juiz de Fora
Juiz de Fora, Brazil

Steven Dutt Ross
Mathematics and Statistics Department
Rio de Janeiro State University
Rio de Janeiro, Brazil

Marco Aurélio Ruediger
Applied Policies Directory
Getulio Vargas Foundation (University)
Rio de Janeiro, Brazil

Luis Flavio Sapori
Graduate Program on Social Sciences
Catholic University of Minas Gerais
Belo Horizonte, Brazil

Joyce Keli do Nascimento Silva
Ph.D. Candidate
Graduate Program on Social Sciences
Federal University of Juiz de Fora
Juiz de Fora, Brazil

Jacqueline Sinhoretto
Graduate Program on Social Sciences
Federal University of São Carlos
São Carlos, Brazil

Wesley G. Skogan
Institute for Policy Research
Northwestern University
Evanston, IL, USA

Letícia Godinho de Souza
Graduate Program on Public Administration
Fundação João Pinheiro
Belo Horizonte, Brazil

André Zogahib
Business Management School
State University of Amazonas
Manaus, Brazil

Police and Society in Brazil

Wesley G. Skogan and
Vicente Riccio

1

Contents

The chapters in this volume examine many aspects of the relationship between policing and society in Brazil. As will become clear, there are very tight linkages between many of the most important features of Brazilian life and the police and their problems. Crime is among the issues facing the police, but the list is much longer. In this essay, we describe this police-society nexus, and examine the possibilities for reform in Brazilian policing. Along the way, we point to specific chapters in this book that address the issues we raise, but in more detail. These chapters are based on research by experienced observers of the Brazilian scene, and much of what they report is presented here in English for the first time.

The first fact about Brazil is that it is very large. At 3.3 million square miles, it is slightly larger than the continental United States. In 2017, the population was just over 207 million, or about two-thirds that of the U.S. It features vast, rolling plains, semi-arid regions, jungle and mountains. Forty percent of the country falls in the Amazon region. The largest state in the area, Amazonas, is featured in several chapters of this book. But while the nation's economy features large agricultural and forest products sectors, Brazil is an urban society. Most of its citizens (about 85%) live in cities. Even in Amazonas, more than 2 million people live in Manaus, its largest city, and they account for about half the state's population. The largest Brazilian city, São Paulo, is home to 12 million people and is the country's economic leader.

Like many physically large countries (ranging from India to Australia and the United States), Brazil has a federal system of governance. The constitution limits the powers of the national government and reserves a great deal of authority for its 26 states and the federal capital district. As we shall see, policing is one of those functions. Rio de Janeiro is another big city (6.4 million) that is featured in this book, but most of its policing is controlled by Rio de Janeiro State, which encompasses the city and its surrounding metropolitan area and includes an additional 12 million residents. There are another 15 cities in Brazil with populations above 1 million, and 24 of the 27 states have populations at least that large. São Paulo State is home to a total of 45 million residents.

Locally and nationally, Brazil has a multiparty political system, a vibrant mass media and a strong civil society, so many policies are hotly contested and fought out in elections at all levels of government. Voter turnout is compulsory, and thus high, at over 80%. There is currently a debate over the country's very fragmented party system. The current party structure inhibits the formation of policy-oriented coalitions in the legislature. Executive branch policies, including those affecting the police and crime prevention, pass through the legislature only after difficult and often corrupt bargains are struck. Legislators themselves often dutifully represent powerful economic elites in their constituencies, especially in rural areas. The federal nature of Brazil also limits the reach of national policies, and bargaining has to take place downward as well if the states are to cooperate with national policy initiatives. One chapter of this book examines the national politics of police reform and the difficulties involved in promoting federal policies among the states.

But an important footnote to the fundamentally democratic character of contemporary Brazil is that in the not-too-distant past the nation passed through an authoritarian abyss that still affects the nature of its institutions, especially the police and the military. April 1964 began with a military coup that was politically aligned with the United States government. This ushered in a 21-year military dictatorship. During this period, most political and human rights were suspended, censorship was imposed and the elected national Congress was shut down. The army took general control of domestic society, and both branches of local policing in Brazil were converted into tools for political repression. Police shared information with army intelligence units. Even today, the Military Police branch of local policing is considered an auxiliary unit of the army, and its military identity is strong even at the state level. During the military dictatorship, thousands of people were tortured and many hundreds are known to have been killed, or they simply disappeared. Civilian rule was restored in 1985, but the overhang of this repressive period—and, until recently, some of those who did the repressing—has lingered on into the contemporary period. Before the military left power, an amnesty law was imposed that protected those in power during the dictatorship period from prosecution, and their immunity was recognized following the handover.

Another feature of Brazil is that it is among the most unequal societies on earth. The gap between those at the very top and bottom of the income distribution is about five times as great as similar gaps in Northern Hemisphere industrial nations. This is despite the fact that economic inequality in Brazil was falling until its recent financial crisis. In Brazil, the richest 10% of households consistently received almost two-thirds of all household income, and they have done so for decades. In some years, the top 0.1% received as much as 15% of total national income (Souza and Medeiros 2015). In early 2017, the *Financial Times* estimated that the wage of Brazilian factory workers was US$2.70 per hour and that it was falling.[1] Inequality spreads beyond income and wealth; other social cleavages are closely linked to them. For example, wage gaps are reflected in educational attainment. Differences in reading and math scores between students coming from households in the top and bottom income groups are larger than in other countries with similar levels of development. The United Nations Development Programme's (UNDP) "Human Development Index" (HDI) assesses three quality-of-life dimensions across many countries: longevity, levels of education and gross national income per capita. In the last HDI global ranking, Brazil scored 75th. It ranked below nations with lower levels of GDP per capita because of violence, health and education issues linked to income inequality. The nation's education, health and security services have not contributed much to a broad range of social inequalities among poorer and richer Brazilians. The country's high violent crime death rate is emblematic of this, and it is discussed in several chapters in this book.

There is also a great deal of inequality among the states. The Brazilian National Institute of Geography and Statistics (IBGE) is responsible for monitoring economic statistics. In a report issued in 2014, the IBGE reported GINI indices for the nation's regions. This indicator rates the distribution of wealth in a society based on the difference in income between the poorest and the richest individuals. It ranges from 0 (an even distribution of wealth) to 1 (highly concentrated wealth). The results showed some progress toward a more equal distribution of wealth in many areas. The Northeast (the poorest region in the country) scored 0.563 in 2004 and 0.509 in 2013; the Southeast (a rich area) scored 0.531 in 2004 and 0.483 in 2013. However, the recession that began in Brazil in 2015 has brought any reduction in inequality across the country to a halt.

A big social fact about Brazil is that it is significantly a mixed-race society. This is deeply linked to the issue of inequality. Long a colony of Portugal, Brazil was a slave-holding country until 1888. Many slaves were imported from West Africa, and there was originally a substantial native population. In contemporary Brazil, the result has produced a very complex racial dynamic.

The 2010 census set the population at about 47% white. The remainder was divided among persons classifying themselves as "black" (8%), "yellow" (1%), or "indigenous" (fewer still), with the largest group (43%) classing themselves as mixed race, or "brown." But all of these categories are situational and shifting, and each subsumes subtly defined subcategories that vary in significance from occasion to occasion. What these categories mean has been contested among Brazilians for almost two centuries. This includes vigorous debates over the role of class versus race in determining life chances in Brazil, a discussion that most recently has begun to feature statistical analyses weighing the significance of the two factors. However, for our purposes, there are two important facts about race. The first is that it overlaps sharply with inequality. The result is that where people live and how they live are clustered both economically and socially, and that clustering has a lot to do with crime. The second feature of race is that it overwhelms virtually every statistic produced by the criminal justice system. Victims, offenders and prisoners—and especially those in each of these categories who *died*—are overwhelmingly persons of color (Cano 2010).

Finally, several chapters in this volume consider the fate of Brazil's *favelas*, or concentrated urban slums. Favelas are one of the places where poor people of color live, and their prevalence and visibility is another of the distinctive features of Brazilian society. Favelas are numerous. In Rio de Janeiro city, there are approximately 800 favelas, and in 2010, about 1.4 million of the city's 6.4 million inhabitants lived there. *Favelados* are not just poor; they are isolated in many ways from mainstream society. Residents often live far from shops or transportation routes. Mostly, these communities have running water, but often there is no provision for the sewage they generate, so health is an endemic problem. Social services may be nonexistent. Electrical service can be sporadic, and there may be few if any streetlights. Few residents have formal claim to the places where they live, and homes are often patched together from cardboard, corrugated iron and scrap wood. The streets are mostly not paved, and buildings have been thrown up without attention to a conventional street grid.

Many favelas are governed not by the formal political system but by criminal gangs that dominate the territory. Governing gangs extort money from residents and the informal businesses that are located there, they fend off incursions by other gangs that want to set up shop, they conduct sometimes large-scale criminal enterprises from their home base, and they form alliances with politicians and corrupt police officials to secure these operations. In a modestly sized area, these gangs might number about 50 or 60 members. Some (but fewer) favelas are under the control of vigilante militia groups. They differ from criminal gangs largely in that they are made up of former or off-duty police officers and other security employees, and they are often under the influence of economic elites and their political allies. They also are in the business of extracting protection money from local people and businesses, and they illegally resell electricity, cable television and other services to residents (see Magaloni, Franco and Melo 2015). No significant inroads into Brazil's crime and policing problems will be made without directly confronting conditions in the favelas. (For a great deal more on favelas, see Jovchelovitch and Priego-Hernandez 2013.)

To be sure, it would also be a mistake to consider favelas as uniformly organized and disadvantaged. Preteceille and Valladares (1999) have questioned the "ideal type" that has been constructed regarding favelas. In fact, there is great diversity among and within them. There are "richer" and "poorer" favelas, and different levels of public services delivered in those areas. The incidence of crime also varies from place to place. The favelas in Rio de Janeiro (featured in several chapters of this book) have been a target of public policies since the 90s, with the *Favela-Bairro* program. It focused on paving the roads, building sidewalks and providing basic infrastructure in those areas. Some of these projects were supported by the Interamerican Development Bank and the World Bank. Understanding this diversity should be important in the design of public policies targeting these areas.

Crime and Policing in Brazil

Violence is endemic in Brazilian society. Most reports on crime in Brazil focus on homicide. These are used to compare Brazil to other countries, or to compare Brazilian cities to each other or over time, because body counts are seemingly the most reliable of the generally unreliable crime statistics produced by the country's police forces. The absence of reliable statistics in Brazil presents a significant obstacle to developing and evaluating the effectiveness of security policies. There is also no equivalent to the National Crime Victimization Survey in the U.S. or the British Crime Survey. The most reliable source of information on violence are mortality data assembled by the Ministry of Health, and these provide the only basis for counting homicide in Brazil. However, there are problems even in that database. "Death by indeterminate causes" is the classification given to over 10% of fatalities registered in this database. Beyond homicide, there is also a lack of systematic information regarding drug dealing, rates of imprisonment and even police personnel (Cerqueira 2013).

Analyses of homicides on a national basis can be found in reports from the Ministry of Health Statistics that are published annually by Sangari Institute in partnership with *Faculdade Latino-Americana de Ciências Sociais* (Latin-American Faculty of Social Sciences). They produce the *Mapa da Violência* (Violence Map). This report analyzes data on homicides and other violent crimes. Each year the report includes a special focus on a specific issue. The

2016 report examined homicides by firearms and documented the spread of gun murders across the Brazilian states. The Northeast region (the poorest in the country) faced the largest increase in violence from 2004 to 2014; it went up an astonishing 124%. Other states showing major growth over this period included Rio Grande do Norte (237 gun homicides in 2004, 1,292 in 2014), Maranhão (up 367%), and Ceará (up 314%) (Waiselfisz 2016). An exception to this trend is the state of Pernambuco, where gun homicides dropped by 25%. This decrease may have been related to a program developed by the state called *Pacto pela Vida* (Pact for Life) that aimed to reduce levels of homicides in Pernambuco. This aimed at integrating the state's police forces, public attorneys and the judiciary to curb the homicide rate. The participation of civil society was also essential to the program. The adoption of formal goals for the program and measures of its success were another salutary feature of the project. The initial results were very positive, and homicide levels began to decrease. Recently, critics have charged that *Pacto pela Vida* has been faltering and needs to regain the resources it needs to reduce violence and fear of crime in the area.[2] However, Pernambuco continues to *not* follow the trend of seemingly intractable increases in violence that characterize many states in the poor Northeast.

The Southeast region in Brazil, which is the nation's richest area, is composed of the states of São Paulo, Minas Gerais, Rio de Janeiro and Espírito Santo. Collectively they have high rates of crime, but they too have witnessed a decrease in homicide. Over the same period we considered above, gun homicides there decreased by 36%. The largest decreases were in the states of São Paulo (down 54%) and Rio de Janeiro (down 42%). These decreases are important, because these are the largest Brazilian metropolitan areas. In general, the rise of violence has occurred in states that have lowered their levels of inequality the most in the last decade (Kahn 2013). In turn, rising crime rates can jeopardize other gains in quality of life that can be observed in Brazil. Chapters in this book address policies dealing with violence and measures to improve the quality of policing and police legitimacy.

Comparatively, Brazil ranks among the violent countries in the world. The United Nations Office on Drugs and Crime's (2014) most recent report rates nations by their homicide rates. They count "homicide related to other criminal activities; interpersonal homicide; and socio-political homicide" (The United Nations Office on Drugs and Crime 2014, p. 11). This definition discounts deaths due to war or suicide, for example. Based on their calculations, the *world* homicide rate is 6.2 per 100,000. In Southern Africa and Central America, the aggregate homicide rate was just over 24 per 100,000, and in South America, Middle Africa, and the Caribbean, it varied between 16 and 23 per 100,000. According to the same report, Brazil stood number three on the list for South America, with a homicide rate of 25 per 100,000 inhabitants. Venezuela was number one by a wide margin, at 54 homicides per 100,000, followed by Colombia at 31 per 100,000. In Central America, Honduras scored

90 per 100,000, and El Salvador 41 per 100,000. Brazil as a whole does not reach these peaks, but its rate has been stable at a relatively high level.

In addition to homicide, other fearsome crimes are not reliably counted, but they are widely reported in the media and discussed in political debates. These include kidnapping, illegal weapons sales, extortion from business, all manner of drug crimes and robberies committed at roadblocks set up between airports and their city centers. Drugs have had a particularly toxic effect on Brazilian society, because the trade is dominated by powerful and violent street gangs. Shootouts between them and the police account for a significant portion of the police-involved killings that are registered each year.

As in many societies, it is those at the bottom of the economic and social ladder who bear the brunt of this violence. Chapter 7 in this volume, by Renato Sérgio de Lima and Jacqueline Sinhoretto, cites figures for inequalities in homicide. Young black males from 12 to 29 years of age are on average 2.6 times more likely to be murdered than young white males, and in some states of Brazil's poverty-stricken Northeast, such as Paraíba and Pernambuco, they are 11 times more likely to be killed. Fatal shootings by police are just as racially disparate. As Chapter 9 documents, in 2011 police in the state of Minas Gerais were twice as likely to kill blacks as whites. This disparity ratio stood at a factor of three in São Paulo, and in Rio de Janeiro police killed blacks at almost four times the rate for whites.

Through 2015, crime had been trending downward in some Brazilian states and for the country as a whole. During the 1990s, Rio de Janeiro was one of the most violent cities on the planet. In the early 2000s, Rio faced about 3,500 homicides per year. This number dropped by about a third through 2008 and 2009, and then dropped significantly more over the next few years. By 2015, the homicide count had fallen to about 1,700 per year. The run-up to the 2016 Olympic Games boosted this total significantly. Homicides peaked earlier in São Paulo (in 1998), and then dropped steadily, to about 50% of its peak. Crime has fallen more in the wealthier areas of the country, which are concentrated in the south, and remain stubbornly high in the poor Northeast. But whatever the trend, the level of homicide in Brazil continues to keep it high on the list of the most violent societies.

An important feature of Brazilian policing is also its violence. The Military Police in particular usually patrol with heavy weapons, and they are quick to use them. They bring heavy weaponry plus armored vehicles and other military equipment to bear during encounters with the criminal gangs that control many of Brazil's favelas. In the next section, we describe policing in those poor communities, and it frequently involves extensive violence. It is widely reported that police perform "extrajudicial" killings of suspects. As a result, the police shoot and wound or kill very large numbers of people. Official reports usually list these as deaths during confrontations or due to resistance to arrest. Fatal incidents involving the police are tracked by various human rights groups, which analyze and report them independently. For example, the Brazilian Forum on Public Safety reports that between 2009 and 2015, Brazilian police killed an average of six persons per day, for a total of 17,688 people over that five-year period (Fórum Brasileiro de Segurança Pública 2016). They report that during 2015, police killed 3,320 people, up from 2,212 three years before. In the state of Rio de Janeiro alone, police killed 563 people in 2014. On a fairly consistent basis, police killings account for about 20% of all homicides each year. Studies examining whom they shoot inevitably conclude that the victims of police violence are overwhelmingly poor racial minorities. Another facet of Brazilian violence is the victimization of police officers. More than 358 police officers were killed during 2014. Among this group, only 91 police officers were killed while they were on duty; the remaining 267 were murdered while they were off duty. Due to their low wages, many police officers work as private guards when they off duty, and this can be a risky assignment. Despite being illegal, this off-duty employment practice is tolerated by police commanders. The number of killings of police in Brazil while they are on duty is 110% higher than the number of police officers killed in the U.S. while they are on duty (41), in 2015 (Fórum Brasileiro de Segurança Pública 2016).

Police are also widely reported to use torture. Torture is employed to extract information from prisoners, retaliate when criminal gangs injure an officer, deter opponents from seeking to harm officers or exact revenge on persons who were uncooperative or who disrespected them. Torture victims may well end up a subject for summary execution as well.[3] Few of these actions result in any judicial review. More than one of the community-oriented policing projects that are described in the next section have blown up following allegations of police torture of residents and indiscriminant police shootings in retaliation for gang violence against them.

For all of this, by the few measures available, the Brazilian police and the criminal justice system are not particularly effective. There are few useful statistics on crime solution rates that could be used to evaluate the effectiveness of police forces and the criminal justice system as a whole. According to the Fórum Brasileiro de Segurança Pública, the solution rate for homicide is below 15% of the cases registered. Only small states such Santa Catarina or the Federal District report better performance measures, with solution rates of 43% and 69%, respectively. In general, the police forces in Brazil do not solve complex cases or those linked to organized crime. The majority of cases solved in Brazil are those in which the perpetrator is easily known, such as in cases involving domestic homicide or disputes between rivals (FBSP 2013).

Another facet of policing in Brazil is corruption. Brazilian police are badly trained and very poorly paid, and many struggle to survive by working off-duty private security jobs or arranging to do paid work while they are on duty. In February 2017, police in the Brazilian state of Espírito Santo went on strike for ten days to protest their wages. Police routinely extract bribes from ordinary citizens in exchange for overlooking offenses, including traffic infractions. Others work for the informal militias that were described earlier. Higher on the earnings scale, they may cooperate with drug traffickers or work with a drug gang in eradicating a rival group. Opportunities for collecting bribes are endemic, because the officers' daily routines provide them access to corrupters, while their managers provide little in the way of supervision, and the organization generally ignores street-level corruption. At the upper echelons, there can be cozy relations between police leaders and local political and economic elites. This is especially true in poorer and more rural states. There, defenders of land rights and environmental activists can find themselves without protection. The public knows of all of this. Davis, Henderson and Merrick (2003) cite surveys from the 1990s indicating that people overwhelmingly believed that police were involved with organized crime and with informal death squads operating within the ranks, and that many Brazilians feared police as much as they feared crime. The Latinobarometro is a survey that is conducted yearly in all Latin American countries. For 2016, they report that the issue of corruption was second on the list of concerns of Brazilians, putting them close to Bolivia and Peru (*Economist* 2016).

Together, these factors describe a toxic combination of police violence, corruption and ineffectiveness, combined with public cynicism. In a society that needs to build confidence in the police, they are most often viewed as corrupt and dangerous. Later sections of this chapter consider what could be done to address these issues.

Chapters in this book also examine some fundamental features of police organization in Brazil. The first is that there is not one body conducting routine policing, but two.[4] Ordinary policing is divided between two distinct bodies: the Military Police and the Civil Police. The Military Police provide the routine street policing familiar to readers from many cultures. They stand by to respond to emergencies, engage in preventive patrol and respond to calls and other forms of complaint. They are organized along military lines and often patrol with heavy weapons. The Civil Police provide what in the Northern Hemisphere is known as "detective work." They investigate crimes and prepare cases for prosecution when they are successfully concluded. Luis Flavio Sapori describes the historical origins of this distinction and some of its implications for practice in Chapter 2 of this volume. In Chapter 4, Eduardo Cerqueira Batitucci and colleagues describe the strong and distinct cultures that dominate each of them. These often impede the kind of routine cooperation that one might expect between policing agencies that share the task of keeping a jurisdiction safe. They frequently engage in turf wars, competing to take credit when trends look favorable, and their relationship is generally one of distrust. Their strong cultures and political connections have also shielded them from efforts to reform police operations, and have forestalled efforts in some states to merge the two into a single police service.

A further feature of both policing branches in Brazil is that there are deep divisions within them, between staff members in managerial positions and rank-and-file officers. In the Military Police, the two groups are recognized as "officers" and "soldiers." Traditional military culture surrounding the division between officers and the enlisted ranks has been imported wholesale into policing as well. In the Civil Police, the split is between unit leaders and lower-level investigators and staff. Chapter 3 in this volume, by Vicente Riccio and colleagues, details the many negative organizational consequences that flow from the strict and impenetrable hierarchy of the Civil Police. Around the world, policing is organized into hierarchical bureaucracies, so these divisions are not a surprise. However, they take on added significance because there is essentially no possibility of advancement between the top and bottom ranks, in either organization. The division between management and street work is both hierarchical and social, based on educational requirements and thus the background of candidates. For the Civil Police, educational requirements to taking the top jobs are even written into the national constitution. Reports by Julita Lemgruber (2002) and chapters in this volume examine some of the pathologies of the resulting divisions between them. These splits undermine internal cohesion and morale, cut managers off from the daily life of street officers, discourage forward thinking among the bottom ranks and create two separate forces with their own cultures inside each of the branches.

A final feature of Brazilian policing is that its military character continues in important ways to resonate with the country's relatively recent experience as an authoritarian dictatorship. During that period, officers policed the people; they were not a police that was *of* the people or *for* the people, which is the tradition of policing that follows the model of Robert Peel's first London police force. Elisabeth Leeds (2007) concluded that, since the return of the country to civilian control, the policing sector has made the least progress toward becoming a truly democratic institution. Chapter 11 in this volume, by Vicente Riccio and his co-authors, described a police training program aimed at democratizing and humanizing the face of the Military Police. They found in their interviews that officers in the higher echelons of the Military Police still thought of themselves as a military rather than a civilian force. They did not see themselves as reflecting civilian society, which they saw as weak and in need of their strong arm.

Policing the *Favelas*

Several chapters of this book focus on policing in Rio de Janeiro's favela communities by Military Police units. Favelas are places that concentrate all of the crime and policing problems we consider in this book. Residents are poor and isolated from many aspects of mainstream society. They are stigmatized because they are favela residents. They are plagued by violent and property crime, and by drug markets which operate openly around them. They frequently live under the control of organized crime groups or armed militias rather than the government. The "taxes" they pay are extortion payments, which bring them little in the form of municipal services. The arrival of the police in their community usually presages an armed struggle between invading Military Police units and heavily armed gang members protecting their turf. Gang members, police and resident bystanders are all at risk of being victims of the resulting gunfire. The gangs themselves frequently have corrupt relations with politicians, economic elites and police officials, so these invasions frequently do not signal any long-term changes in the conditions of residents' lives.

Before about the mid-2000s, the major actors in Rio's favela policing were Special Operations Battalions (or BOPE, in their Portuguese acronym). They are heavily armed military units trained in counter-insurgency warfare. Their approach to policing the favelas could be described (as above) as a "clear and leave" strategy for repressing crime. Their crime-fighting approach was to crash into these communities, engage with the heavily armed gangs that claimed them, spread as much terror of policing as they could among the residents, and pull away. Their occupation duties were few.

But beginning in the late 2000s, Rio's government pressed for a new approach to favela policing, one a bit more in accord with the principles of community policing. This became the task of UPPs (or, Pacifying Police Units). In contrast to the BOPE, they pursued a "clear and hold" strategy. BOPE units were still employed to gain control of a targeted area, but then new special teams of officers were to remain behind. Their task was to build relationships with the community and engage in crime prevention and civic education projects. There was also the promise that successful pacification would bring with it new public services, such as better schools and health clinics. The UPPs presented a new approach to policing in Rio's poor communities. Their strategies were actually markedly different from those of BOPE units alone and the crash-in tactics of others that preceded them. In their 2015 report, Magaloni, Franco and Melo reported that since 2008, UPP projects had been launched in over 100 favelas. Chapter 9 in this volume, by Vicente Riccio and Wesley G. Skogan, describes in detail the origins and evolution of the UPPs and many organizational details regarding their pacification activities.

Inevitably, the UPPs had mixed results, for theirs was a hard target. Some evaluations were conducted of their impact on crime, using the best data that could be assembled—which are often not very good. For example, many observers cited the visible decline in violent crime in Rio during the post-2009 period as evidence of the impact of the UPPs in favelas. One of the best actual studies of the impact of UPP interventions in favelas in Rio de Janeiro was conducted by a research team from Stanford University in the United States.

They carefully assembled and analyzed official records on homicides of all kinds, including those perpetrated by police. They examined before-and-after changes in homicide in targeted favelas (depending on the analysis, as many as 155 favelas), and compared them with changes over the same period in matched parts of Rio that were not involved in the effort. They also reported on three in-depth analyses of specific UPP interventions that they could carefully document on the ground, through interviews and field observations (Magaloni, Franco and Melo 2015).

The findings were striking. They found that the UPPs had no direct effect on overall homicide. Crime trend lines did not correspond to the entry of the BOPE and UPP teams across their large sample of areas. However, they did identify a dramatic reduction in a particular form of homicide—killings by police officers. These went down by an estimated 60% following BOPE plus UPP interventions. As we noted earlier, by changing the nature of their work, it was hoped that UPP officers would adopt and practice a more community-oriented, democratic style of policing. The UPP interventions seemed to have this desired effect, as measured by a very important statistic in Brazilian society, homicides by the police. The research team also reported another, less surprising, finding: the UPP interventions worked better at reducing homicide in better-off favelas. In Brazil, as elsewhere, one effect of social programs is that the (slightly) better off become better off.

Chapter 10 in this volume, by Vicente Riccio and colleagues, found parallel evidence of a reduction in police violence. They surveyed residents of two Rio de Janeiro favelas that had been occupied by UPP teams. They found a very strong link between resident's satisfaction with the community policing program that they had introduced and the belief that police violence had gone down significantly in their community. In these areas, positive assessments of the UPPs were also linked to the view that homicide in general had declined, and residents of all backgrounds thought that open drug dealing had diminished. Those who thought police were doing a good job also reported feeling safer and that they could more easily come and go in their community.

However, having developed, pilot-tested and fielded a highly visible and apparently successful new approach to dealing with crime in its favela communities, Rio's attention to the program faltered, and currently it is at risk of collapsing. The proximate causes of this lapse were two: money and the 2016 Olympic Games. The Games consumed the city's cash, and during the run-up to the Games, they could not even pay the police. Only an emergency infusion of federal funds kept officers on the street. Official attention shifted to providing security to better-off parts of the city where tourists would gather and around Olympic venues. Further, the collapse of the international price of oil in the mid-2010s hit Rio de Janeiro State's revenues hard. In Chapter 9 of this volume, Riccio and Skogan assess future prospects for UPP, and they stress the resource-intensive nature of the UPP project. Even in better times, there was never a realistic prospect that Rio de Janeiro could mount similar operations in a significant fraction of the city's 800 favelas. Even more discouragingly, it turns out that there was no money—or political will—to actually deliver on the promise that new education and health services would be delivered to targeted communities as part of the follow-up, consolidation stage of UPP's pacification model. Further, Magaloni, Franco and Melo (2015) report that, into the 2010s, drug traffickers had adapted to UPP strategies. They spread their operations to more corners of the city, found unpacified turf to control and eventually began to move back into previously reclaimed areas.

Paths to Reform: Organizational Restructuring

A question addressed by many chapters in this volume is what their findings suggest regarding police reform for Brazil. Here we address several main pathways to reform, applying what police researchers suggest could be done to promote reform to the situation in Brazil.

Among reformers, there often is an instinct to force change by reorganizing established institutional arrangements. Police agencies have been amalgamated while others have been split up; they have been centralized, with control shifted to the national capital, and they have been decentralized to the localities; some lost their insularity while others were largely freed to control their own agenda. With few exceptions, there has been little research on what is the best model of police organization, or even how much of a difference such changes in organizational arrangements actually make.

In particular, observers have been quick to point to inefficient and ineffective features of Brazil's distinction between the Military Police and the Civil Police. Julita Lemgruber (2002), an experienced student of the Brazilian policing scene, suggests that this jurisdictional split has hindered the development of a more comprehensive perspective in law enforcement planning and budgeting, and has forestalled comprehensive criminal justice reform by dividing the authority over large swaths of the case processing cycle among the two. The two institutions

> duplicate efforts, activities, and resources. They frequently engage in turf wars, struggling with each other over space and competing to take credit for results. Their organizational cultures are very distinct and their relationship is generally marked by distrust, if not open hostility.
>
> (p. 4)

In Chapter 2 of this volume, Luis Flavio Sapori also notes that the two have become opposing organizations, vying intensively for resources and power. He describes how they lobby against each other in the state and federal legislatures and the dysfunctional effects this competition between them have on their crime-fighting effectiveness. He later documents the failure of attempts to merge the two branches in several states, and the negative political consequences that reverberated from this effort.

There may indeed be inefficiencies in case processing, but this may not be among the largest issues facing Brazilian policing or a solution to any of its most fundamental problems. As David Bayley (2006) points out, there usually is no clear link between any common form of police organization and the exercise of effective democratic policing. The extremely decentralized model of American policing rates high on achieving political accountability at the local level, but in truth the results of that are not always attractive. It certainly has stymied the spread of innovation and limited the extent of professionalism in police management. Like Brazil, German police are organized at the state level. They are both effective and efficient, and they have never notably overstepped the bounds placed upon them by their relatively new democratic institutions. Sweden's single national police force is held in high regard, while Italy has multiple and often competing national and local police forces that operate with mixed results. In the last two decades, Dutch police have gone from being highly decentralized and locally oriented bodies that were directly responsible to their mayors to a group of regional forces, and then to an even more consolidated number of agencies that are run nationally. Most recently, municipal councils have gotten back into the local policing business, hiring their own supplemental officers. The Dutch people seem not to have been much affected by these changes. Even more recently, the British have begun electing police commissioners to provide popular political oversight over their very professional regional agencies, but without giving them much say over the levels of funding they will receive. Bayley would argue that it is really the missions assigned to them and what police *do* that are central to their democratic prospects, not the details (within limits) of how they are organized.

Paths to Reform: Internal Accountability and External Oversight

Matters involving external and civilian oversight of the police, and their accountability to the rule of law, are a more serious matter. These relate to identifying, investigating and disciplining officers who breech the boundaries set by law and the constitution. Of course, among the issues facing policing, these are among the hardest to resolve. The perennial question, "Who will watch the watchman?" has never successfully been answered in a general way; any solutions are always local and perhaps temporary. Police are the armed wing of the state, and the appropriate use of their lethal and non-lethal powers will always be contested territory.

Internal accountability involves vigorous internal investigations and levying of punishments in response to documented misconduct. Officer misconduct covers a broad range of issues, and inevitably, the police themselves will have to take responsibility for investigations and disciplining for many kinds of cases. In the police reform literature, a distinction is usually made between infractions of agency rules (e.g., being late for work) and state criminal statutes (including bribery and theft) on one hand, and complaints from the public regarding police misconduct that involves the public on the other. Agencies typically treat these as separate streams of problems to be dealt with. In unpublished research on Chicago, the first author found that about half of all reports and complaints of rule and law violations were generated internally, by supervisors and managers within the organization, and about half came from the general public. In Chicago's system, the former were dealt with internally, and the latter were investigated by an external civilian agency.

How internal issues are handled is actually a topic of great interest in policing. Clearly, one goal of internal accountability is to deter future misconduct. If the mechanism for doing so is to be individual punishment, the first goal would be individual deterrence; managers could conclude "they won't do that again" after passing judgment. It is hoped that most managers would take a larger view, one of general deterrence. They could hope that punishing individual officers will send a message to the organization's employees that clarify management's expectations regarding their behavior. If successful, a general deterrent message could ensure that many other officers would not consider breaking the rules in the first place. In addition, active internal accountability processes could send a message to the community the agency serves, one that action can successfully be taken when employees misbehave. Because some of the most economically significant issues dealt with by departments are internal—a big one is abuse of medical leave—investigations and their resulting actions also send a message to political leaders that the agency is acting on behalf of the voters and taxpayers.

In even larger scope, internal rule enforcement raises questions about the functions of punishment itself. If the goal of the organization is to guide the behavior of its employees and set the bounds that define unacceptable behavior, is punishment always the best way to do that? For example, an alternative to punishment could be training. In some agencies, officers who drop their Taser in the locker room and it discharges are sent immediately to intensive Taser training; when they return they are among their district's experts on Taser deployment. Officers who are perennially late for work and inattentive to duty may need counseling regarding problems that they are having at home, or with alcohol. In the 21st century, agencies' human resources departments (now frequently called "talent managers" in the private sector) could play a significant role in advancing the goals of the organization, as an alternative to placing a letter of reprimand in their file or denying them some of their pay.

Current thinking is that external oversight and control procedures in agencies should incorporate at least two functions. The first is to monitor the outcomes of the vigorous internal investigations of police misconduct that we have already described. As an external body, much of this work could be to serve as the final "appeals court" for the final conclusions of internal agency investigations. Second, an important role for external oversight agencies is to monitor agency practices and patterns of officer behavior. Rather than just focus on individual cases, their remit should include data analysis and management review. The role of the external watchdog should include monitoring patterns of misconduct and the effectiveness of the internal investigations being conducted by the police. Among the questions they should ask are, "Which units are causing the most problems with the public, and why?" and "How long are investigations taking, and why?" In addition, current thinking about best practices recommends that an external body be charged with ensuring effective management and efficient performance by their policing counterparts. The questions they should address include, "How are the agency's resources being allocated?" and "Are they getting the most bang for their buck?" Policing is a governmental function, and attention needs to be paid to its effectiveness and efficiency as well as to its fairness. This is usually referred to as an "auditing function" in discussions of external review.

One of the most thoroughgoing reform efforts in recent history has been the reform of policing in Northern Ireland. This project followed decades of tense Protestant-Catholic tension and intercommunal terror campaigns in that part of Great Britain. In the eventual political settlement between them, two bodies were created that carry out external oversight functions. A police board was created that focused on the effectiveness of the new Police Service for Northern Ireland. It was charged with monitoring trends in agency activity and crime and reporting out its findings and management recommendations. This was coupled with the designation of a policing ombudsman, who receives and investigates complaints about police misconduct. Together, these bodies speak to the most important external and internal oversight issues facing policing, and they provide an effective example of how to "watch the watchman."

Brazil's police ombudsman offices were created in a few states in the late 1990s, and since then about half the states have instituted a version of this office in order to receive and process complaints from the community. They independently investigate the complaints that are brought to them, but then pass them on to the internal affairs units of the departments that are the target of the complaints. Police ombudsmen were not charged with the responsibility of auditing patterns of police practice or dealing with inefficiencies or their managerial problems. And, like external review bodies around the world, police ombudsman have been met with hostility and even outright resistance by the agencies they oversee. Ignacio Cano (2006) observed that in actual operation they were falling far short of expectations. They rarely had their own staff and had to borrow workers from other parts of state government. They were not effective at following up with complainants or in communicating with the general public about their efforts, and the reports they released indicate that few cases that were concluded led to any punishment for the accused.

Internally, Brazilian police forces typically have only weak organizational controls. Cases against individual officers are rarely pursued by prosecutors, who almost always decline to carry them forward. Lemgruber (2002) concluded that one of the main limitations to the prevailing Brazilian oversight model is its dependency on what are known to be biased and ineffective internal affairs mechanisms within the police forces, coupled with the reluctance of prosecutors to proceed independently and ombudsman offices with little actual influence.

Bayley (2006) further cautions that there are prerequisites for ensuring that accountability and review functions are carried out effectively. One is that the external monitors are independent of both the police and the political branches of government. This is a difficult issue, for someone must appoint the watchman. A second requirement is that they are adequately funded. Both in the U.S. and Australia, there have been examples of politicians creating external oversight bodies in response to crisis, and then ensuring that they remain largely ineffective by starving them of staff and funding. Caps on their budgets have been one of the obstacles faced by many of Brazil's police ombudsmen. The instinct of many in the political system will be to avoid earning the wrath of organized police officers and their friends and relatives, for they can be a significant political force in local politics.

Paths to Reform: Finding a Community Focus

In a democracy, police must maintain the confidence of the people. In the Northern Hemisphere, one common approach to building this confidence has been community policing. In the North, Bayley (2006) deems community policing to have been the most popular police reform of the 20th century. There are many definitions of community policing, but at root, it requires responsiveness to input by the public concerning both the needs of the community and the best ways by which the police can help meet those needs. It takes seriously the public's definition of its own problems. Community policing requires that departments develop new channels for learning about neighborhood problems, and when they learn about them, they have to have systems in place to respond effectively. Civic engagement could also extend to involving the public in some way in efforts to enhance community safety. Community policing promises to strengthen the capacity of communities to prevent crime on their own. In the United States, the idea that the police and the public are "co-producers" of safety, and that they cannot claim a monopoly over fighting crime, predates the community policing era. The community crime prevention movement of the 1970s was an important precursor to community policing.

Finally, community policing may need to be supported by new organizational structures and training for police officers. Departments need to reorganize in order to provide opportunities for citizens to come into contact with their officers under circumstances that encourage these exchanges. There has to be a significant amount of informal "face time" between police and residents, so that trust and cooperation can develop between the prospective partners. In the U.S., many departments hold community meetings and form advisory committees, establish storefront offices and survey the public. However, it is important that community policing is an organizational strategy but not a set of specific programs or structures. How it looks in practice should vary considerably from place to place, in response to unique local situations and circumstances. Remaining flexible about the exact organizational forms that are required is particularly important when we consider transplanting the philosophy of community policing to distant places and cultures.

There have been transplantation efforts in a number of places around the globe. Davis, Henderson and Merrick (2003) described several of them in Brazilian cities. Among the goals of the projects were to improve community relations with the police and to infuse more cooperative, democratically compatible values within the police force. In Rio de Janeiro, an NGO (nongovernmental organization) with external backing partnered with one police battalion serving favelas near a better-off area of the city. Officers were assigned to regularly patrol particular neighborhoods. They worked on foot, and they were to try to foster good relations with residents and business operators they encountered during their shift. Police also met with local community groups. In a São Paulo experiment, officers were specially selected and trained for a similar effort. They were assigned to small community stations, and they worked with resident groups and the media to encourage dialogue about safety issues and to facilitate community involvement in crime prevention. In Belo Horizonte, a project involved more intensive crime analysis and a problem-solving orientation by police, coupled with community meetings to elicit the public's concerns.

Evaluations of these efforts found some evidence of their effectiveness in addressing crime, but none of them could be sustained. They were all conducted by state Military Police forces, and top officials remained nervous about giving up control to working officers on the street. "Compromising the police hierarchy" is how the authors put it (Davis, Henderson and Merrick 2003, p. 289). Vocal opponents of the concept within the force dismissed community policing as soft and easy policing and "women's work." While there were NGOs fostering these efforts, little grassroots support developed among ordinary people in the areas being served. Surveys of officers and residents found that few even knew there was a program going on.

In Chapter 4, Eduardo Cerqueira Batitucci and his colleagues describe how the organization and culture of the Military Police in the state of Minas Gerais derailed efforts to establish community policing units there. Their organization, culture and military tradition all worked against efforts to create local community councils and engage in problem-solving policing. The Military Police of Minas Gerais never really understood the concept or the values it represented, and they were not in favor of the operational changes that would be required to promote any real change in their policing style. They were also unwilling to give up their heavy weapons while engaging in community-oriented contacts.

Paths to Reform: Building Legitimacy

Our final point relates to the importance of legitimacy in securing democracy, and the role of the police in that. What is legitimacy? Legitimacy is one of the fundamental cornerstones of democracy. It underlies obedience to the law and to the requests or commands of the authorities who protect it. Legitimacy is a belief in the rightness of the state. Legitimacy supports an *obligation* to obey, one that is based on citizens' duty. Where police are viewed as legitimate, people will defer to their authority and to the law, because the police are viewed as generally trustworthy. They can hope that when they stop people or give them instructions they will obey quietly, so that officers can do their jobs efficiently and safely. Police also hope that when they make decisions, the public will accept them as the right decisions. They also rely on most of the people obeying most of the laws, most of the time. There is some evidence that legitimacy beliefs are linked to reduced levels of offending, and particularly lower levels of youth delinquency. Societies with sufficiently high levels of legitimacy do not need an officer on every street corner in order to secure order.

How can police build their legitimacy? Research suggests that there are three major pathways to legitimacy, and this section will briefly examine each of them. First, legitimacy can be built through procedurally fair treatment by the police, or "procedural justice." Second, it can be enhanced through policies and practices that demonstrate adherence by the police to norms regarding equal treatment of social groups (e.g., "people like me") in society. This is usually known as "distributive justice." Finally, police have to be sufficiently effective at providing security. They must be able to protect the public and provide a sufficiently orderly environment, so that democratic processes can prosper. Most researchers would place these factors in this order: fair treatment followed by distributive justice, with effectiveness coming up last. However, most of their research has been conducted in Northern Hemisphere countries where many neighborhoods are already fairly safe, force policies are professional and police are general well-meaning. Conditions in Brazil differ significantly on all three of these dimensions, and it is unclear how each of them would fare when it comes to setting priorities for police reform.

A large body of survey research supports the view that it is *procedurally fair treatment* that generates trust in the police, because citizens infer from how they are treated whether or not the police have good intentions—that they are trustworthy. Treating people in ways that are recognized to be fair and respectful, and making fair and neutral decisions, strengthens the social bonds between individuals and the police. Trust is evidenced when citizens believe that police try to do the right thing, acting on behalf of the best interests of the people they deal with. In this view, people may trust police if they seem to embody the norms and values of the community and when they think police are sincere and well intentioned (Van Craen 2016). The latter means that they have the community's interests at heart and respond to the needs of the community (Jackson, Bradford and Hohl 2012). In Tyler's (2004) view, the resulting trust is one of the most crucial components of procedural justice theory, because it underlies legitimacy. The more people trust the police, the more likely they are to support them and act in accordance with their requests. Trust is also easier to achieve where police are seen as honest and concerned about the well-being of the people they deal with.

Of course, achieving procedurally fair policing is linked to other police reform issues discussed already. One is confidence that the police organization takes officer conduct seriously and acts when its rules are breached. Strong, independent police oversight can help build legitimacy and public trust, through increased transparency and accountability to the public that the police serve. As we have seen, oversight fosters this accountability through both independent investigations and systematic analyses of police operations. These can identify needed changes in police practices and training and provide a meaningful voice for the public in ensuring community safety.

Another set of popular concerns is linked to the idea of *distributive fairness*. There are fairness concerns at the level of groups and society, as well as within individuals. Distributive fairness relates to perceptions that the outcomes people receive—for example, to be arrested or ticketed, or to be the target of abuse or humiliation—are distributed appropriately across groups. This might involve comparisons between rich and poor, or between ethnic and racial groups. They will often involve fairness judgments between the treatment of "my group" and "others," although distributive concerns can also arise from analyses of patterns of operational practice. Distributive fairness also is involved in the perceived allocation of police resources.

Being under (or over) policed, or living in a neighborhood where police seem to come more slowly when they are called, can be seen as distributive fairness issues.

In Brazil, most research linked to legitimacy has focused on distributive justice. In 2010, Cano summarized what was known regarding racial disparities in the operation of the criminal justice system. As he noted, as in many societies, the criminal justice system is a venue in which biases can openly present themselves. In summary, this research found that, in the judicial system, blacks are least likely to be represented by a private attorney and more likely to be convicted and get stricter sentences if they offend against whites. Official data on police violence in Brazil are mostly terrible, but independent surveys find that blacks are more likely than whites to be stopped and searched. They are also most likely to report being assaulted by police, even more so than they are disproportionately victimized by conventional assaultive violence. Blacks are most afraid of the police, and the only group to be more afraid of the police than they are of crime. Cano's own study of fatal police violence in Rio de Janeiro and São Paulo combined data on police use of force from multiple sources, including autopsy and ombudsman records, and also compared them to population statistics for the city and for the demographics of the local convict population. He found that blacks were more likely to be targets of police violence, and they were more likely to be injured accidently during shootouts involving others. When they were wounded, blacks were more likely to die of their injuries.

A third pathway to legitimacy is police *effectiveness*. This relates to their ability to secure acceptable levels of community safety and order. Where police are effective enough that everyday life can be conducted safely, concern about the quality of police service may shift to other, customer-oriented dimensions, such as politeness and showing respect. But where effectiveness seems wanting, an emphasis on improving the professional crime-fighting capabilities of the police and associated agencies may be included on the legitimacy-building agenda. Being able to protect its people is a bedrock feature of a legitimate state. As Justice Tankebe (2013, p. 112) put it,

> When citizens demand that the police demonstrate effectiveness in tackling crime and disorder in their local areas . . . they are not simply making crude instrumental demands; on the contrary, they are expecting the police to fulfill a normative condition for their legitimacy.

While research conducted in wealthy Northern Hemisphere countries typically finds that the effects of effectiveness are overshadowed by concerns about procedural justice, Tankebe's (2011) work in Ghana found a much stronger relationship between perceived police effectiveness and judgments regarding their legitimacy. This could be taken as evidence that a modicum of effectiveness, and thus personal security, is required before demands for other kinds of reforms emerge.

Of course, this point links to the extremely high rate of violence in Brazilian society, coupled with the ineffectiveness and corruption that characterizes local law enforcement. Effectiveness is important because Brazil is a vibrant, if flawed, democracy. Views of police effectiveness can make a difference. Crime is always on the political agenda when elections are contested. The public's understandable concern about crime is backstopped by the nation's feisty mass media, which is quick to highlight security lapses. Leeds (2007) notes how the press drives cycles of crisis and demands for quick reform. But as she notes, media-driven crises, when combined with aggressive office seeking, tend to generate only short-term solutions to problems, including crime. Almost inevitably, this quick-fix political environment fosters repression. The get-tough policies that follow range from invasions of favelas that seem threatening to surrounding areas to vehicle checkpoints and aggressive stop-and-frisk operations. This in turn escalates resistance by the powerful gangs that are inconvenienced by these tactics, which next sparks retaliatory violence by police.

One factor behind the almost inevitable repetition of this cycle is the fact that there is a significant pool of at least tacit support for repression among better-off voters. Tough talk wins elections. In Chapter 7 of this volume, Lima and Sinhoretto cite a common Portuguese-language expression, that "good criminals are dead criminals—*bandido bom é bandido morto*." They note that many Brazilians at least tacitly support the use of violence in order to guarantee peace for law-abiding citizens. In a recent survey conducted by Fórum Brasileiro de Segurança with DataFolha, more than 3,600 respondents were interviewed around the country. In that survey, 57% of the respondents supported this statement (FBSP 2016). Reviewing survey findings, Magaloni, Franco and Melo (2015) set the number of supporters for repressive crime policies at about one-third of Rio de Janeiro's population. On the other hand, in Chapter 7, Lima and Sinhoretto cite polling evidence that Brazilian society is "split down the middle" over this issue.

In turn, these political instincts can undermine attempts to change policing. As Bayley argues (2006, p. 69), "In political life, the requirements of security trump aspirations to reform, a pattern to be found in stable as well as struggling democracies." At some level of concern, crime may crowd out concerns about the niceties of law enforcement practices. In the political realm, it is common to pit lawfulness (or "legal nit-picking") versus effectiveness. There is ample evidence that this is a false choice, at least in the developed Northern Hemisphere (Skogan and Frydl 2004). However, where effectiveness is currently low, the choice may seem like a real one. "Unleashing" the police may seem to be the best that can be accomplished. Police resorting to violence can be seen as the inevitable collateral damage of effective crime control. Efforts to get them to organize their work in a different fashion can be seen as putting the public at risk in some untried social experiment, and police will be quick to support that concern.

Discussion

As the essays in this volume document, Brazil is a large country facing large problems. At the core lies some of the basic features of Brazilian life: poverty, inequality, racial divisions, debilitating levels of violence and a state that cannot protect large segments of its people. Individually, each of these problems presents a daunting challenge to reformers; collectively, addressing them will require heroic levels of policy effort, coordination and investment.

It has been tried. In 2007, the administration of President Luiz Inácio Lula da Silva (known to all as "Lula") mounted a well-financed and broadly conceptualized reform effort at the national level. It was aimed at all of the security services of Brazil, so it included prisons and prison guards, firefighters and others, in addition to the police. On the crime prevention front, elements of the program addressed police hiring, training and equipment; organizing in poor communities; social programs for youths; education and employment opportunities for offenders; and special programs for favelas. It promised to increase police pay. And it failed. Chapter 12 in this volume, by Marco Aurélio Ruediger, examines the policy system in Brazil. It identifies the key structural features that stifled reform there. These ranged from bureaucratic resistance within the federal government to turnovers in leadership of the project and the limits that Brazilian federalism place on change efforts originating at the center. The states resisted the new state-federal relationship imposed by the program, with its rules controlling spending and (this was new) actual monitoring of program implementation at the local level. When the new president's attention to the project waned, well-organized interests in the bureaucracy and legislature gutted the budget. It was a top-down program that never developed a constituency at the grass roots.

There is nothing unique about this failure of reform. While researchers working in the United States write frequently about innovations in policing, in truth many of them are not widely adopted or well implemented, and too many are just press releases. The obstacles to police reform are formidable even in Northern Hemisphere countries. In the end, over a modest period of time, many reforms fail and most disappear. This is true even though they may seem to be successful; that is not a determinative fact in the policy process (Skogan 2008).

So, it should be no surprise that we anticipate that reform in Brazil will take time. Change will be at best slow, and success uncertain. Reform must involve changing the habits and mindsets of many actors throughout the criminal justice system and in political life. Fostering public trust in the police will be at least as hard.

Notes

1. www.ft.com/content/f4a260e6-f75a-11e6-bd4e-68d53499ed71
2. http://jconline.ne10.uol.com.br/canal/politica/pernambuco/noticia/2016/09/24/pacto-pela-vida-morreu-diz-mentor-do-programa-254101.php
3. These and other analyses of Brazilian police violence can be found on the Human Rights Watch and Amnesty International web sites. The web site for the Fórum Brasileiro de Segurança Pública has some English-language pages.
4. In addition to state police forces, there is a national policing body that broadly resembles the scope and duties of the Federal Bureau of Investigation in the United States, and other forces guard the nation's borders and perform specialized functions. Many cities also employ Municipal Guards to perform watchman duties; since 2014, they have also been armed.

References

Bayley, D. 2006. *Changing the guard: Developing democratic policing abroad.* New York: Oxford University Press.

Cano, I. 2006. Public security policies in Brazil: Attempts to modernize and democratize versus the war on crime. *SUR: International Journal on Human Rights* 3: 136–155.

Cano, I. 2010. Racial bias in police use of lethal force in Brazil. *Police Practice and Research* 11: 31–43.

Cerqueira, D. 2013. Mapa dos Homicídios Ocultos no Brasil [Map of Hidden Homicides in Brazil]. Text for discussion 1848. Brasília, IPEA. Available at http://www.ipea.gov.br/portal/index.php?option=com_content&view=article&id=19232 on 15th June 2017.

Davis, R., Henderson, N., and Merrick, C. 2003. Community policing: Variations on the western model in the developing world. *Police Practice and Research* 4: 285–300.

Economist. 2016. The Latinobarometro Poll. September 3.

Fórum Brasileiro de Segurança Pública. 2013. A Investigação de homicídios no Brasil. Available at http://www.forumseguranca.org.br/publicacoes/a-investigacao-de-homicidios-no-brasil/ on 15th June 2017.

Fórum Brasileiro de Segurança Pública. 2016. Anuário Brasileiro de Segurança Pública 2016, v. 10. Available at http://www.forumseguranca.org.br/publicacoes/10o-anuario-brasileiro-de-seguranca-publica/ on 15th June 2017.

Jackson, J., Bradford, B., and Hohl, K. 2012. *Just authority: Trust in the police in England and Wales.* London & New York: Routledge.

Jovchelovitch, S., and Priego-Hernandez, J. 2013. *Underground sociabilities: Identity, culture, and resistance in Rio de Janeiro's favelas.* Brasilia: UNESCO Office in Brazil.

Kahn, T. 2013. Crescimento econômico e criminalidade: uma interpretação da queda de crimes no Sudeste e aumento no Norte/Nordeste. *Revista Brasileira de Segurança Pública* 7(1): 152–164.

Leeds, E. 2007. Serving states and serving citizens: Halting steps toward police reform in Brazil and implications for donor intervention. *Policing & Society* 17: 21–37.

Lemgruber, J. 2002. *Civilian oversight of the police in Brazil: The case of the ombudsman's offices.* Rio de Janeiro: Center for Studies on Public Security and Citizenship, University Candido Mendes.

Magaloni, B., Franco, E., and Melo, V. 2015. *Killing in the slums: An impact evaluation of police reform in Rio de Janeiro.* Stanford University Center on Democracy, Development and the Rule of Law, December.

Preteceille, E., and Valladares, L. 1999. *Favelas no plural.* Caxambu; paper presented at the XXIII Annual Meeting of National Association of Post-Graduates on Research in Social Sciences: Anpocs.

Skogan, W. 2008. Why reforms fail. *Policing & Society* 18: 23–34.

Skogan, W., and Frydl, K. 2004. *Fairness and effectiveness in policing: The evidence.* Washington, DC: National Academies Press.

Souza, P., and Medeiros, M. 2015. Top income shares and inequality in Brazil, 1928–2012. *Sociologies in Dialogue: Journal of the Brazilian Sociological Society* 1: 119–132.

Tankebe, J. 2011. Explaining police support for the use of force and vigilante violence in Ghana. *Policing & Society* 21: 129–149.

Tankebe, J. 2013. Viewing things differently: The dimensions of public perceptions of police legitimacy. *Criminology* 51: 103–135.

Tyler, T. 2004. Enhancing police legitimacy. *The Annals of the American Academy of Political and Social Science* 593: 84–99.

United Nations Office on Drugs and Crime. 2014. *Global study on homicide.* Vienna: Author.

Van Craen, M. 2016. Understanding police officers' trust and trustworthy behavior: A work relations framework. *European Journal of Criminology* 13: 274–294.

Waiselfisz, J. J. 2016. Mapa da Violência 2016. Homicídios por Armas de Fogo no Brasil. Rio de Janeiro FLACSO.

Section I

The Organization of Brazilian Police

The Dual Civil and Military Models for Policing in Brazil

2

Luis Flavio Sapori

Contents

Police systems around the world display a diversity of institutional designs. In comparative perspective, national police systems are distinguished by (a) the level of fragmentation, which may be local, regional or federal; (b) the diversity of responsibilities conferred upon them; (c) their degree of professionalism; (d) their level of accountability; and (e) their degree of autonomy from the political system. The form that each system takes is generally evolutionary rather than planned. Police systems are products of the history of each country, reflecting their singular political and social dynamic (Bayley 1975).

The Origins of the Brazilian Dual Model

In Brazil, the police acquired its first institutional features at the beginning of the nineteenth century, when the country was still a colony of Portugal. In 1808 and 1809, the "Intendance General of Police and the Military Division of the Royal Guard Police" was created in Rio de Janeiro. It was organized along the lines of the system prevailing in Lisbon, the capital of Portugal, at that time. However, in parts of the country there already existed military units that conducted surveillance of the streets. In fact, the origins of the Brazilian police system could also be seen in the gold and diamond mining regions of the late eighteenth century, when the Regular Regiment of Minas Gerais Cavalry was created with the mission of keeping justice and the "good order and public safety" (Cotta 2012, p. 316).

After independence in the 1830s, Brazil briefly experimented with an alternative police model, one that lasted less than ten years, during a historical period known as the Regency. At that time, local municipalities were authorized to exercise police and judicial powers, and a justice of the peace took center stage when it came to public safety. From 1840, however, the provinces—now Brazil's states—assumed control of their police forces, a model that prevails in Brazilian society to this day. In 1871, the Police Inquest, a public notarial body charged with prosecutorial powers, was established by the reform of the Criminal Procedure Code. This consolidated responsibility for conducting the investigation of crimes to delegates of the police (Holloway 1997).

Importantly, at this time Brazil established a dual model for policing. Each state formed an investigative police, commanded by delegates responsible for the criminal investigation. Initially called Judicial Police, over time they became known as the Civil Police. The other wing of policing is militarized, with a structure and discipline similar to that of the army. They provided services that today we call "street policing." In some states, this militarized police was called the Military Brigade and in others, the Public Force. In the state constitutions developed during the twentieth century, the term Military Police came to be their common name (Batitucci 2010; Ege 2013).

A fundamental aspect of the institutional history of the police in Brazil is the fact that, from the mid-nineteenth century until the late 1960s, the Military Police acted more as state armies than what in other parts of the world would be considered as police organizations. Street patrolling existed, but the organization maintained large contingents of officers quartered in barracks. In important moments in history, the state Military Police forces fought as if they were engaged in warfare. These moments included the constitutional revolution of 1932 and the military coup of 1964. In the first case, the state of São Paulo rebelled against President Getulio Vargas, who came to power in 1930 promising to hold a national constituent assembly. When by 1932 this promise was not fulfilled, large segments of the population mobilized in resistance, leading to an armed confrontation with federal forces. In 1964, in turn, amid the political crisis of President João Goulart's government, the armed forces succeeded the federal executive and imposed serious restrictions on Federal Congress. They ruled Brazil until 1984.

As a result of their emphasis on military duties, some Brazilian states created new uniformed police departments that did engage in "conventional" policing; often they were called Civil Guards.[1] This lasted until 1969, when the Civil Guards were abolished and their staff and responsibilities were taken over by the Military Police during the military dictatorship.

This brief historical narrative helps us understand how Brazil has become one of the countries in the world that maintains a police system separating criminal investigations (by the Civil Police) and street policing (by the Military Police). This in turn has led to chronic conflict between the two policing models, and it is also a source of inefficiency in actually responding to crime. These issues are the main issues examined in this chapter.

Institutional Design of the Police

The current Brazilian institutional design for policing was established by the Federal Constitution in 1988. At that historic moment, the country was redefining the institutional parameters of a new democracy that was being launched. After 20 years of military dictatorship between 1964 and 1984, Brazilian society was able to overcome its authoritarian past and formed a Constituent National Assembly.

The new Federal Constitution addressed public safety in Article 144. It distinguished it from national security. For the first time in the constitutional history of Brazil, safety was conceived as a right of citizenship, requiring the protection of life and property, and assigned this responsibility to domestic police. The defense of the country and state institutions were the sole responsibility of the armed forces, and any involvement by the armed forces in domestic public safety matters was placed under very strict restrictions. Despite these changes, the 1988 constitution maintained the same police system prevailing since the military dictatorship.

The Brazilian police system is structured as follows:

a) at the federal level there are two police organizations: the Federal Police (PF) and the Federal Highway Police (PRF). Both fall under the Ministry of Justice. It is the responsibility of the PF to patrol national borders and investigate interstate and international crimes, such as drug trafficking and smuggling, as well as crimes against property of the federal government. The PRF is responsible for patrolling federal highways and cannot investigate other crimes that may occur. A Federal Railroad Police is also constitutionally provided for, but has not been instituted to date;

b) at the state level there are two police organizations: the Military Police and the Civil Police. Every state, including the Federal District (Brasilia), is organized following this dual model. Both branches fall under the authority of the state governors and are overseen by state boards of public safety. The Military Police are responsible for street policing and cannot investigate criminal offenses, with the exception of military offenses. The Civil Police are limited to investigative activity and work at collecting evidence concerning crime. As judicial police, they are also responsible for preparing cases for prosecution;

c) at the city level municipalities can create Municipal Guards. They are restricted to minor watchman roles, acting largely as security guards. The authority to create Municipal Guards rests in the National Status of Municipal Guards legislation, which was enacted in 2014;

d) the Fire Brigade is also mentioned in Article 144. They are responsible for fire and civil defense activities and are seen as an integral part of Brazil's public safety establishment. In many Brazilian states, the Fire Brigade is organized along military lines.

The Military Police also serve as auxiliary armed forces, and they have constitutional permission to act in situations threatening national security. The Military Police are subject to their own disciplinary legislation, the Military Penal Code. Disciplinary and possibly criminal offenses committed by their officers are investigated, prosecuted and judged in accordance with the Military Criminal Procedure Code. The hierarchy of the Military Police is pyramidal, incorporating the rank nomenclature of the army. There is a broad divide between the careers of lower-ranked officers (soldier, sergeant) and the careers of the top officers (lieutenants, captains, majors, lieutenant colonels and colonels). There is little or no mobility across these two career paths.

The Civil Police are subject to the Criminal Code and the Code of Criminal Procedure, like any Brazilian citizen. The main feature of the organizational hierarchy of the Civil Police is the supremacy of delegates. They hold bachelor of law degrees, which are required for this position. Others in the organization are subordinate to them, like investigators, registrars and coroners.

Brazil has at present 56 police organizations, including 54 state police forces and two federal police. In some Brazilian states, a third force was created, called the Scientific Technical Police. These divide the responsibility for criminal investigations and coroner's work. In most of the country, however, both of these functions remain the job of the Civil Police, composing the Criminal Expertise Department.

Policing: A Loosely Coupled System

The first impression one gets of the Brazilian police system may be that these divisions of responsibility are complementary and rational. Military Police officers maintain their presence on public roads, perform overt uniformed surveillance and detain criminals. They manage call centers, and when citizens dial the 190 emergency number, they are connected to the Military Police. The main product of all of this activity is a formal record of crimes committed and some arrests at the scene.

The Civil Police, in turn, do their work from police stations. They act in response to reports of criminal activity brought by the Military Police and

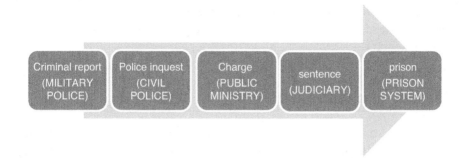

Figure 2.1 The criminal justice system in Brazil

collect evidence regarding what happened. Their product is inquests that are referred to the courts. The Public Ministry and the judiciary are organizations that then take over the flow of cases. The Public Ministry has the prerogative of charging the individual investigated in the police inquest. The judge, in turn, accepts the prosecutor's charge and coordinates the criminal proceedings when the defense has active participation. The product of this phase is the court judgment. Upon conviction, the defendant may go on to serve time in the prison system, administered mainly by the states.

As noted, there is a clear division of functions between these organizations, forming a seemingly continuous and interdependent flow of activity. In its formal representation, the criminal justice process could be described as a "system." However, the daily functioning of the criminal justice system in Brazilian society actually is characterized by chronic conflict and breakdowns in coordination. In reality, it should be considered a "loosely coupled" system (Sapori 2007b; Paixão 1982). Importantly for us, it is the organizational segmentation between the Military and Civil Police that creates this loose linkage. In past decades, they have become opposing organizations, vying intensively for resources and power. This conflict pervades the performance of both groups on a daily basis.

Outsiders visiting Brazil and walking the streets of its big cities will not notice this conflict. It generally is not visible, and it is unknown even to most Brazilians. However, there have been occasional physical confrontations between branches of the police, such as the confrontation between the Civil Police of São Paulo who went on strike and the riot squad of the Military Police that protected state buildings, in October 2008 (Rede Record 2011). At least 25 people were injured in that episode. In the city of Belo Horizonte, the capital of Minas Gerais State, Civil and Military Police officers argued, shoved and threatened to attack each other in February 2011 (UOL Notícias 2008).

Situations like those described are not everyday occurrences. The main contest between the Military and Civil Police takes place backstage, in the offices of governors, and is invisible to the public. It is present in all Brazilian states to a greater or lesser extent. This is never publicly recognized by their leaders. Instead, they hew to the line that the police are "sisters" and wholly complementary.

The Corporatist Dispute

The rhetoric that they are "sister organizations" hides antagonism between the Civil and Military Police, a tension that has grown in the last 20 years. The instigators of this antagonism are the elites of both organizations: the delegates of the Civil Police and high officers of the Military Police.

These organizational elites lobby the national Congress intensively, defending their corporatist interests through representative bodies such as the National Association of Police Delegates of Brazil and the National Federation of State Military Officers Entities. At the moment, the main clash between delegates and military officials is over their ability to attain a legal career status, so that their salaries would be equivalent to the salaries of judges and prosecutors, who are among the most highly paid civil servants. Civil Police delegates have claimed this status for many years, and military officers are also pleading for the same benefit. As one outcome of this struggle, several state Military Police agencies changed their statutes, requiring undergraduate degrees in law as a prerequisite for hiring. Formal legal training has historically been required only of the delegates, who publicly express disagreement with this political move by military officers. The political confrontation between organizational elites pervades the everyday activities of both organizations. The dispute between Civil Police delegates and military officials has become a dispute between the police as a whole.

This is only one of the factors that has led to the decoupling of the Brazilian police system. There is also intense competition between them for power, especially with regard to the scope of their duties. Military police claim the authority to create Detail Occurrence Terms (TCO), which have been conceived as the exclusive responsibility of the Civil Police. The TCO is simply formal recording of the occurrence of lesser offenses, so-called misdemeanors. According to the Law on Special Criminal Courts, promulgated in 1995, the TCO should be referred directly to the judge of the criminal special court, which then proceeds to scheduling a hearing for the case. The task of the police is simply reporting the TCO as much detail as possible, collecting information about the crime that has occurred, including about victims and offenders.

Military Police want to take charge of TCO and the Civil Police do not agree. The delegates believe that they alone constitute what the law defines as "police authority," and thus only they are legally competent to take such an action. Military officials, in turn, are severe critics of any monopoly of TCO by the Civil Police. In other words, the Military Police want to add to their constitutional allocation of authority the competence to act as the investigative police in misdemeanors. The Civil Police, in turn, understand this as breaking their monopoly of criminal investigations under the Federal Constitution.

In the background of this competition for assignments is vagueness of the legal boundary between street and investigative police. Complaints that the "other police" are going beyond their competence are recurrent. The Civil Police has expressed dissatisfaction with the strengthening of the intelligence arm of the Military Police, called P2. Civil delegates understand rightly that this sector often performs criminal investigations, identifying alleged perpetrators and enabling their arrest. P2 is composed of military officers working undercover. It is not uncommon for both branches of the police to be involved in the investigation of the same crime, usually ones of great public impact. The Military Police, in turn, complain that the Civil Police unduly invest in tactical street operations using uniformed officers with military training and escalating crisis situations, such as bank robberies with hostages and riots in prisons. It is not uncommon for tactical forces of both police organizations to present themselves in these situations, prompting long discussions about who should manage the crisis.

These chronic disputes between the Military and Civil Police make routine cooperation between them an exception, not the rule. It is true that some street-level officers in both organizations are friends and even develop working relationships over time, enabling cooperation in some situations. However, this cooperation is based strictly on low-level personal relations, and they last only as long as "police friends" find themselves working on the same problems. Conflict at the organization level confounds the solution of some crimes, leads to turf wars over geographical areas, makes intelligence gathering more difficult and even affects the training of police officers and operational planning. Every aspect of this institutional dysfunctionality deserves greater attention in Brazil.

System Dysfunctions

There are two sources of reported crimes in Brazil: (1) reports completed by Military Police officers when they are contacted by the public or they view events while on patrol (called here "BOs"); and (2) investigations initiated by the Civil Police, of incidents referred to them by the Military Police or reported to them directly by the public. The numbers reported by the Military Police and Civil Police are always different. This presents problems in diagnosing crime problems, because these figures are inconsistent and duplicative with regard to both time and space.

Each of these organizations reassures everyone that their data are the most correct and tries to discredit criminal statistics produced by their competitor. Homicide data in Brazil, for example, varies between BOs and Civil Police inquests, with the incidence of homicides always higher in the Civil Police database. The reason is simple: attempted homicides recorded in BOs commonly turn into homicides in inquests, because victims frequently die in the days after being registered by the Military Police. In the case of robberies, in turn, the numbers of the Military Police are always higher than those of the Civil Police. There is evidence that the latter initiate criminal investigations in this crime category only when the Military Police have arrested an offender in the act, which happens in only a small percentage of occasions (Lima 2011; Costa 2004).

Another disjunction resulting from the dual Brazilian system of policing is the lack of overlap between the geographic areas their respective units serve. The Military Police are organized as battalions and then in companies, and both serve very precise territorial boundaries, which may include a number of cities or even neighborhoods in the same city. The Civil Police, on the other hand, are organized around regional police offices that coordinate work in smaller district police stations. Similarly to the military, their regional and district police stations have territorial boundaries. However, in many Brazilian states, the subunit boundaries of the Civil Police do not match those of the Military Police. This often disrupts the daily work of both agencies, for example in the delivery of BOs to police stations. In the early mornings, weekends and holidays, when the district police stations are closed, the time spent on this by the military is quite high, requiring traveling tens of kilometers. This waste of resources occurs because the location of investigative police stations and their opening hours do not match the needs of the street police (Muniz and Paes-Machado 2010).

Not only that, but the Military and Civil Police rarely share information and background knowledge about crime. Both agencies have IT systems that optimize their administrative and operational activities. Both organizations have banks of qualitative and quantitative data on crimes and criminals. However, their bureaucratic stance is to restrict as much as possible access by their counterparts to these databases. They often resist implementation of information systems that threaten to integrate their respective data and activities. It is common, for example, for traffic control crackdowns by the Military Police to identify suspicious vehicles and individuals. However, investigation of vehicle registries and databases recording outstanding arrest warrants can only be performed in consultation with the central office of their state's Civil Police. The Military Police thus depend upon the goodwill of the civil officer to be able to make a query of the organization's database. The Military Police, in turn, hold databases on criminals, their modes of action and areas of operation, and they are often concentrated in the P2 sectors. They use this data sporadically to monitor contacts with hardened criminals, but do not automatically provide information to the Civil Police, which need to request information through formal channels. Criminal investigation could be enhanced if such data access were available on a shared computer system (Sapori and Andrade 2008; Misse 2010).

Not sharing information leads the two agencies in the direction of completely uncoordinated operational planning. Military and Civil Police allocate their staff and resources to the cities and areas they are responsible for without considering each other's plans. Their tactical operations in various places and at various times are also treated as independent issues. One organization does not know how the other plans to deal, for example, with crises of violence plaguing a particular city. This operational disarticulation often leads to public disputes between them, with Military Police leaders claiming they are acting repressively in the arrest of many criminals but that Civil Police inquests are not being initiated. The Civil Police, in turn, accuse the military of inefficiency in street policing and failing to prevent the occurrence of crime, which thus ends up overloading their investigative capacity (Kant de Lima 1995; Sapori 2007a).

Another example: the Civil and Military Police have their own teaching academies, with distinct training courses and curricula. They are very resistant to suggestions that they integrate some or all of their training efforts. Training of mixed groups of Military and Civil Police officers happens only occasionally, depending on the initiative of one or another state. However, the prevailing view is that Military and Civilian officers should not mix and should retain their distinct identities. They are like "oil and water" (Riccio, Meirelles and Muller 2013;Santos 1997;Poncioni 2005).

Attempts to Reform the Dual System of Policing

The operational pathologies that result from the decoupling of the Military and Civil Police, and the obstacles that it creates for effective crime control, have been pointed out by scholars since the late 1980s. Only in the next decade, however, were these problems perceived as a public issue. By the second half of the 1990s, the integration of the police rose to the agendas of state governments (Sapori 2007b).

The state of Pará, at the north of the country, was the first to move (from 1995 to 2002) toward the integration of their police in the areas of information systems, training and the geographical boundaries of the two units. These efforts were implanted in the state capital, Belém, creating an Integrated Center of Operations (CiOp) that brought together the radio dispatching operations of the Military and Civil Police and the fire department. In addition, Pará created the Safety Training Institute of Pará(IESP), integrating the academies of the two agencies.

The state of Ceará, in northeastern Brazil, also made reforms in the public safety sector in the late 1990s, doing so in response to serious allegations of corruption within the police. Ceará created a Model District in Fortaleza, the state capital. It brought together subunits of the Military and Civil Police in the same building, standardized their geographical areas, and—like Pará—integrated policing operations.

In the same period, the state of São Paulo, in the southeast of the country, formulated a comprehensive crime control policy that, among other things, created a criminal justice information system (INFOCRIM) that integrated the databases of their Military and Civil Police.

In 2003–2010, the state of Minas Gerais, also located in the Southeast, implemented the most audacious police integration policy to date in the country. It could serve as a model for the other states. The integration model designed by Minas Gerais created integrated communications and information centers as strategic bodies to integrate police organizations. They oversee geographically integrated territorial areas, and their central role in controlling communications and information systems was designed to facilitate joint operational planning regarding street policing and investigative activities. Integration revolved around three projects: information integration (Integrated System of Social Defense, or SIDS); geographical integration (Integrated Areas of Public Safety, or AISP); and operational integration (Integrated Management in Public Safety, or IGESP). Alongside this followed the integration of prison personnel and integrated police training (Sapori and Andrade 2008).

At the end of the 2000s, the states of Pernambuco (Northeast) and Rio de Janeiro (Southeast) were inspired by these projects, particularly Integrated Areas of Public Safety and Integrated Management in Public Safety, to develop their own police integration initiatives. This also happened in the state of Espírito Santo (Southeast), which since 2012 has invested in police integration as one of the core elements of its public safety policy.

Throughout this period, other Brazilian states incorporated some of these integration models in their respective police systems. Two initiatives were the most widespread: (1) integrated operations centers, assembling radio communications by the Military and Civil Police in the same building; and (2) the creation of integrated geographies for all policing, so that branches of the two agencies began to work in common territorial spaces. In practice, this means that each Military Police battalion or company has a regional or district Civil Police station sharing its territory, bringing together street policing and the further investigation of crimes.

Moves toward integrating policing in the states received a direct contribution from the federal government, through the National Public Safety Secretariat (SENASP), which is embedded in the Ministry of Justice. The first national public safety plan formulated by the federal government was launched in 2000 during the government of Fernando Henrique Cardoso. It proposed 124 discrete actions, one being the integration of the Military and Civil Police. In 2003, the first Lula government released a public safety plan for Brazil, which provided basic guidelines for the reform of the police system. The integration of the police was again contemplated, under the label of the Unified Public Safety System. This plan included the creation of unified police academies, unified intelligence units, joint internal affairs bureaus and an independent police ombudsman. It called for the further coordination of police with other organizations in the criminal justice system, particularly the judiciary and prosecution, to be facilitated by the creation of state-level integrated management offices. In 2007, during the second Lula government, another national plan was released, the National Safety Program with Citizenship, or PRONASCI. Once again, the integration of police was considered one of the pillars of this plan (Soares 2007). In every case, the federal government promised funds for state governments once they satisfied the guidelines established by the national government.

Conclusion: The Failure of Reform

However, efforts to integrate Brazil's Military and Civil Police have not been able to fundamentally alter their dual structure and chronic dysfunctions. National efforts to do so since the mid-1990s were not sustained. The states of Pará, Ceará, São Paulo and Minas Gerais proved unable to institutionalize the relationship they tried to develop between their policing agencies, particularly in the areas of training and operational planning. After an initial period of cooperation, antagonism and corporatism continued to prevail. Efforts to accomplish something continue in Pernambuco State, but these also threaten to fail, and those in Espírito Santo are only in their infancy.

The case of Minas Gerais is emblematic of this failure of reform. The police integration policies adopted by this state involved the preparation of a complex framework for coordinating their activities, and this led to a tangle of new nomenclatures and acronyms that have become part of the dynamics of the current police system (SIDS, IGESP, AISP, SICODS, TPI). There was to be an intense formalization of procedures and the development of joint standards, resolutions and decrees. All of this was to be accomplished by government and police agency representatives.

However, what looked like progress toward the institutionalization of reform began to fall apart when events in the political sphere renewed the classic corporatist dispute between police organizations. In 2010, controversial laws were passed, the first of which (as described earlier) was the redefinition of Civil Police delegates as legal professionals in the state civil service. Months later, a second law granted similar legal status to high officers of the Military Police of Minas Gerais. Union leaders in the Civil Police questioned in court the constitutionality of this new civil service legal status for Military Police officers, on the grounds that street policing did not require the legal training that their new status made mandatory. Another achievement of the Civil Police was months later also obtained by their military counterparts, namely the requirement of higher education for entry into higher police careers. This led to further dissatisfaction among delegates within the Civil Police. Since then, delegates have tried to break agreements that had been reached regarding integration policy, which included calls for wage parity between police, especially between Civil Police delegates and higher military officers. In short, the Civil Police continue to defend their more advanced professional status, while the Military Police persist in claiming the higher wages this would imply.

The result of this corporatist struggle was the loss of legitimacy of the joint bodies that had been established by the state government. The goal of integrated operational planning, which was the initiative that promised the best hope for reducing crime, did not happen, and provisions for the coordination of the efforts of the two agencies on a daily basis no longer are in effect.

The decisive political reality that underlay this collapse of police integration in Minas Gerais was the weakening of the authority of the governor. Police integration was an agenda item established by the governor, and while he was at his most powerful the police were collaborating with each other. When that political leadership faltered, old antagonisms resurfaced (Sapori and Andrade 2013).

This example suggests that the Brazilian dual system of police and its resulting problems will not easily be overcome. Across all of the states, the separation of street policing and investigative assignments in different organizations invariably has fostered competition for resources. Competition and antagonism between police agencies is not unique to Brazil, but the uniqueness of the Brazilian case seems to be the operational inefficiency generated by such a system. Disjunctions between the Military and Civil Police have not led to virtuous competition for better results, leading to public benefits. On the contrary, the more the police compete with each other, the greater the tendency toward increased inefficiency in both patrol and criminal investigation. The ability to prevent and suppress crime is inevitably weakened.

This situation also reflects a major shortcoming that characterizes the governance of Brazil, one with implications for the high crime levels observed there in recent decades. The problem is the limited effectiveness of the state in ensuring public safety, which manifests itself in the low degree of certainty of punishment facing potential criminals. Available data show that the chances that someone committing a robbery or murder will be investigated by the police, prosecuted, judged and found guilty are very small in Brazil (Sapori and Soares 2014;Beato 2012).

A recent victimization survey conducted by the Center for Public Safety of Federal University of Minas Gerais (CRISP-UFMG; DATAFOLHA/CRISP 2013) in partnership with the Datafolha Institute shows, for example, that more than half the Brazilians who are victims of thefts and robberies do not report this to the police in the first place. They do not do so because they do not believe in the ability of the police to take effective action. This mistrust has foundation. A report of the National Council of the Public Ministry in 2012 estimated that only 8% of homicides annually registered in the country are solved by the police with an identification of the perpetrator (ENASP 2012). In robberies, this gap is even greater, according to a survey conducted by Sou da Paz Institute in São Paulo city from 2009 to 2011. Only 6% of robberies recorded by the Military Police were thoroughly investigated by the Civil Police and only 4% were solved by the identification of an offender.

The realization that the Brazilian police system needs to be reformed is spreading. There is a growing conviction that the Federal Constitution needs to be changed, redefining at that level how policing and the criminal justice system are organized. However, the likelihood of constitutional change is low for now, for the corporate interests of the Military and Civil Police currently prevail in the Federal Congress.

Note

1. In São Paulo State, the Civil Guard was established in 1926, exclusively dedicated to street policing, and was subordinate to the chief of the Civil Police. In the following years, this model was copied by other states. The Civil Guard was uniformed and worked independently of the Military Police, performing foot, vehicle and horse patrols. Later, the Civil Guard used radio dispatching. It was disbanded by Decree Law No. 667 of 2 July 1969, in the government of General Costa e Silva.

References

Batitucci, E. 2010. A evolução institucional da Polícia no século XIX—Inglaterra, Estados Unidos e Brasil em perspectiva comparada [The institucional development of the police in the nineteenth century: England, United States and Brazil in comparative perspective]. São Paulo. *Revista Brasileira de Segurança Pública* 4(7):30–46.

Bayley, D. 1975. The police and political development in Europe. In *The formation of national states in Western Europe*, ed. C. Tilly, 328–379. Princeton, NJ: Princeton University Press.

Beato, C. 2012. *Crimes e Cidades* [Crimes and cities]. Belo Horizonte. Federal University of Minas Gerais Press.

Costa, A. T.C. 2004. *Entre a lei e a ordem: a reforma das polícias do Rio de Janeiro e de Nova Iorque* [Between law and order: Reform of the police of Rio de Janeiro and New York]. Rio de Janeiro: Fundação Getulio Vargas Press.

Cotta, F. A. 2012. *Matrizes do sistema policial brasileiro* [Brazilian police system matrices]. Belo Horizonte: Crisálida Press.

DATAFOLHA/CRISP. 2013. *Survey Nacional de Vitimização* [National victimization survey]. São Paulo: Author.

Ege, F. T. 2013. *Uma breve história da Polícia no Brasil—revisão da militarização e do caráter oligárquico* [A brief history of the police in Brazil—review of militarization and its oligarchic character]. São Paulo: Clube dos Autores Press.

ENASP. 2012. *Estratégia Nacional de Justiça e Segurança Pública. Relatório Nacional de implementação da Meta 2—um diagnóstico da investigação de homicídios no país* [National strategy of justice and public safety: National report of the implementation of the goal 2: A diagnosis of homicide investigation in the country]. Brasília: Conselho Nacional do Ministério Público [National Council of the Public Ministry].

Holloway, T. H. 1997. *A polícia do Rio de Janeiro: repressão e resistência em uma cidade do século XIX* [Police in Rio de Janeiro:Repression and resistance in a city of the 19th century]. Rio de Janeiro: Fundação Getulio Vargas Press.

Kant de Lima, R. 1995. *A Polícia da cidade do Rio de Janeiro: seus dilemas e paradoxos* [Police in the city of Rio de Janeiro: Their dilemmas and paradoxes]. Rio de Janeiro: Forense Press.

Lima, R. S. 2011. *Entre palavras e números: violência, democracia e segurança pública no Brasil* [Between words and numbers: Violence, democracy and public safety in Brazil]. São Paulo: Alameda Editorial Press.

Misse, M. 2010. A investigação policial no Brasil: resultados gerais de uma pesquisa [The police investigation in Brazil: General results of a research] *Dilemas: Revista de estudos sobre controle social e conflitos. Rio de Janeiro* 3(7):35–50.

Muniz, J., and Paes-Machado, E. 2010. Polícia para quem precisa de Polícia: contribuições aos estudos sobre policiamento [Police for who need police: Contributions to studies on policing]. Salvador. *Cadernos CRH* 23:437–447.

Paixão, A. L. 1982. A organização policial em uma área metropolitana [The police organization in a metropolitan área]. *Dados: Revista de Ciências Sociais Rio de Janeiro* 25(1): 63–85.

Poncioni, P.2005. O modelo professional de Polícia e o modelo de treinamento profissional da futura academia de polícia do estado do Rio de Janeiro [The professional police model and professional training of future police academies in the State Police of Rio de Janeiro]. *Sociedade e Estado* 20(3): 585–610.

Rede Record. 2011. *Video mostra briga entre policiais civis e militaris em Minas Gerais*, February 3. Retrieved from http://noticias.r7.com/cidades/noticias/video-mostra-briga-entre-policiais-civis-e-militares-em-mg-20110203.htm

Riccio, V., Meirelles, M.R., and Muller, A. 2013. Professionalizing the Amazonas military police through training. *Police Practice and Research: An International Journal* 14(4): 295–307.

Santos, J. V. 1997. A arma e a flor: treinamento da organização policial, consenso e violência [The gun and the flower: Training of police organization, consensus and violence]. São Paulo. *Tempo Social: Revista de Sociologia da USP* 9(1): 38–64.

Sapori, L. F. 2007a. *Os desafios da polícia brasileira na implementação da ordem sob a lei* [The challenges of the Brazilian police in the implementation of the order under the law]. In *Polícia, Democracia e sociedade* [Police, democracy and society], ed. Ratton, J. L. and M. Barros, 97–137. Rio de Janeiro: Lumen Juris Press.

Sapori, L. F. 2007b. *Segurança pública no Brasil: desafios e perspectivas* [Public safety in Brazil: Challenges and perspectives]. Rio de Janeiro: Fundação Getulio Vargas Press.

Sapori, L. F., and Andrade, S. C. 2008. A integração policial em Minas Gerais: os desafios da governança da política de segurança pública [Police integration in Minas Gerais: Governance challenges of public safety policy]. *Civitas* 8(3):428–453.

Sapori, L. F., and Andrade, S. C. 2013. Os desafios da governança do sistema policial no Brasil: o caso da política de integração das polícias em Minas Gerais [Governance challenges of the police system in Brazil: The case of the police integration policy in Minas Gerais]. *Revista Brasileira de Segurança Pública* 7(1):102–130.

Sapori, L. F., and Soares, G.A. 2014. *Por que cresce a violência no Brasil?* [Why is violence growing in Brazil?] Belo Horizonte: Autêntica Press.

Soares, L.E. 2007. A política nacional de segurança pública: história, dilemas e perspectivas [The national public safety policy: History, dilemmas and perspectives]. *Estudos Avançados* 21(61):77–97.

Sou da Paz Institute. 2013. *Investigação e esclarecimento de roubos em São Paulo* [Research and clarification of robberies in São Paulo]. 7th Encontro do Fórum Brasileiro de Segurança Pública [7th Meeting of the Brazilian Forum on Public Safety], Cuiabá, July.

UOL Notícias. 2008. *Tropa de choque da PM em confront com policiais civis em grave em SP*, October 16. Retrieved from http://noticias.uol.om.br/cotidiano/2008/10/16/ult5772u1118.jhtm

Hierarchy, Career and Professional Advancement in the Civil Police

3

Vicente Riccio,
André Zogahib,
Janaína Lawall and
Mario Aufiero

Contents

Police in Brazil are a target of constant criticism. Their ineffectiveness is widely recognized, including by public administrators, academics, human rights activists and even police officers who can take a critical view of the status quo. To a great extent, this criticism is levelled at the daily practices of the police, with special emphasis on abuses committed against the population and misconduct by its members. Critics emphasize the low efficiency of the police forces in the prevention, repression and solving of crimes, as well as their low degree of legitimacy in the eyes of the public.

Among the problems listed by these various groups, the question of the organizational model of the Brazilian police stands out. In general, the dichotomy of a police force intended to patrol the streets (the Military Police) and another focused on criminal investigations (Civil Police) does not make for coordinated and effective action. Problems such as conflicts of jurisdiction and overlapping actions occur constantly in their work. Critics also point out that the Military Police have adopted an organizational structure that mimics the Armed Forces, while the Civil Police acts like a legal bureaucracy, which reduces their ability to solve crimes. These problems reflect the norms established by the Brazilian Constitution of 1988 (Article 144), which regulates public safety in the country. Despite these criticisms, counterpressures from the police have prevented the approval of major changes to the current model (Azevedo and Vasconcellos 2011).

Among the criticisms of the organizational model of the Brazilian police are the hierarchies and career paths within them. In Brazil, there are parallel careers within the two branches of policing. The Military Police reproduce the military distinction between officers and the enlisted ranks, commonly called "soldiers." The former are responsible for management, with the highest rank being that of colonel. Ordinary soldiers rank between private and sergeant, and they work on the street. There is no mobility between these two groups, and conflicts between them can be intense. For example, a 1997 strike of the Military Police in Minas Gerais was led by a corporal, and it questioned the existing career structure. The strike arose when salary increases were awarded to officers while the salaries of soldiers remained frozen.

In the case of the Civil Police, the division is between inspectors, who hold bachelor's degrees in law and are responsible for conducting criminal investigations, and investigators and clerks, who carry out the tasks of checking facts and recording the details of cases under the supervision of the inspectors (Lino 2004). In general, entry to this latter career depends on finishing high school, but some Civil Police agencies have started to demand higher education for entry into the career. This depends on the criteria established by each state.

The existence of dual career tracks in policing has been widely questioned in Brazil. Scholarly studies of this issue are recent and seek to explore the contradictions and flaws in the model. The problems that have been identified are not just a matter of administration or human resources. Rather, they are issues of an institutional nature related to the distribution of power within the police, which are also directed at the other organs of the criminal justice system (the judiciary, the public prosecution and the prison system). The model adopted in Brazil defines competences and spheres of power between the two types of forces that are marked by internal disputes between different hierarchical levels of the police, overlapping of responsibilities between them, and conflicts regarding police investigations that are manifested in disagreements between the prosecutors' office and the Civil Police (Sapori 2007).

This chapter examines the Civil Police, which is responsible for investigating crimes in Brazil. The organization adopted by the police in Brazil is based on a very particular model of criminal investigation. Unlike most Western countries, whether of Roman-Germanic or Anglo-Saxon legal tradition, in Brazil there is no clear separation between the phases of investigation and adjudication. In the Brazilian system, the Civil Police both conduct investigations of criminal activity and generate final reports concerning guilt. In this model, there is not only investigation, but also decisions regarding "guilt" with regard to the facts (Misse 2011; Azevedo and Vasconcellos 2011). This dual competence defines the power of the police inspector, with regard to its internal aspect in relation to his subordinates and in relation to the other institutions of the criminal justice system, particularly the public prosecutor.

The aim of this study is to analyze how hierarchy, career aspirations and job satisfaction affect the operations of the Brazilian Civil Police. The research was conducted among the Civil Police of the Amazon region, as part of a project supporting their effort to realign themselves strategically. The chapter examines how these issues are perceived by the members of the force, bearing in mind the different roles performed by the organization. It describes how hierarchical divisions within the Civil Police affect perceptions of the police belonging to the two levels. This analysis allows us to observe the extent to which hierarchy shapes perceptions concerning members' chosen careers and their commitment to the profession. Therefore, it is possible to see the role of this institutional arrangement in the adherence of the police to their professional career. At the end, we discuss issues for further research on the subject in Brazil.

Who Are the Civil Police?

The architecture of the Brazilian security system is defined in Article 144 of the constitution. It establishes the powers of federal entities in the field of public safety (the nation, states and municipalities) and the functions of the Brazilian police forces, by defining their spheres of activity.[1] As regards the Civil Police, they have jurisdiction to investigate criminal infractions, except for military and federal ones, in the various states. Moreover, the constitution itself identifies police inspectors as being responsible for managing the institution.[2]

The main responsibility of the Civil Police is conducting criminal investigations. Its characteristics do not reflect just a way to organize police work; they also reflect the distribution of power within the Civil Police institution and in relation to other organs of the criminal justice system. The outcomes of their investigations provide "instructions" for the other actors, which elsewhere would be typical of the work of prosecutors and judges. The final judgments of the Civil Police on cases have come to dominate their interest, instead of valuing criminal investigations themselves. Their decisions become the first judgment by the state regarding a crime, since the analysis contained in their reports will be reproduced at the judicial stage (Azevedo and Vasconcellos 2011).

The role of the police inspector reflects this arrangement, since the course of his or her work is not only administrative but also "judicial." The work carried out is considered to be part of the judicial process. The criminal investigation model in Brazil contributes directly to this portrayal. The police inspector has a higher position in the hierarchy in relation to others involved in the criminal investigation process.[3]

The division of labor within the Civil Police is also a way to distribute power vertically. All other employees involved in the investigation of crimes, including investigators, clerks responsible for recording what is found and scientific experts[4] are subordinate to the police inspector. The police inspector is responsible for presiding over the investigation and determining final judgments against suspects. Upon completion of their work, they decide whether to send the case on to the public prosecutor. After analysis, prosecutors decide whether to initiate a criminal case against a suspect.[5]

Mostly, this is the model of how investigations work in Brazil. Police inspectors value their total control over cases and insist on retaining superior bureaucratic status in their organization. In the Civil Police, this superiority of inspectors is reinforced by a constitutional requirement regarding educational qualifications for entry into the career: they must have a law degree. This differentiates theirs from any other career path in the institution. In turn, this requirement has favored the "legalization" of decision-making within the Civil Police and contributed to a low-level effectiveness of the core business of the Civil Police: criminal investigations.

Organizational conflicts arising from this model emphasize even more its inefficiencies. But how is this division expressed within the police force? What is the resulting contrast between the perceptions of employees in the "superior" and "inferior" levels of the organization? How are they expressed within the police institution? Does this hierarchical distinction affect perceptions of career paths and commitment to the profession? Our research sought to answer these questions, based on interviews among the Civil Police in the State of Amazonas.

Public Security in Amazonas

The Amazon region covers a great part of Brazil (40%) and is marked by great complexity. While home to the largest forest and the greatest biodiversity on the planet, the region lacks adequate development policies reflecting its size and diversity. The Amazonas has an area of 1,559,161.68 square kilometers and 3,905,483 inhabitants.[6]

The Civil Police of Amazonas, responsible for investigating most crimes affecting the region, has approximately 2,465 employees carrying out their work in 62 municipalities. They are divided among inspectors (332), criminal experts (194), clerks (388), investigators (1,295) and administrative assistants (256). The latter includes career civil servants hired through public competitions and employees hired temporarily by the state government.

Despite great world interest in the Amazon region, criminological studies on the region are few and recent. This is also true of research on policing there. Existing studies on the questions of violence and crime generally cover issues such as the environment, land disputes and issues involving the rights of indigenous people (Loureiro and Guimarães 2007; Sant'Anna and Young 2010; Rabello 2013). These issues are important, but the complexity of the state, whose capital is an industrial hub and has a mining economy in most of its territory, faces many other issues. Moreover, Amazonas borders on Colombia and Peru. They are cocaine producers on a global scale, and many of their export routes pass through Amazonas. As a result, challenges to security institutions are immense. Amazonas, like the whole region, has suffered a significant increase in violence in recent years. The homicide rate has nearly doubled in the region in the last decade due to increased drug trafficking. For example, in 2004 the level of homicides was 16 per 100,000 inhabitants. This number grew to 32 in 2014. Considering the entire country during this period, the homicide rate grew only 10%, from 26 to 29 homicides per 100,000 inhabitants.[7] So, in Amazonas difficulties observed in the country's more populous regions are present, plus there are additional challenges imposed by its vast and varied character and geographical location. But while the workings of the Civil Police take place in a distinctive context, the institutional model of policing in the state is the same as that adopted across the country. Thus, analysis of career-related issues is still likely to reveal issues common to the Brazilian police forces.

The Civil Police of Amazonas

The Civil Police of Amazonas is the arm of the Amazonas State government responsible for the investigation of criminal offences. At their historical origin in the monarchical period, Brazilian police were highly centralized around the royal court based in Rio de Janeiro. The position of police inspector was created in 1841, as part of a move to impose administrative centralization based on court dictates and to control local populations. The police power was essential to this strategy (Bonelli 2009). With the advent of the Republic in 1889, there came a need to organize the police institutions along more republican lines. The Civil Police of Amazonas was officially established only in 1922 (Law 3052/22) in order to adapt to national requirements of the criminal code and criminal procedure of the republican period. In this period, it was not obligatory to have a law degree to hold the position of inspector, since the lack of qualified professionals made it difficult to appoint graduates in remote and isolated regions of the country.

The shift toward current arrangements took place with a constitutional amendment in 1971, which reserved the position of inspector for graduates in law. However, at this time there were still exceptions to the rule, with the so-called *provisionado*, or commissioner, who could carry out the functions in a specific location in the absence of a qualified professional. In the Amazon region, marked by vast areas with difficult access, provisionados were widely employed. The 1988 constitution abolished the provisionados. To hold this position it is required to have a law degree and to pass a competitive public examination (Dantas 2009). The requirement for higher education in order to enter into upper-level career tracks in the Civil Police was now only for inspectors and scientific experts.

However, the organization of the Civil Police of Amazonas underwent a major change in 2009. In that year, further requirements for higher education were adopted for entry into the posts of detective and clerk.[8] Thus, the demand for university education—but not necessarily a law degree—has become common for investigators and clerks. From then on, many professionals with university degrees entered the Civil Police lower down in the formal hierarchy. There are now two career tracks in the institution that require university education, but they have different duties, status and levels of power.

Although the expansion of higher education requirements drew positive responses among the public and security professionals, there is no definitive conclusion about its effectiveness. Other research has concluded that skill among police is based primarily on experience, which is why higher education does not have a significant impact on actual practice (Bittner 1990). Moreover, practice is much more important in the construction of the identity of the police than is academic training (Bayley and Bittner 1984; Oberweis and Musheno 2001). Additionally, it should be noted that the evidence on educational requirements in policing is still insufficient for making more definitive recommendations as to its adoption (Skogan and Frydl 2004).

The point relevant to the current study is that new demands for educated employees have blurred somewhat old distinctions between the two major levels of hierarchy within the Civil Police. Before 2009, there was no requirement of higher education for the careers of detective and clerk in the Civil Police of Amazonas. The change to the established criteria makes it possible for more qualified professionals to conduct investigative work and the administrative routines of police inquiries. However, these more qualified professionals cannot aspire to the organization's management posts, which are in the hands of the police inspectors. Thus, we see in the Civil Police a process of renewal that started with the competition for entry into the ranks of clerks and investigators being reserved for those with higher education. This group of newcomers with greater cultural capital may have more critical views, in comparison to those who came before them. This raises the question of how the two groups perceive their satisfaction with and appreciation of careers in the Civil Police.

The Amazonas Survey

Our research with the Civil Police of Amazonas was conducted between November and December 2013, in the context of an effort by the organization to realign itself strategically. The research focused on employees of all levels. The survey was conducted with the authorization of the institution and by means of a web survey, which could be completed using the Internet. Web administration of the survey was chosen due to the vast size of the state and budget constraints on carrying out a traditional survey. It enabled us to (a) increase the number and geographical diversity of staff members who would be able to participate, (b) expedite the work of collecting and tabulating the data, and (c) reduce costs. Web administration is often recommended when the study population is well known, all potential respondents have access to the network and they have email addresses. Of course, web administration also has limitations that merit attention, in order to avoid jeopardizing the survey (Joncew et al. 2014).

The questionnaire distributed to members of the Civil Police was based on a survey developed by Skogan (2015) for research in the Chicago Police Department. It focused on relationships between police and the community, especially minorities, as well as problems of procedural justice involving police officers and their superiors. The questionnaire was translated into Portuguese and adapted to the Brazilian scene. The questionnaire included questions concerning (a) officers' demographic profiles, (b) their views of violence, justice and crime, (c) perceptions of their relationship with the community, (d) their views on the use of force, (e) assessments of the structure of the Civil Police, (f) reports of relationships with other components of the criminal justice system and (g) measures of career satisfaction.

This chapter examines aspects of professional development in the Civil Police. The independent variable considered here is our respondent's position in the institutional hierarchy, while the dependent variables measure issues related to job satisfaction, job commitment and satisfaction with working conditions. Respondents are divided into two groups: those in the upper hierarchical level (level 1), composed of inspectors and experts, and those in the lower hierarchical level (level 2), who are investigators and clerks.

Data collection took place in November and December 2013. Responses were obtained from 287 participants from a universe of 2,465 employees, for a 12% response rate.[9] Based on administrative data on characteristics of Amazonas Civil Police, respondents to the survey were broadly representative with respect to gender, function/position and length of career. However, while this survey provides a useful portrait of Civil Police employees in Amazonas, further research will be required to speak more generally about Brazil as a whole.

Profile of Participants

Members of the Civil Police in Amazonas are young. This was the result of reforms culminating in the hiring of many new employees beginning in 2009. Overall, 65% of respondents were under 40 years of age. As this implies, many respondents were in the early or middle stages of their careers. Among the respondents, more than 90% had been in the Civil Police for no more than 15 years. (These figures match administrative data.) There was a significant female contingent as well; 34% of respondents were women. The effects of reform can also be seen with regards to education: 96% of those responding held higher education degrees and 80% reported post-graduate training. In Brazil, a bachelor's degree involves four years of study. There is a further, intermediate level between a bachelor's degree and the equivalent of a master's degree, which is a course of study providing specific occupational training after completion of a bachelor's degree, but is not a master's degree.[10] In the Civil Police of Amazonas, many employees have attained this further level of education because it can be a requirement for further promotions; this was also established in 2009.

As regards to race, a majority (55%) declared themselves mulatto, and 39% as white. Others identified themselves as Afro-Brazilian (3%), Oriental (2%) and indigenous (11%). In short, in Amazonas the Civil Police is a young force, with a high level of education, it is majority male, and it is majority mulatto.

Hierarchy and Career Satisfaction

For this analysis, ranks in the Civil Police were divided into hierarchical level 1 (inspectors and experts) and level 2 (clerks and investigators). The former group included 51 inspectors (18%) and 12 experts (4%), and they constituted 22% of the total sample. The second-level group of respondents was composed of investigators (46% of the total) and clerks (31%).

The survey included several questions gauging the career commitments of staff members. They were asked to rate their overall job satisfaction with the question "How do you rate your level of satisfaction with your career in the Civil Police?" They could do so on a five-point scale, with responses ranging from very satisfied to totally dissatisfied. Many respondents clustered near the middle of this range. Overall, 25% were very or fairly satisfied, and 31%

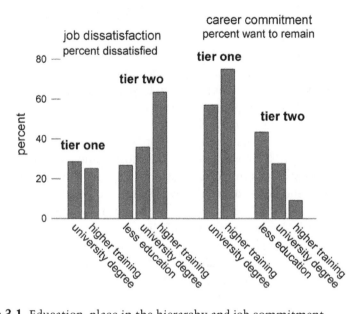

Figure 3.1 Education, place in the hierarchy and job commitment

reported being largely or totally dissatisfied. Not surprisingly, top managers—the inspectors and experts who run the organization—were more satisfied than those below them in the hierarchy. However, across all employees, those with *more* education were *more dissatisfied* with their careers, by a notable margin. This stems from the organizational dilemma described above, that created by changes in the recruitment of investigators and clerks, the line staff who actually conduct and document investigations. The results of this can be seen in Figure 3.1.

As Figure 3.1 documents, new and more educated line staff members dominate the pool of disgruntled employees. Many are now university educated, but they are excluded from opportunities for advancement by the two-tier hierarchy that dominates the Civil Police. Among investigators and clerks, the more educated they are, the more unhappy they are about their career prospects. Among the most educated, those with some post-university qualification, more than 60% of the second-tier staff indicated that they were largely or totally dissatisfied with their careers. They have nowhere to go.

The organizational dilemma created by the post-2009 reforms in hiring for the Civil Police is illustrated even more starkly in the right-hand panels of Figure 3.1. It charts responses to the question "How do you evaluate your desire to continue in the career of the Civil Police of Amazonas?" Respondents could choose among a number of categories designed to elicit the strength of their commitment to remaining on the job. Possible answers to the question (there were five possible responses) ranged from "I wish to continue in my job" to "I sometimes think of leaving my job" and others indicated their intention to eventually leave.

In this instance, there were very large differences in career commitment between first- and second-tier employees *and* among educational groups. The two factors worked quite differently, as can be seen in Figure 3.1. Among the leadership, more than 85% planned to stay on the job or on occasion "considered" leaving; the comparable figure for detectives and clerks was about 65%. Also among senior managers, the more educated they were, the more committed they were to their career. In the most highly educated category, 75% of tier-one managers intended to stay on the job. However, among the second-tier staff, the more educated they were the more they wanted to leave. At the maximum, among line staff with a post-university university qualification, only 9% wished to stay in the Civil Police.

Some of this dissatisfaction was about their salaries. This can be seen in responses to a third question regarding their satisfaction with their paycheck. Respondents were asked to rank their satisfaction with their pay on a five-point scale ranging from very satisfied to totally dissatisfied. Many were fairly dissatisfied with their economic situation. Overall, about 55% of those surveyed were "slightly" satisfied or worse on the five-point scale. Top-tier managers were somewhat happier than lower-level staff, by about 10 percentage points. Again, the striking finding with regard to pay was the high level of dissatisfaction with their pay among detectives and clerks (this is not shown in Figure 3.1). Second-tier employees with less than a university degree were the most likely to say they were very satisfied with their salary, but among the others hardly anyone did. Among university graduates slotted into the second level in the hierarchy of the Civil Police, more than 60% were largely or totally dissatisfied with their pay. They find themselves perpetually confined to the lower ranks of the organization, with no real opportunities for advancement, while holding university degrees (and many had more training than that) yet not making a satisfactory salary.

Conclusion

Our survey uncovered marked discrepancies among the career prospects of members of the Civil Police. Senior managers were largely satisfied with their careers, a situation that was created by ensuring that they will always dominate the top-level positions in policing. They were less happy about their salaries, which are considerably higher than those of second-tier staff members, but perhaps they were comparing their civil service pay with that of the managers of comparably large organizations in other sectors of society. A big majority of senior managers were committed to remaining in their careers.

At the bottom of the hierarchy, Civil Police employees were more dissatisfied on every measure, and their level of dissatisfaction was tied to their training. The more educated they were, the more dissatisfied they were with their jobs. The more education they had, the more unhappy they were about their salaries. And the more educated they were, the more they hoped to leave.

This organizational dilemma seems *constitutionally* constructed. In the Civil Police, the superiority of inspectors is reinforced by the constitutional requirement that top managers have special qualifications that reserve top management slots for themselves. Others must remain on a career path that does not promise a bright future. When after 2009 the Amazonas Civil Police began hiring large numbers of seemingly "more qualified" second-tier staff, they filled those positions with employees who can see no path forward in the organization. This was further encouraged by national policies, which paid for the courses that advanced the educational level of the staff, but supported them to take this training in fields that did not qualify them for advancement up the management ranks. The hierarchical model that characterizes the Civil Police in Amazonas, and perhaps elsewhere in Brazil, has "built in" a level of organizational dysfunction that may limit its effectiveness in its core tasks.

Notes

1. Article 144 of the Federal Constitution establishes the existence of five types of police force in Brazil—(1) the Federal Police, (2) the Federal Highway Police, (3) the Federal Railway Police, (4) the Civil Police, and (5) the Military Police—and the Fire Brigade. The Federal Police are responsible for crimes related to the nation and its public institutions, as well as interstate and international infractions. It acts in cases involving international drug trafficking and carries out policing of borders. The Highway and Railway Police are the federal government's responsibility and they patrol the roads and railways. The Civil Police investigate crimes and the Military Police conduct public patrolling; both are the responsibility of state governments.
2. Pursuant to Art. 144, paragraph 4: "§ 4 The civil police, under the direction of career police inspectors, are responsible for, subject to the competence of the Union, judicial police functions and the investigation of criminal offenses, except for military ones."
3. This characteristic of the Brazilian model inspires police inspectors to seek the same bureaucratic status as prosecutors and the judiciary. Belonging in a legal career rather than a police career leads them to claim parity in salary with the public prosecution and the judiciary: the best-paid sectors of the Brazilian public service. However, this is unlikely to happen because of budget constraints in the states.
4. Experts are responsible for producing scientific evidence in police inquiries and attend to inspectors' requests. Although they are at a higher level of the Civil Police career, experts do not have the same power as the inspectors, who are responsible for the management of the organization.
5. The power of the police inspector can be seen also in the fact that the position of Police Chief or Chief Inspector, responsible for the management of the institution, is only accessible to career inspectors.
6. Available at www.ibge.gov.br on 02/05/2016.
7. Available at www.ipea.gov.br/portal/images/stories/PDFs/nota_tecnica/160322_nt_17_atlas_da_violencia_2016_finalizado.pdf on 03/22/2016.
8. In Brazil, a higher education degree is the equivalent of a bachelor's degree in the United States.
9. Of the 287 respondents, five were administrative assistants and one contributed no responses; they are not considered in the analysis presented here, reducing N to 281. Skips in

the questionnaire were allowed for some questions, so the number of valid responses varies according to the question. Also, some police officers found selected questions to be very sensitive and chose not to respond.
10. In the survey, 6% of employees reported holding a master's degree, 1% (three employees) reported having a doctorate.

References

Azevedo, R. G., and Vasconcellos, F. B. 2011. O Inquérito Policial em Questão—situação atual e a percepção dos Delegados de Polícia sobre as fragilidades do modelo brasileiro de investigação criminal [The police inquiry under Question: The current situation and the perception of police inspectors about the fragilities of the Brazilian model of crime investigation]. *Revista Sociedade e Estado* 26: 59–75.

Bayley, D., and Bittner, E. 1984. Learning the skills of policing. *Law and Contemporary Problems* 47: 35–59.

Bittner, E. 1990. *Aspects of police work.* Boston: Northeastern University Press.

Bonelli, M. G. 2009. Perfil Social e Carreira dos Delegados de Polícia [Police inspectors' social profile and career]. In *Delegados de Polícia* [Police inspectors], ed. M. T. Sadek, 22–50. Rio de Janeiro: Centro Edelstein de Pesquisas Sociais.

Dantas, H. 2009. A Formação Acadêmica dos Delegados de Polícia [The academic formation of police inspectors]. In *Delegados de Polícia* [Police inspectors], ed. M. T. Sadek, 51–71. Rio de Janeiro: Centro Edelstein de Pesquisas Sociais.

Joncew, C., Cendon, B. V., and Ameno, N. 2014. Websurveys como método de pesquisa [Websurveys as research methods]. *Informação & Informação* 19: 192–218. www.uel.br/revistas/ informação.

Lino, P. R. 2004. Police education and training in a global society: A Brazilian overview. *Police Practice and Research* 5: 125–136.

Loureiro, V., and Guimarães, E. C. 2007. Reflexões sobre a Pistolagem e a Violência na Amazônia [Reflections about hired killers and violence in the Amazon]. *Revista Direito GV3* 1: 221–246.

Misse, M. 2011. O Papel do Inquérito Policial no Processo de Incriminação no Brasil: algumas reflexões a partir de uma pesquisa [The role of the police inquiry in the Brazilian incrimination process: Some reflections based on research]. *Revista Sociedade e Estado* 26: 15–27.

Oberweis, T., and Musheno, M. 2001. *Knowing rights: State actors' stories of power, identity and morality.* Aldershot: Ashgate.

Rabello, A. C. 2013. Amazônia: uma fronteira volátil [Amazon: A volatile frontier]. *Estudos Avançados* 27: 213–235.

Sant'Anna, A. A., and Young, C. E. F. 2010. Direitos de Propriedade, Desmatamento e Conflitos Rurais na Amazônia [Property rights, deforesting and rural conflicts in the Amazon]. *Economia Aplicada* 14: 381–393.

Sapori, L. F. 2007. *Segurança pública no Brasil: Desafios e perspectivas* [Public security in Brazil: Challenges and perspectives]. Rio de Janeiro: Editora Fundação Getulio Vargas.

Skogan, W. 2015. Surveying police officers. In *Envisioning criminology: Researchers on research as a process of discovery*, ed. M. Maltz and S. Rice, 109–118. New York: Springer.

Skogan, W., and Frydl, K. 2004. *Fairness and effectiveness in policing: The evidence.* Washington: National Research Council.

Police Culture and Organizational Reform in Brazilian Policing[1]

4

Eduardo Cerqueira Batitucci, Marcus Vinícius Gonçalves da Cruz, Amanda Matar de Figueiredo and Letícia Godinho de Souza

Contents

This chapter examines policy and strategic decision-making in the Brazilian police. It focuses on the operational and institutional characteristics of the Civil and Military Police of the state of Minas Gerais, and how those characteristics affected the planning and implementation of reforms in the areas of community policing and criminal investigations. In the Brazilian system, police are organized at the state level, which means that they are usually very large organizations with employees numbering in the thousands. The Military Police are responsible for street patrol, while the Civil Police investigate crimes and report their findings to state prosecutors. But while they are distinct organizations, both share the cultural and organizational characteristics that are conventionally labeled as the "professional-bureaucratic model of policing." This is especially true in terms of their shared crime-fighting ideology and use of technological approaches to crime control (Batitucci 2011).

In this chapter, we examine these characteristics of police occupational culture as they impact the implementation of community policing and criminal investigation initiatives. These responsibilities represent two of the strongest challenges facing Brazilian police today—their legitimacy deficit, from the community perspective, and their inefficacy with regard to fulfilling the obligations of the criminal justice system.

Dilemmas of the Incorporation of the Professional-Bureaucratic Model

Walker (1977) details the principal elements of the professional-bureaucratic model of policing, as it is known in the United States. These include the development of a professional self-awareness, through the production of professional literature and the foundation of police associations and unions; militarization as a control strategy, with an emphasis on discipline; administrative reform, with the introduction of Taylorist and Fordist principles common in the private sector; the bureaucratization of police organizations; professional improvement through police academies and the use of institutional criteria for the recruitment and promotion of officers; and the intensive use of technology, especially that which enhances police mobility and communication (e.g., automobiles, telephones and radios).

It is without a doubt that police activity in contemporary Brazil, especially where the Military Police are concerned, was strongly influenced by this model and its organizational and technological elements. Some of the greatest innovations the Brazilian police have experienced in the last 50 years were based on those strategies. For instance, throughout the 1980s, the Military Police in Brazil heavily invested in the creation of command and control systems, usually based in computerized dispatch communication centers, that increased their mobility and accessibility while maintaining the logic and values of the military structure they inherited from the Brazilian colonial past.

In this period, discretion by frontline officers was not considered a problem, since the police elite believed in the force of the military values and the symbolic control exercises by their military-style hierarchy. Police officers were encouraged not to fraternize with civilians, and the job was perceived as simply a matter of following orders. Routes and patrol locations were predefined and crime-oriented, and most of the everyday work of officers was confined to responding to incidents called in through a centralized dispatch service. "Radio-patrol," as police slang calls it, contributed to the construction, by the frontline police culture, of the distorted view of the community that comes of dealing continually only with crises throughout their whole working day.

In the American context, Wilson and Kelling (2000, p. 10) suggested that this model of professionalization completely changed the relationship between officers and the communities they serve. Professionalism contributed to minimizing the importance of everyday contacts between officers and the community, and maximizing a rational, "scientific" approach to management that stressed officers' accountability to objective indicators and not to the experiences relayed upwards by officers themselves. In the Brazilian case, the institutionalization of this model strengthened a pre-existing characteristic of policing. This was a culture marked by the prevalence of the discipline of law in the training of the officer corps, and militarism in their ideology and operational structure. As cultural components born from the historical traditions of the Brazilian police, these two frameworks intersect to create an abstract conception of the police role, which symbolically devalues the operational activity of frontline officers. Their knowledge and experience is often considered irrelevant. Instead, police leaders hold a quasi-aristocratic view of policing, one in which "management cops" (Reuss-Ianni 1993) are considered superior vis-à-vis frontline police, when it comes to professional competence and dealing with complexity (Batitucci 2015).

According to Walker (1977, p. 64), the long-term result of the spread of this model of policing in America was a fundamental shift in the nature of the police mandate. It became one of the ideological and operational dominance of the notion that the role of the police is to fight crime. Greater reliance on seemingly objective, tangible measures of their effectiveness, including statistics such as reported crimes and the number of arrests, reinforce this definition of effectiveness. Activities dedicated to "community service" lost importance to the police, who saw themselves engaged in an endless war against an invisible enemy.

In Brazil, the police mandate as defined in legislation and in public opinion (Muniz and Proença Jr. 2007; Muniz and Silva 2010) is vague. This has widened and made contestable the boundary between what is and what is not appropriate policing. This has in turn allowed police to meet a very wide range of demands in Brazil, including those centered on the idea of fighting crime and those that are relevant to the mediation of everyday conflicts, civil defense, traffic control and even social assistance, among many others. Their movement into all of these social spaces has given police an overwhelming presence in the Brazilian society. On the other hand, openness in the definition of what policing should be has sidestepped clarifying debate over what professional policing should look like in 21st-century Brazil, both conceptually and in operational practice.

This problem becomes evident in discussions of how police can police in a way that enables them to regain their legitimacy, and how they can enhance their technical proficiency in addressing conventional crime problems. To illustrate this, we examine issues surrounding the adoption of community policing by the Military Police and new investigative procedures by the Civil Police.

Community Policing and the Military Police

The idea of community policing in the Military Police dates back to the early 1990s. The thinking at that time focused on the need for "a police that contemplates the attitudes of partnership, cooperation and interaction with community leaders," and to seek to offer a new focus on policing which, instead of solving "random problems," would work within priorities established in partnership with the community (PMMG 1993). The main justification for adopting community policing practices was to meet the needs of the police in dealing with social changes, in particular the end of the dictatorship and the implementation of a new Brazilian federal constitution. Another objective was to secure through these partnerships new and alternative sources of funding to sustain the police. From a policing standpoint, the Military Police during that period did not make any substantive changes that would institutionalize these initiatives. There was at first no movement toward creating community councils nor any special training for officers responsible for community policing. Any changes in policing in this early period were confined to thinking about the police role in a newly re-created democracy and not in any concrete institutional changes. The Military Police lacked, at that time, the cultural and professional elements necessary for adopting these kinds of innovations, especially any changes involving frontline police officers. This was due in part to the prevalence of a military culture in the organization (FJP 2014).

By the end of the 1990s, the Military Police did formalize the creation of community councils within their regional commands. However, the councils that were created functioned as organizational "add-ons," created by regional commands in order to satisfy guidelines established by their organization. This did not bode well for the councils, for the regions were not driven by a conception of why and how there should be community involvement in public safety (PMMG 1999). In practice, the Military Police did not recognize any autonomy exercised by the community in their participation, and instead accepted them solely as a legitimizing device that could not challenge the institutional assumptions of the police. Souza (1998) observed that, in a broader perspective, there was no institutionalization of community policing as a philosophy and a community safety strategy. The Military Police were not able to internalize the concept, the values it represented and the operational activities required to promote any real change in their policing style. In her opinion, community policing remained isolated within the organization, any successes it showed were dependent upon the initiative of specific commanders, no attention was paid to challenging cultural views and operational practices that ran counter to a community-oriented philosophy, and it faced a low acceptance among both frontline officers and managers.

But by 2002 there emerged a new perspective on community policing. It emphasized the creation of cooperative partnerships through active community participation in all aspects of policing processes, from planning to action. The public would have an autonomous role and would not be tied to the police or their programs or be dependent on police funding. This was seen as speaking to the legitimacy problems of the police. A Military Police memo explained, "community participation in planning and decisions improves the technological and professional profile of the police, because of the improvement in the levels of satisfaction, sense of security, quality of life and reduction of crime and disorder" (PMMG 2002). The new guidelines advised special attention to the great challenges that these new perspectives implied, especially concerning the police themselves: their culture, methods and management processes. The guidelines were presented with a clear normative focus and did not prescribe specific structures, organizational change strategies, training content or allocation of police officers and other resources. For example, in addition to the community councils, the new perspective on policing included reference to stations designed from the experience of Japanese *Kobans*. Adopting these would call for the long-term assignment of officers, involving them in continuous and ongoing community policing activities in order to reinforce the relationship between police and community. However, as FJP (2014) observes, the Military Police ended by suggesting that the community would be responsible for the construction of the stations, creating a virtually insurmountable obstacle to their implementation, especially where they would be needed in the poorest and most vulnerable communities. To date, not a single police station has been built following this model.

From 2004 onwards, new operational tactics were developed, based on specialized patrols or squadrons. "Active Prevention Patrols" (PPA) were the first, conceived of to

> work under the primary objective of reinforcing the population's ties of reciprocity, solidarity and participation, through continuous visits by the police to the population most in need of the police services (vulnerable citizens and victims of crimes), surpassing the traditional concept of an "abstract consumer for the police Service."
>
> (PMMG 2004, p. 12)

However, the guidelines suggested, paradoxically, that PPAs should be "preferably equipped with heavy weapons" to be able to meet its "secondary missions," which were described as "repressive actions and support to tactical squadrons."

GEPAR, jargon for "Specialized Patrol Squadrons for Vulnerable Communities," was created in the early 2000s. This unit was developed to accomplish two missions: community policing and the prevention of homicide in violent slums. They were described as complementing preventive action through social policies. In 2005, the Military Police broadened the field for GEPAR, describing it as a "new form" of policing within the favelas, using a problem-oriented approach. Note that, despite endorsing the concept of a "problem-oriented policing," some "problems" were predefined in guidelines for the program. They prioritized violent crimes, drug trafficking, the seizure of illegal firearms and control of wars between juvenile gangs. Moreira and Godinho (2010) examined the connection between GEPAR and social policies in favela areas in the city of Belo Horizonte. They conducted a survey of all of the officers involved in GEPAR until that time, some 230 of them. They concluded that a major problem with the program was that only the commanders of GEPAR had regular contact with social service agencies. They reported that there was great difficulty in arranging interactions with the community and mobilizing community leaders to get them involved in partnership projects, as well as a number of deficiencies related to specific training and logistical issues.

By the end of the 2000s, problem-oriented policing had become the overall conceptual framework for the institutionalization of community-based policies within the Military Police. However, it was defined in a particular way. "Problem-oriented policing recognizes that criminal behavior is a result of an interaction between the individual and the environment. This highlights that opportunity can be considered the main cause of crime" (PMMG 2011). Thus, by identifying the problem as opportunity and the solution its management, the program's guidelines skewed problem solving toward a specific set of social dynamics and to a specific conception of policing based in situational crime prevention (Felson 1996) and the routine activities approach (Cohen and Felson 1979). Lost from view was community involvement in the development of priorities and solutions for those problems.

In conclusion, the Military Police invested a large institutional effort in the design, development and implementation of community policing in order to deal with the legitimacy questions facing the police in Brazil. This effort, however, was hampered by their institutional legacy, rooted as they were in a legalistic and militaristic framework for actually conducting operations.

Criminal Investigations in the Civil Police

For Roberto Kant de Lima (Kant de Lima 1995, 1989) the Brazilian legal tradition has two main features. On the one hand, it is an accusatorial system that publicly investigates while preserving a role for defense of the accused. The accused is presumed to be innocent, and the function of the legal process is to draw together information enabling the court to be convinced of his or her guilt or innocence while protecting the accused. On the other hand, the Brazilian tradition also has the features of an inquisitorial system. This in one in which, before the prosecutor's complaint is filed with a court, the Civil Police performs an investigation. The legal system does not state the fact, but assumes its probability, that the accused is guilty, and the *inquisitorial* phase constitutes a search for evidence by the police to ensure that this presumption is true. From this vantage point, the system's concern is with injury to the public interest and not with the rights of the accused. So, the Brazilian Code of Criminal Procedure, despite claiming that the process is accusatorial and conforming therefore to the constitutional provisions of equality and balance between the parties and the due process of law, states that the judicial process may be preceded by an extrajudicial procedure, conducted by the Civil Police, of an inquisitorial nature supposedly under the supervision of the prosecutor and the judge.

The pioneering research on the modern Civil Police in Brazil is that by Paixão (1982), Paixão, Martins and Sapori (1992), Kant de Lima (1989, 1995), Oliveira (2004) and Mingaardi (1992). All of them rely on ethnographic projects conducted in units of Brazilian Civil Police during the 1980s. Their work identified two strands of work within the Civil Police, responsibilities which have historically been described as a dichotomy that is contradictory: on one hand, there is the conducting of criminal investigations, and on the other, dealing with the formal and legal requirements of the police report that is made to the prosecutor, the *inquérito policial* (IP). With slight variations, the workflow in a Civil Police precinct is described as follows: the victim or the Military Police registers a complaint. Next, the *delegado*[2] (the person in charge of the case) becomes aware of the incident and dispatches a group of police investigators. Once they have verified the appropriateness of proceeding formally, an IP is initiated. This is usually under the coordination of an *escrivão*, always formally presided over by the *delegado*. The *escrivão* sends work orders to the investigators, and coordinates interviews with victims, witnesses and suspects. Usually, he is also in charge of gathering together the pieces of evidence and organizing the information that is collected. Once the investigation is over, the *delegado* prepares a final report, which is forwarded to the court. He may request more time for investigation, suggest that the suspect is guilty of specific offenses, or suggest that the IP be terminated in the absence of sufficient evidence to pursue the case further.

However, in his research in the field, Paixão (1982, p. 74) found that these formal procedures did not describe accurately the actual practice of police investigations. Instead, they were oriented "on the one hand, by organizational assessments of the actual legal aspects of the case, and on the other, by the police theories knowledge about the nature of crime and its perpetrators." The result was that, as one police investigator affirmed, "when the investigation is initiated, it is almost ready. We already know who the criminal is" (1982, p. 74).

This highlights the important role played by stereotyping and the symbolic construction of the prototypical criminal, and his contrast to the "good" citizen (Paixão 1982, pp. 74–76). In the everyday practice of the police, there is a great deal of "correctional detention," in which people are arrested for a reason that is tangential to an actual offense. For example, officers do this "to give a lesson" to someone who is improperly behaving or to extract information from them about other ongoing criminal activities. This serves a second feature of actual police investigations, which is their reliance on networks of informants who feed them with insider information about the world of crime (see Bittner 1967). This often uncorroborated intelligence also leads to arrests and detention.

Therefore, there can be a constant tension between what is "legal" and must be required and what is "possible" to require in a case. In some instances, the police select where the law can be applied and where it should not be applied. By doing so, the police protect the image of the judicial and legal systems, which remains seemingly "within the law," while the police are seen to constantly violate or distort it (Kant de Lima 1995, p. 52). The apparent criminal's confession becomes a key element justifying the stereotypes that drive investigations, leading it, in the author's view, to legitimize the use of physical violence as a method of investigation. A consequence is that the police turn into an agency that unofficially arbitrates or tries and punishes sectors of Brazilian society for whom the formal judicial process is often unavailable (Kant de Lima 1995, pp. 84–85). As a result, some of the most important issues concerning the Civil Police in Brazil arise from the daily activities that make up criminal investigations. They reveal important elements for understanding the place investigations occupy in the criminal justice system.

Civil Police define in their everyday practices who are the suspects, and they often do so based on stereotypes mainly when dealing with poor people. Then the important aspect of their job is to find them guilty. In a culture based on an inquisitorial model, this is an open road to arbitrary practices. Rodrigues (2011, p. 90) illustrates this, in the words of a PCMG police investigator she interviewed: "here the goal is to find a criminal and that he makes a confession. That is what is important. The soul of the investigation is this." Thus, establishing guilt of those caught up in this process is the endpoint of the police investigation. Miranda, Oliveira and Paes (2010, p. 134) made the same point in research with police in Rio de Janeiro. For those interviewed, "Suspects are guilty *a priori*, because they will not confess, or will lie to protect themselves." The presumption of guilt orients expectations by the police of a truth that they only need to "confirm."

All of this points to a large degree of ritualism in the investigations of the Civil Police. Rodrigues (2011, p. 91) draws attention to the irrelevance associated with actual investigations, since any substantive aspects related to it as a means to solving a crime is replaced by a systematic production of reports (field communications, interviews, confessions, service orders). Zilli and Vargas (2013, p. 630) highlight the same point, pointing the "notarial character of the IP, which overlaps the dynamism and technicality of investigations—relegating to testimonial evidence much greater importance than to the so-called technical evidence."

This problem tends to become more severe where demands for productivity and efficiency result in performance appraisal management systems that push for finalistic results—such as reported IPs and other indicators of crime management. In this situation, it is common to press for "productivity over quality of investigation and the substitution of the discretionary power of the police by the detailed specification of its performance." Thus, as pointed out by Rodrigues (2011, p. 126), it is common to find investigators spending more time writing field reports than conducting field investigations. There are *escrivães* who carry out four, five hearings per day; and *delegados* only dealing with writing IPs' conclusions and losing any real connection to the actual crime investigation. So, as noted by Misse et al. (2010, p. 84) and Azevedo and Vasconcellos (2011, p. 73), the actual police investigation becomes a ceremonial and bureaucratic act, to the detriment of investigative and analytical evidence gathering, through prioritizing the search for a suspect and only secondarily actually conducting investigations.

Our research on the Civil Police was conducted during 2013–2014 and involved systematic observation of the day-to-day activities in police units and focus groups with *delegados*, *escrivães* and field investigators. This revealed that the course of action in police investigations is an intuitive one. There is no procedural guidance for officers enforced by the organization that leads them to apply any standardized institutional expertise to work in complex cases. The "vision" and "experience" of the individual police officer, driven by community pressure and dynamics of crime in the area, guide institutional priorities and work process. There is no institutional knowledge management, and oral tradition and on-the-job learning are the dominant forms of socialization of new police officers. Criminal stereotypes and work guidelines are informally generated by the local culture of police districts, and are informally passed along to new police officers through socialization. The central Civil Police Academy exerts just a secondary level of socialization, and largely a ceremonial one with little substantive grip on actual practice.

Observations of field investigations and interviews with police investigators instead reveal practice that fails to recognize and treat the crime scene as its central focus. In homicide cases, for example, it was unusual that one police team concentrated on solving a particular crime. Instead, there was institutionalized detachment between the teams responsible for preliminary investigations (those related to the crime scene) and the teams responsible for the follow-up investigations based on later developments. *Delegados* usually were not present at crime scene investigations and knew about them only through police field reports. But another theme that emerged from interviews and focus groups was the limited effectiveness of the reports that were produced. They tended to meet formal requirements but had marginal utility in actually clarifying the dynamics of the crime they described. At the crime scene, as well as in other areas of the investigative process and the routines of operational units, there was a great deal of improvisation and a lack of dialogue between investigators. Actually, secrecy among them was the more dominant mode, since information and knowledge was hoarded by individual investigators, not shared professionally.

Aware of this criticism, in the second half of 2014 the chief of the Civil Police established an experimental police unit that was to test new approaches to investigations. It focused on homicide cases arising in a specific area of the city of Belo Horizonte, a city of three million that is the capital of the state of Minas Gerais. The innovations to be tested included systematic crime analysis in their area of responsibility, focusing on the construction of network maps of drug and gang-related activity, and a team approach to the investigative process. For the first time, *delegados*, investigators, *escrivães* and crime-scene investigators were to work together on particular homicide cases. Each team was solely responsible for their case, from beginning to end. They were to share all of the information they collected and the responsibility for all the reports they produced.

The experimental unit worked on 18 homicide cases in a four-month period, during which we were able to follow their work. We concluded that teamwork among the police officers had positive effects on the routines and work processes of the experimental unit. They also focused more on the specific facts and circumstances of their cases. The knowledge they exchanged proved crucial to the performance of the individuals involved and on their understanding of the collective benefits of investigative work. Their formal duties were conducted with greater quality, and the investigators perceived an increase in their understanding of the complexities involved in the cases they investigated. This shift in the focus of their work encouraged quality investigations and less focus on the bureaucratic formalities of the IP process. There was consensus among all officers involved that they were doing better police work.

Although the majority of opinion inside and outside the organization was positive, the initiative lasted only four months and was then discontinued. This was largely due to the opposition of the prevailing traditional culture of the Civil Police. To date, no substantive changes have been made in the way in which investigative units work in Minas Gerais.

Conclusion

The dual goals of building legitimacy and increasing efficacy remain a problem for police in Brazil. From a cultural standpoint, it is clear that the Military Police is not convinced of the necessity or operational utility of community policing, despite great discussion and broad support for it. There remains a clear disconnection between policy discussion and daily policing. The actual implementation of programs and policies is often discontinuous, faced with competition for resources with traditional police activities. The Civil Police have not been able to allocate needed personnel and other resources. Even in the case of police officers who are directly involved, there is great suspicion about community policing, and even ignorance of its conceptual underpinnings. On a day-to-day basis, many of the activities that are described as community policing are actually traditional police practices, especially those directly related to the professional model. Implementation of most community policing policies is in the discretionary hands of local commanders, who by virtue of a more or less personal attachment to the proposals, either boost it or not. To the extent they are driven by performance management indicators and evaluated based on them, it is very difficult for managers to cope with the resource demands of community policing programs at the operational level. Few officers are motivated to participate in community policing activities.

Thus, our conclusion is that, despite apparently large efforts to implement a robust community police program over the past 15 years, to the Military Police these activities still face ritual, cultural and institutional difficulties. As is evident in our analysis, efforts in Minas Gerais toward organizational decentralization of command have not reached frontline officers and have not affected the core activity of police. It is a movement restricted to the management level of the organization, a movement with the objective of increasing its capacity for command in an increasingly complex environment. The discretion of the frontline police officers to carry out community-oriented activities has never been emphasized.

These findings support the thesis of dissociation between control and discretion advanced by Kelling and Moore (1988); or, to put it in another way, between planning and operational activity. By discussing elaborately the academic and technical aspects of community policing without developing organizational mechanisms to connect theory with practice, the leadership of the Military Police deepened the void between concept and action, and limited the breadth and depth that central office policies could have. In this context, community policing could be understood through the concept of institutional isomorphism. DiMaggio and Powell (2005) suggest that innovations are more often put forward to construct political and normative legitimacy for the organization and leaders rather than to actually impact operational efficacy or effectiveness.

On the problem of efficacy, the experimental homicide investigation initiative that we evaluated illustrated that, although it was a relative success on the field, it was not able to confront the traditional culture of the organization regarding how investigative police work should proceed. Detective work continues to feature a disconnection between the actual investigation and the formal demands of the IP, and the latter remains central on the radar screen of Civil Police officers and in their professional identity. *Delegados, escrivães* and investigators see their respective work as if they were in opposition to one another. Rather than seeing investigations being built from the contributions of the team, from the perspective of their own careers each member remains compartmentalized and self-centered, reflecting the internal conflicts and the demands of their relationships with the other actors in the criminal justice system.

All of this is widely recognized by those within the police, and not just by researchers. An important question, then, is the possibility that this realization will promote institutional change in the Civil Police. Were claims that there would be reform just ceremonial speeches in response to critical questions regarding the investigative inefficacy of the Brazilian Civil Police?

Meyer and Rowan (1977, pp. 342–344) argue that it is usually assumed that a rationally constructed, formal organizational structure is the most effective form of coordination and control of complex technical activities in the modern world. This view is based on the assumption that organizations work according to their organizational design—"coordination is a problem of routine, rules and procedures are followed and operational activities conform to what the formal structure prescribes." Meyer and Rowan argue, however, that empirical research often contradicts this model, pointing to the importance of parallel informal organizations that are as or more important than the formal ones. Also, the structural elements of formal and informal organizations can be disconnected from each other, and from the practical activities they are intended to promote: "rules are violated, decisions frequently go unimplemented and, if implemented, bring out uncertain consequences, the technologies used have an efficacy problem and the evaluation and inspection systems are subverted, offering little coordination" (1977, pp. 342–344).

Thus, to keep in ceremonial conformity with external pressures, organizations tend to disconnect their formal structures from the uncertainties of their technical tasks (and, therefore, the demands of efficiency and efficacy), becoming instead loosely articulated. That is, there is a disconnect between the formal structure visible from the outside and actual operational activities. Many of their visible structural characteristics become the product of organizational conformity to myths that are institutionalized in the social environment, and work as "rational and impersonal mandates that identify several social goals as technical in nature and specify, imperatively, appropriate and rational means to reach those goals" (Meyer and Rowan 1977, p. 344).

It is possible a robust community policing program could correspond to the "correct" or "appropriate" manner of conducting police work, given the values it reflects (Crank 2003)—values that, to achieve legitimacy, officers must share. In investigations, information and knowledge emerged as key elements of effective police work. Using them effectively would require dissemination of knowledge and experience within police organizations, which could only be accomplished by governance mechanisms making this happen on a day-to-day basis. But as yet neither of these reforms, one aimed at securing legitimacy and the other at enhancing the effectiveness of traditional policing, has taken root in the Brazilian police.

Notes

1. This research was partly financed by *Conselho Nacional de Desenvolvimento Científico e Tecnológico* [National Counsel of Technological and Scientific Development] CNPq and *Fundação de Amparo à Pesquisa do Estado de Minas Gerais* [Research Support Foundation of Minas Gerais' State] FAPEMIG.
2. The *delegados* team is usually made up of investigators who have a law degree and are empowered to carry out the field work. The reports produced by the field agents are organized by an *escrivão*, which has the function to collect and organize the field reports, and usually cross-examine victims, witnesses and defendants. The *delegado* has the final word on all investigations, as well as drafting the conclusions, which are forwarded to prosecutors and the judges.

References

Azevedo, R. G., and Vasconcellos, F. B. 2011. O Inquérito Policial em Questão—situação atual e a percepção dos Delegados de Polícia sobre as fragilidades do modelo brasileiro de investigação criminal [The police inquiry under question: The current situation and the perception of police inspectors about the fragilities of the Brazilian model of crime investigation]. *Revista Sociedade e Estado* 26: 59–75.

Batitucci, E. C. 2011. A Polícia em transição: O modelo profissional-burocrático de policiamento e hipóteses sobre os limites da profissionalização das polícias brasileiras [The police in transition: The bureaucratic-professional policing model and hyphotesys of Brazilian police profissionalization]. *Dilemas: revista de estudos de conflito e controle socia* 4: 65–96.

Batitucci, E. C. 2015. Polícia de Ciclo Completo e as Reformas no Aparato Policial e na Segurança Pública Brasileira [Complete cycle police and the reforms of police apparatuses and public security in Brazil]. In *Caderno Temático Seminário Internacional de Segurança Pública*, ed. *Câmara Dos Deputados* [The Brazilian House of Representatives], 41–43. Brasília: Câmara dos Deputados.

Bittner, E. 1967. The police on skid-row: A study of peace keeping. *American Sociological Review* 32: 699–715.

Cohen, L. E., and Felson, M. 1979. Social change and crime rate trends: A routine activity approach. *American Sociological Review* 44: 588–608.

Crank, J. P. 2003. Institutional theory of police: A review of the state of the art. *Policing: An International Journal of Police Strategies and Management* 26: 186–207.

DiMaggio, P. J., and Powell, W. W. 2005. A Gaiola de Ferro Revisitada: isomorfismo institucional e racionalidade coletiva nos campos organizacionais [Iron cage revisited: Institutional isomorfism and colective rationality in organizational fields]. *Revista de Administração de Empresas* 45: 74–89.

Felson, M. 1996. Preventing retail theft: An application of environmental criminology. *Security Journal* 7: 71–75.

FJP. 2014. Análise dos Programas e das Ações de Policiamento Comunitário na Polícia Militar De Minas Gerais (1980–2010) [Community policing programs and actions analzis at military police of minas gerais]. *Relatório apresentado à FAPEMIG, projeto APQ-01212-11* [Final Report Fapemig Project APQ-01212-11]. Mimeo.

Kant de Lima, R. 1989. Cultura jurídica e práticas policiais—a tradição inquisitorial [Legal culture and police practices—the inquisitorial tradition]. *Revista Brasileira de Ciências Sociais* 4: 65–84.

Kant de Lima, R. 1995. *A polícia da cidade do Rio de Janeiro—seus dilemas e paradoxos* [The police of the city of Rio de Janeiro its dilemas and paradoxes]. Rio de Janeiro: Editora Forense.

Kelling, G. L., and Moore, M. H. 1988. *The evolving strategy of policing.* Washington, DC: Perspectives on Policing, National Institute of Justice, United States Department of Justice, N°4.

Meyer, J. W., and Rowan, B. 1977. Institutionalized organizations: Formal structure as myth and ceremony. *American Journal of Sociology* 83: 340–363.

Mingardi, G. 1992. *Tiras, gansos e trutas: segurança pública e polícia civil em São Paulo (1983–1990)* [Cops, Snitchers and Punks: Public security and civil police in São Paulo]. São Paulo: Página Aberta.

Miranda, A. P. M., Oliveira, M. B., and Paes, V. F. 2010. A reinvenção da "cartorialização": análise do trabalho policial em registros de ocorrência e inquéritos policiais em "Delegacias Legais" referentes a homicídios dolosos na cidade do Rio de Janeiro. [The reinvention of "notarization": An analysis of crime reports and police inquiries in "Legal Police Precincts" concerning voluntary homicides in Rio de Janeiro]. *Pesquisas Aplicadas em Segurança Pública*, Ministério da Justiça, Brasília 2(4): 119–152.

Misse, M., Costa, A.T., Vargas, J.D., Ratton, J.L., and Azevedo, R.G. (eds.). 2010. *O inquérito policial no Brasil: uma pesquisa empírica* [Police inquiry in Brazil: An empirical research]. Rio de Janeiro: Ed. BookLink.

Moreira, H. W., and Godinho, L. 2010. Estudo de caso: uma comparação da influência do programa Fica Vivo e do GEPAR na redução dos crimes de homicídio na 1ª. RPM [Case study: Comparing the influence of the Fica Vivo program and GEPAR in homicides reduction at 1° RPM]. MBA Dissertation. Fundação João Pinheiro, Belo Horizonte.

Muniz, J. O., and Proença, D., Jr. 2007. Muita politicagem, pouca política os problemas da polícia [Too much politcking and few policies and the problems for police]. *Estudos Avançados* 21: 159–170.

Muniz, J. O., and Silva, W. F. 2010. Mandato Policial na Prática: tomando decisões nas ruas de João Pessoa [Police Mandate in use: Making decisions in the streets of João Pessoa]. *Cadernos CRH* 23: 449–473.

Oliveira, L. 2004. *Sua Excelência o Comissário e outros ensaios de Sociologia Jurídica* [Your highness the comissar and other essays of legal sociology]. Rio de Janeiro: Ed. Letra Legal.

Paixão, A. L. 1982. A Organização Policial numa Área Metropolitana [Police organization in a metropolitan area]. *Dados—revista de Ciências Sociais* 25: 63–85.

Paixão, A. L., Martins, H. T., and Sapori, L. F. 1992. Métodos e acidentes de trabalho: violência, legalidade e polícia [Methods and work incidents: Violence, legality and police]. *Análise e Conjuntura* 7: 76–91.

PMMG. 1993. *Diretriz de Policiamento Ostensivo 3008/93* [Guidelines for ostensible policing]. Belo Horizonte: Imprensa Oficial de Minas Gerais.

PMMG. 1999. *8ª Região da Polícia Militar. Instrução 01/99-8°CRPM* [8th military police region—instruction 01/99-8th CRPM]. Belo Horizonte: Imprensa Oficial de Minas Gerais.

PMMG. 2002. *Diretriz para a Produção de Serviços de Segurança Pública n° 04/2002—CG* [Guidelines for the delivery of public security services]. Belo Horizonte: Imprensa Oficial de Minas Gerais.

PMMG. 2004. *Região da Polícia Militar. Instrução 01/2004-8ªRPM. Cria e regula as Patrulhas de Prevenção Ativa, para emprego na capital do Estado* [8th military police region—instruction 01/2004-8th RPM—creation and regulation of active prevention patrol to be deployd at State's capitol]. Belo Horizonte: Imprensa Oficial de Minas Gerais.

PMMG. 2011. *Diretriz para a Produção de Serviços em Segurança Pública nº 3.01.06/2011—CG* [Guidelines for the delivery of public security services]. Belo Horizonte: Imprensa Oficial de Minas Gerais.

Reuss-Ianni, E. 1993. *Two cultures of policing: Street cops and management cops.* New York: Transaction Publishers.

Rodrigues, J. N. L. 2011. O inquérito policial para o crime de homicídio: inquisitorialidade, discricionariedade e conflito em busca de verdade e de culpados [The police inquiry in homicide cases: Inquisitorial shape, discretion and conflict in the search of truth and guilts]. Master's Degree Dissertation on Sociology, Federal University of Minas Gerais, Belo Horizonte, Brazil.

Souza, E. 1998. Polícia Comunitária em Belo Horizonte: avaliação e perspectivas de um programa de segurança pública. [Community policing in Belo Horizonte: Evaluation and perspectives of a public security program]. Master's Degree Dissertation on Sociology, Federal University of Minas Gerais, Belo Horizonte, Brazil.

Walker, S. 1977. *A critical history of police reform.* Lexington, MA: Lexington Books.

Wilson, J. Q., and Kelling, G. L. 2000. Broken windows: The police and neighborhood safety. In *Community policing, classical readings,* ed. W. M. Oliver. Upper Saddle River, New Jersey: Prentice Hall Ed.

Zilli, L. F., and Vargas, J. D. 2013. O trabalho da Polícia Investigativa face aos homicídios de jovens em Belo Horizonte [Investigative police work in relation to youth homicides in Belo Horizonte]. *Ciência & Saúde Coletiva* 18: 621–632.

Managing Gender Relations in the Brazilian Police

5

Ludmila Mendonça Lopes Ribeiro

Contents

Studies discussing the gender dimensions of the daily operation of police forces have been growing steadily in number over the past decades (Mourão 2015). One way to classify the approaches of these studies is to note that they differentiate between biological dimensions (sex) and their social significations (gender), dimensions that show variation from one society to another. From the advent of theories of modernity, the main category taken for analysis has been how biological sex plays a prominent role in social life and privileges males as agents of transformation. In contrast, women were assigned a secondary role, confined to the domestic environment and to caring for the home and the children—who in turn would be educated by her in accordance with their gender. From sex, two clearly distinct genders (here "role-assigning cultural categories") would be defined: masculine and feminine. Any disconnection between sex and gender was treated as dysfunctionality, either social or medical (Giddens 2001).

The concept of gender arises from the need to address the differences between the sexes and how their construction defines social relations (Küchemann et al. 2015). While sex relates to the biological aspect, gender is a cultural construct directly related to a given society, specifically defined in both time and space. This perspective stresses the fact that the same biological sex originates various genders, depending on how the individual recognizes and inserts him/herself into the social order (Hirata et al. 2009). Thus, femininity and masculinity are cultural constructs learned during the socialization process; they are not unchangeable but in constant transformation.

71

We will use the construct *gender* to understand differences between individuals in Brazilian police organizations. While the 1988 Federal Constitution of the Brazilian Republic (CR/1988) barred any discrimination based on differences between the sexes,[1] the inner workings of the institutions in charge of public security reinforce a myriad of social roles according to an individual's biology, which contributes to reproducing unequal gender relations.

The Survey

The data analyzed in this chapter derives from a research project on women in police institutions, carried out by the Brazilian Forum on Public Security (*Fórum Brasileiro de Segurança Pública*—FBSP) and by the Center for Studies on Organizations and People (*Núcleo de Estudos de Organizações e Pessoas*—NEOP) of the Getulio Vargas Foundation (FGV), with support from Brazil's Ministry of Justice and CRISP (*Centro de Estudos de Criminalidade e Segurança Pública* or Center for Studies on Crime and Public Security) of UFMG (Federal University of Minas Gerais). This study seeks to understand how gender relations are constructed inside various Brazilian law enforcement agencies.

The institutional arrangement of public security in Brazil is governed by Article 144 of CR/1988. According to the provisions therein, the task of keeping order and combating crime shall be carried out by the following organizations: 3 Federal Police agencies, 27 Military Police organizations (performing ostensive policing duties) and 27 Civil Police forces (the latter with judicial police powers). In addition, there are 1,081 Municipal Guard bodies (FBSP 2015)—formerly assigned to public asset protection and currently engaged in crime prevention, as their statutes have been approved. These total 1,138 policing agencies staffed by 648,000 professionals (FBSP 2015). Each type of agency follows very distinct *modus operandi*, so any research focused on individual officers and their gender relations must consider the specificities of these institutional arrangements.

In order to reach this huge group of officers in their entirety, online questionnaires with password-controlled access were made available to all registered public security professionals listed in the Ministry of Justice's database. The Internet option for conducting the survey is justified by the huge size of Brazil and our intention to reach the largest possible number of police officers, ranging from those working in state capitals to those based in the country's most remote locations. The resulting sample broadly reflects the wide diversity of policing in Brazil today. Of the total number of questionnaires distributed in this way, there were 11,982 valid returns, or about 2% of all those performing police duties throughout Brazil. The distribution of respondents was broadly in proportion to the distribution of organizations and the numbers of police officers—male and female—currently active in Brazilian territory. The data from this online survey is representative of each police institution, with resulting estimates boasting a 99% confidence level and sampling margin of error of 1.17% in each stratum. This analysis excluded respondents belonging to fire departments, who for organizational reasons were also included in the survey.

The survey included questions differentiating between the concepts of sex and gender. However, few transgender respondents identified themselves, and otherwise there was a high correspondence between complete responses to the sex and gender items. So despite our more comprehensive understanding of gender, responses to the sex-category question are utilized in this analysis of power relations between men and women.

Female Participation in Policing

In many places around the world, policing is understood stereotypically as being a male's job, since it involves protecting the population against crime and criminals while also maintaining order. Thus, the actions carried out by police forces are seen as men's roles in traditional societies (Soares and Musumeci 2005). In Brazil, this scenario is not different, which would explain that the overwhelming majority of police officers in our sample (81%) are male. The gender distribution of Brazilian police forces is described in Figure 5.1, which depicts this by type of agency.

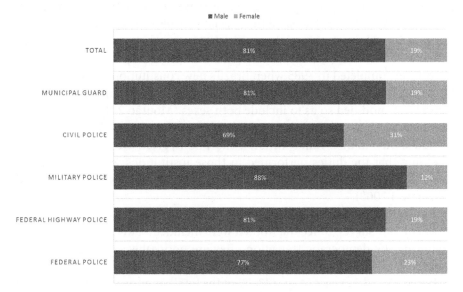

Figure 5.1 Distribution of respondents by sex and type of police force

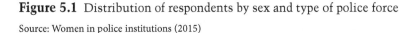

Source: Women in police institutions (2015)

This virtually 80–20 split raises the question of what 19% female participation in policing means in the context of police organizations and in Brazilian society. According to the Brazilian census of 2010, economically active women represent 43% of the working population, which means that they are underrepresented in police institutions. This number is low in comparison to some other societies, even though surveys conducted by UNODC show that policewomen hardly ever reach 30% of the policing labor force anywhere in the world.[2] Even seeing it from this perspective, Brazil falls short of the world's average.

Nonetheless, if we compare 19% female participation in policing to the results of an earlier survey, one conducted in 2000, we have much to celebrate. At that time, females did not exceed one digit as a percentage of the Military Police force. This was also true of the Civil Police, where there were positions that were somewhat guaranteed for women. This was the result of the creation of Special Police Stations for Assistance to Women (DEAMs, with the Portuguese initials) in the 1990s. The DEAMs were intended to provide specialized assistance for women, and they ended up being populated largely by female police, who would in principle be more capable of listening to female victims (Musumeci and Soares 2004). However, in that period the percentage of female officers overall still fell short of our 20% figure for 2015. Over the past 15 years, the proportion of females engaged in Brazilian police forces has grown at an accelerated pace, causing even the Military Police—the most resistant to gender equality—to include more than 10% of women in its ranks.

Women started joining the Brazilian police corps in 1955, as São Paulo State's Decree no. 24.548 created the Special Female Policing Corps (Donadio 2009, p. 91). However, it was during the 1980s that their presence was intensified as the country slowly moved from authoritarianism to democracy, a transition completed in 1985 when Brazil's new constitution (CR/1988) came into effect. This provided the constitutional basis upon which police structures were modified so as to include both sexes (Mourão 2015, p. 215). Until the Federal Constitution was enacted in 1988, Brazilian police forces only included men in their ranks, with few exceptions, given the prevailing understanding that the duties performed in those institutions were associated to male physical strength and therefore were men's exclusive right (Soares and Musumeci 2005).

Table 5.1 presents a demographic profile of male and female officers, based on our survey. Since the women were included in the police forces only following the democratic transition, they are noticeably younger than their male peers. While women police are an average 36 years old and mostly are between 26 and 35 years of age (43.2% of the total), men are an average 38 and highly concentrated within the age group from 36 to 45 (42.9%).

Another difference between men and women in the police has to do with skin color, something that is always a flashpoint in Brazilian society.

Table 5.1 Percentage distribution according to age, skin color, marital status, children and schooling, per sex

	Males (%)	Females (%)
Age		
18 to 25	2.9	3.9
26 to 35	32.9	43.2
36 to 45	42.9	36.2
46 to 55	18.8	14.5
Above 56	2.4	2.3
Total	100.0	100.0
Skin color		
White	44.4	50.7
Black	9.3	8.9
Brown	44.3	37.9
Yellow	0.8	1.5
Indigenous	0.4	0.2
Other (please specify)	0.8	0.8
Total	100.0	100.0
Marital status		
Single	15.8	31.6
Married/in Steady Union	79.5	57.6
Divorced	4.6	9.9
Widow(er)	0.2	0.9
Total	100.0	100.0
Children		
Yes	72.9	52.8
No	27.1	47.2
Total	100.0	100.0
Schooling		
First grade—completed	1.0	0.1
Second grade—incomplete	1.5	0.3
Second grade—completed	20.1	8.3
Higher Education—incomplete	20.9	14.4
Higher Education—completed	32.6	35.1
Post-graduation—*lato sensu* (specialization) complete or incomplete	20.8	36.3
Post-graduation—*stricto sensu* (M.A./Ph.D.) complete or incomplete	3.0	5.5
Total	100	100

Source: Women in police institutions (2015)

As noted by Muniz (2012), depending on the classification methodology adopted, the results of surveys can vary widely, as the way each individual perceives himself or herself as to color is very much related to their socio-economic status. Far from indicating the respondent's race, skin color classification rather reveals how he or she sees him/herself in terms of social standing, as whites have traditionally been this country's elite. In our survey, we adopted the same methodology as the IBGE census, which involved asking respondents to classify themselves in terms of skin color. It should be noted that, among Brazilian police, females are the majority among whites (50.7%) and males among dark skin color (53.6% are browns or blacks), despite this not being reflected in the country's wider population.

Does this mean that our policewomen are part of Brazilian elite, whereas male police officers originate from the lower social strata? In order to answer this question, one must unveil the relations between sex, schooling and skin color. Outside the walls of police institutions, numerous studies highlight the fact that school failure is more prevalent among black men (Carvalho 2004). At the other extreme, women represent the majority of higher education students. Male police tend to report fewer years of schooling than do their female peers—on average, women tend to be one grade above men. While males are the majority among those who have at most completed high school, women are the majority of those with a postgraduate degree, either complete or incomplete, *lato* or *stricto sensu*. Thus, the presence of more women among police whites means that those with a more solid education background are the ones electing to pursue a career in the police, as previous surveys had already indicated (SENASP 2013).

With regard to marital status, the highest percentage of both sexes was concentrated in the "married or in steady union" category: 79% of men and 58% of women were in that category. This distinct pattern in marital status seems to have impacted childbearing rates, as the percentage of women with children is smaller than that of men: 73% against 53%, respectively. These differences may be interpreted as a consequence from the prevailing age range in each of the two groups, as the women are somewhat younger than men in the force. But they can also be understood as associated with women's choice for the career at the expense of having a family—which should be postponed to a later age, or even altogether discarded in favor of a more satisfactory professional and personal life (Lima 2012).

Nevertheless, being a policewoman does not seem to mean being free from duties considered "feminine" in Brazilian culture: 66% of female respondents indicated they dedicate their free time to domestic chores (as against 50% of the men) and 31% never perform remunerated activities in their off time, in contrast with half of their male peers (51% of whom always perform paid activities in off hours). Therefore, being a policewoman is to take on a double shift, as it happens with 88% of working women, according to IBGE data.[3]

Gender Relations in Brazilian Policing: Towards Sex Equality?

If gender is a cultural construct on a sexually differentiated human body understood as a field in which power is articulated, and serving as a mechanism for organization of equality and inequality, how then are men's and women's places determined in Brazilian police forces?

The incorporation of women into Brazilian police forces coincides with the experiences of several other Latin American countries. The notable exceptions would be Chile and Uruguay, where females were included in the 1930s (SENASP 2013, p. 16). The admission of women happened along with a redefinition of the way police forces are expected to act within a democratic context, as their presence in the ranks was seen as an opportunity for reform, for humanizing the forces with a new emphasis on "preventive—less truculent—policing strategies", thought to be typical of the feminine role (Calazans 2005, p. 2). Starting from the principle that "the condition of police, in the case of men, would only accentuate the worst attributes of masculinity", the arrival of women would mean a humanization of the institutions, a way of "completely removing the remnants of the police's dictatorial past" (Soares and Musumeci 2005, p. 118).

This assumption may be questioned at its origin, given that this opening to women was not wide, unconditional and unrestricted. Rather than a reformulation of assumptions on how police should act, what actually happened was the establishment of mechanisms confining women to some defined spaces within the institution, including assigning them welfare work focused on domestic violence—especially when involving children and the elderly, given the presumed feminine character of such activity (Mourão 2015). In the Military Police, for instance, the place of women was marked by a differentiated career path, with distinct promotion criteria from their male peers (Musumeci and Soares 2004).

This selective incorporation of women into the policing profession continues to the present day and guides distinct admission criteria according to sex, such as with the system of quotas—which sets a predefined percentage of positions for females. Support for this quota system among officers themselves is documented in Figure 5.2. Support for quotas was strongest among the powerful Military Police. While the quotas were initially a demand of the feminist movement—for they would secure at least a required minimum access to the profession (Araújo and AlvesAlves 2007)—as women went on

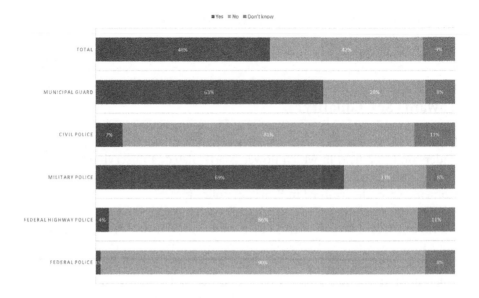

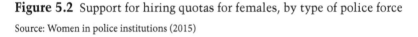

Figure 5.2 Support for hiring quotas for females, by type of police force

Source: Women in police institutions (2015)

gaining an ever larger field in the marketplace this system turned into a hurdle on their way towards reaching higher percentages than those imposed by the quotas (Calazans 2005). Indeed, the quotas are a limiting factor to women wishing to join the institution.

As noted, support for selection by means of quotas was most widely supported among the Military Police (69%) and Municipal Guard (63%). These two forces look to the armed forces for their structural and operating models (Souza 2011). In these institutions, restricted access is justified by the physical differences between men and women. If "one must run after bandits",[4] women would lack the required competence for such (Soares and Musumeci 2005, p. 12), and so it is imperative to establish the number of positions each sex is legally entitled to at the first stage of the selection process.

The quota system for police hiring is a controversial measure, as it implies a situation in which "women and men are in conflict, as they vie for scarce resources" (Abreu 2011, p. 9). On the other hand, setting a threshold percentage for women "interferes with that dispute seeking to prevent the scale from tilting too much to the men's side" (Abreu 2011, p. 9). In the case of police, this quota cap for women is widely accepted internally—which may be seen as an obstacle to change: in total, 48% of the interviewees are in favor of keeping or setting quotas for admission of women; 52% of the men believe that the incorporation of females should not exceed certain parameters. Women, in turn, support that policy in lower percentages (31%), given their understanding that they would have better chances to join the ranks if not for those caps (Soares and Musumeci 2005), as the first stage of selection is a general knowledge test—at which they could take advantage of their longer school years.

Despite the fact that their arrival occurred by means of a quota system, "bit by bit, the policewomen moved from exclusive units to join the wider force, through a process that unified male and female staff" (Mourão 2015, p. 20). In our survey, only 5.3% of respondents reported the existence of differentiated careers according to sex, all of whom belonged to Military Police and Municipal Guard ranks.

We see that nowadays the functional gap between sexes is narrower than it was 30 years ago—when women were exclusively assigned support/office duties, thus reinforcing the stereotype according to which only men rather than women should be out there in the streets (Musumeci and Soares 2004; Calazans 2005). Figure 5.3 depicts the distribution of job assignments by sex. As it reports, even today, a larger percentage of women (33% versus 22% of the men) are deployed in the administrative sector, and fewer serve in operational units. However, based on other research, the latter is in fact an improvement over past practice (SENASP 2013).

As Figure 5.3 further illustrates, at higher positions in the hierarchy, such as strategy and direction, the differences between men and women are smaller, as schooling and specialization are somewhat more valued than the individual's sex in those functions. Moreover, 39% of all interviewees agree

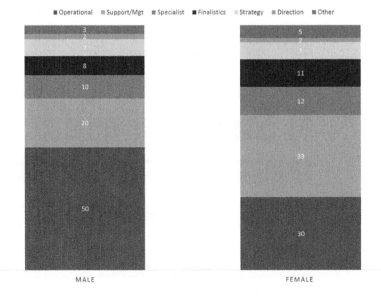

Figure 5.3 Distribution of duties performed by police, by sex

Source: Women in police institutions (2015)

that, in order for a woman to fill a hierarchical position above men, she should have a wider academic background. However, another 14% (16% of the men and 4% of the women) still believe that policemen and policewomen should perform different activities as suited to their sex, a view perhaps reinforced by stereotypical differences that are in fact socially constructed over the biological element.

Another way of verifying the stereotypical basis of continuing gender inequalities is to examine whether mounting numbers of women are accompanied by changes in the physical structure designed for them, such as bathrooms, lodgings, locker rooms and even nurseries (Mourão 2015). Such equipment is intended to offer women more privacy, away from male eyes, in addition to ensuring their return to work after childbirth, as caring for small children is seen as a typically female task (Freitas 2001). It turns out that workplace infrastructure adapted to women is very much institutionalized in Brazilian police organizations: 86% feature differentiated bathrooms, 66% specific accommodations and 7% have nurseries. In only 12% of them are there no such items. These details are summarized by type of force in Figure 5.4. The Civil Police are among the institutions where this latter percentage is higher, despite the fact that it operates police stations specializing in assistance to women. At the other extreme is the Federal Police, with 95% of its units fitted with at least a minimally adapted infrastructure to cater for both sexes.

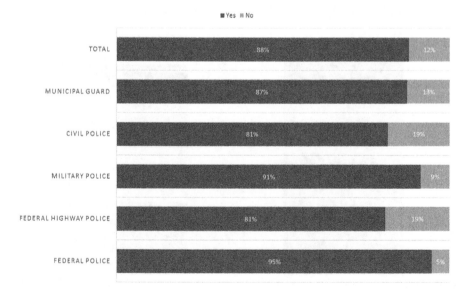

Figure 5.4 Availability of facilities for exclusive use by women, by type of force

Source: Women in police institutions (2015)

The adoption of new personal protective equipment has been one of the adaptations Brazilian police have made to confront the more structured and lethal criminality that they now face in urban areas. Police forces set up Internal Occupational Accident Prevention Committees to consider these and established "the mandatory use of personal protection equipment by any police officer on duty" (Sandes 2007, p. 35). Personal protection equipment (PPE) ergonomically adapted to women represent the other side of the coin in terms of adapting the institutional culture for receiving the feminine, given that body anatomy is the main element of sex differentiation. Thus, feminine molding of bulletproof vests and belts/holsters is an indication that the police organization acknowledges—and is willing to adapt to—feminine morphology. According to 42% of the interviewees, PPE are not available to women. The Federal Police count on a high percentage of PPE adapted to women, whereas the Municipal Guards cope with equipment shortage, with at least half of the corps lacking it.

As Figure 5.5 documents, the Civil Police, which in principle should pose fewer obstacles to the admission and promotion of female police, are instead among the institutions with the lowest percentage of PPE ergonomically adapted to women (47%). Next follows the Military Police (39%) which, although essentially intended to patrol the streets, do not count on enough PPE adapted to the woman's body for all their female police officers—the

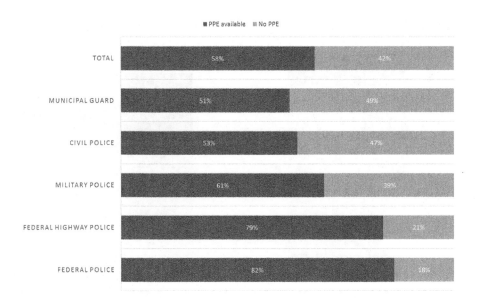

Figure 5.5 Availability of personal protection equipment ergonomically adapted to women, by type of force

Source: Women in police institutions (2015)

apparent rationale being that only men are physically and morally able to work out in the streets, and so only they should need the PPE.

A less visible aspect of gender relations among police is the so-called glass roof (Silveira 2004), or the existence of subtle criteria applied when acknowledging men and women as part of the institutional dynamics. Women find these symbolic barriers hard to overcome, for they involve informal, often unwritten rules, though recognized by members of the organization in the performance of their functions. Examples would include statements like "the individual will only make good progress in the career if it is a man" (validated by 12% of interviewees) or "the men who joined the force with me are in a better position now, even though the institution does not define separate career paths" (confirmed by 28% of the women interviewed).

Another representation of that "glass roof" is the resort to "jokes" or derogatory innuendos seeking to belittle women in the exercise of their professional activities. This happens occasionally or even frequently, with notorious differences between men and women as to that behavior, as documented in Figure 5.6. The more accentuated it is, the larger the percentage of female respondents reporting this dynamic in the workplace. In total, 14% of the women report the constant occurrence of such practice versus 5% of the men.

Further, almost half of the interviewees have already been a target of chauvinist jokes with a sexist character or of inappropriate comments on their

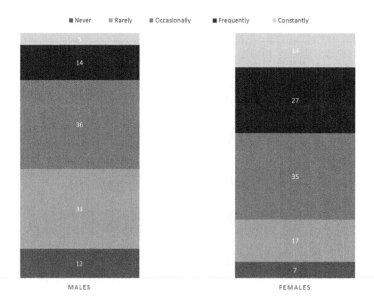

Figure 5.6 Victimization by inappropriate comments by peers with regard to sex/ gender or sex orientation, by respondent sex

Source: Women in police institutions (2015)

physical appearance or about cognitive differences supposedly determined by sex. Women are more often targeted (66% at least once). Nonetheless, the percentage of men affected by this misconduct is also rather high (44%) when considering that police forces are male-dominated institutions, and therefore one would not expect their prevailing gender to be victimized by these informal practices. There is a culture of disrespect in the police environment of which women are the preferred target, but which will also not overlook any weakness in men when dealing with the "different", i.e., those who do not fit the masculine standard.

Derogatory jokes "constitute a veritable psychic murder, however it may present itself as an indirect form of violence; with regard to it, and under the pretext of tolerance, many of us become complacent, indifferent and neglectful" (Freitas 2001, p. 9). When it comes to police organizations, their notorious male chauvinism—deeply rooted in society and present in workplace interactions—lead to blaming women for an uneven power dynamic between the sexes. The aggressor's strategy is to disqualify the victim and thus justify his own inadequate behavior. Testifying to that is the fact that for 57% of the women and 63% of men, among respondents, feminine behavior may indeed entail chauvinist jokes. The highest degrees of agreement are found in institutions with military characteristics—which are precisely the ones posing greater difficulties to the admission of women. Nonetheless, as Figure 5.7

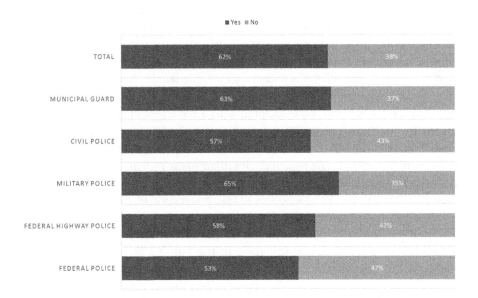

Figure 5.7 Agreement with the statement: "Women's behavior may entail inappropriate comments with regard to sex/gender or sexual orientation", by type of force

Source: Women in police institutions (2015)

illustrates, other forces also display high percentages in that regard, always above 50% of the interviewees, confirming the fact that playful devaluation of women is a fruit of an inadequate attitude rooted in the police imagination.[5]

Jokes of this nature are indeed forms of discrimination and coercion, and can cause real harm, if not to the personality, at a minimum to the person's dignity. The associated suffering is often coupled with a lack of understanding of what is causing it. Even so, police culture typically does not see this pattern of behavior as a violence, which prevents it from being treated appropriately (Lima 2002). For 48% of the policemen, jokes or malicious comments about physical appearance, affective-sexual orientation or cognitive capacity are not forms of gender-related violence. Women see such attitude as violence more often (55%), although only 6% of them have formally reported incidents of that nature.

Discrimination, humiliation, disrespect or coercion all have a name: "moral harassment", an attitude that is as old as work itself. In the 1990s, this was identified as a form of violence capable of generating pathologies that can manifest themselves in absenteeism and psychological leave (Freitas 2001). In the police forces, it is still a sort of taboo theme, with only a few programs focusing on discussing the matter more seriously. How does moral harassment come to be? Disqualifying the victim is the most common strategy, somehow causing the other's humiliation—either actual or symbolic—to be naturalized (i.e., seen as natural) and understood as a phenomenon that is part of life in society and therefore also in organizations (Freitas 2001, p. 11). In the case of Brazilian police forces, moral harassment is institutionalized by practices and comments, which stress the view that those who are discriminated or humiliated somehow "earned" it. As jokes make people laugh, they tend to disguise their violent dimension.

If moral harassment is "associated with a recurrent effort by a person to disqualify another" (Freitas 2001, p. 9), the same is true of sexual harassment. Sexual harassment is part of uneven relations between men and women: as in the case of the *senhores de engenho* (Brazilian sugar mill and plantation owners, who during colonial and slavery times had power of life and death over their families and servants) who would take possession of women slaves' bodies to satisfy their lust without that being considered a crime (Freyre 2000). The problem is that practice survived to the end of slavery in Brazil in the form of a naturalized sexual initiation of the family's boys by their housemaids. "Until not long ago, a woman who worked out of the home was seen as a 'slut', for a woman who subjects herself to the world of streets must be prepared to 'submit to the casting couch'" (Freitas 2001, p. 13). It would be naive to believe that this imagery has just vanished as redemocratization took place in Brazil, for it is deeply rooted in the social practices that pervade our history as a society.

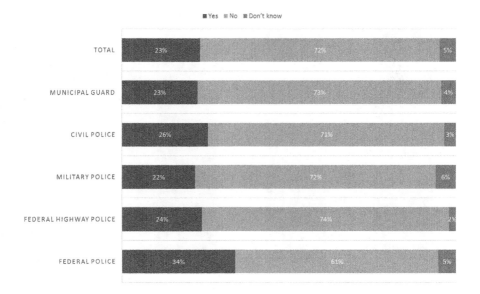

Figure 5.8 Direct victimization by moral or sexual harassment, by type of force

Source: Women in police institutions (2015)

Among the officers we interviewed, 23% had been victims of moral or sexual harassment, representing 42% of the women and 21% of the men. These percentages are presented, by type of force, in Figure 5.8. Female victimization was almost twice as high as male victimization, thus confirming the hypothesis according to which discriminatory practices tend to reinforce sex differences, as the police forces replicate domination patterns prevailing in the wider society (Soares and Musumeci 2005, p. 138). In other words, sexual harassment will hardly ever happen among equals. It simultaneously reasserts sex and power differences, by ascribing to people the connotations that gender presupposes. Among the institutions surveyed, respondents serving in the Federal Police reported the highest percentage of victims of moral or sexual harassment, 34%. By contrast, the Military Police is the force with the lowest percentage of cases, which either indicates that not always does the popular imagery find resonance in police practices, or perhaps that the policewomen in such institutions find it harder to speak up about the theme even through online surveys.

The frequency of moral harassment is described in Figure 5.9, and it is considerably more frequent than sexual harassment (89% versus 11%). However, the distribution of moral harassment varied considerably from that of sexual harassment. Fully 96% of victimized men suffered moral harassment, whereas 26% of women with sexual harassment. The frequency with which victimization happens shows differences both in terms of sex and type of harassment.

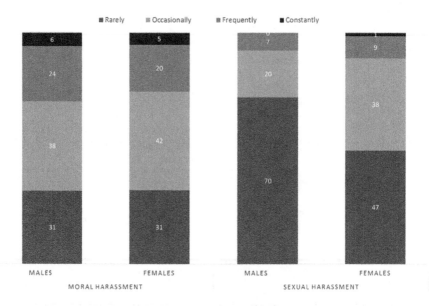

Figure 5.9 Direct victimization by moral or sexual harassment, by sex

Source: Women in police institutions (2015)

With regard to the moral type, differences between men and women are very subtle: 70% recognize that this type of violence is a daily routine in their lives. As for differences between the sexes, female victims declared that this sort of "indecent proposal" tends to happen at times, whereas the men said it rarely happens.

While moral and sexual harassment are encountered frequently inside police institutions, especially when the victim is a woman, only 12% denounced the violence they suffered in headquarters and police stations, and only 1/4 of these were satisfied with the developments triggered by their reporting. Women are more prone to suffering moral harassment in silence: despite being more frequently victimized than men are, they break even when it comes to denouncing abuse, at 12% for both sexes. The figures change when it comes to sexual harassment, as more women than men file a formal complaint (12% versus 7%), probably because for men sexual harassment is seen as a double humiliation: violation of gender role (given that sexual harassment is traditionally seen as an offense by men against women) and violation of equal condition terms (as it debases the one being harassed).

In this context, there is a pressing need for policies capable of preventing gender violence in Brazil's police forces, so that policewomen that assist members of the public in similar circumstances will not assume the normality of the experience and thus revictimize those who—differently from what the police normally do—are willing to pursue a suitable treatment of the issue. Several studies of the performance of DEAMs point at the fact that the very policewomen in charge of providing that specialized assistance often blame the women for the violence of which they are victims, by dismissing it as part of the female condition. About this, see Durão (2013).

The Importance of a Gender Policy

The incorporation of women into the police institutions of Latin America is a product of the continent's democratic transition process. It took place as local police (in particular) started being seen as service providers rather than political armies. In that context, women were included with the aim to democratize the institution by contributing their femininity—which was expected to neutralize masculine brutality—and by performing essentially social work, based on the belief that policewomen could establish a closer relationship with the community while performing a pacifying, protective role (Donadio 2009, p. 82). The more visible consequence of adopting this new way of engaging females in the police was the associated differentiation in what it means to be a man or a woman police officer (Lima 2002).

Being a police officer in Brazil is by no means an easy task. It involves undergoing a series of tests for admission, to be exposed to one of the highest homicide rates in the world (UNODC 2014) and to put one's own life at risk, given the high percentage of police that die in the exercise of the profession (FBSP 2015). Being a policewoman is even harder in a country that fails to appropriately discuss the admission of females in the force and to develop gender policies capable of shedding light on the symbolic violence pervading institutional life and preventing gender violence, such as in the form of moral and sexual harassment.

In the survey, we can see that women participate in policing at lower percentages than those seen among the economically active population generally. In view of the difficulties faced when trying to join the ranks, and subsequently to rise to the same posts as their male peers, women end up giving priority to their professional career to the detriment of marriage and children, while substantially improving their own education. Although more educated than men, a higher percentage of women take up tasks seen as less important, such as those of the support staff. While today there are no longer separate careers for men and women in the police forces, females keep being symbolically confined to defined spaces demarcated by male chauvinist jokes seemingly intended to remind women of their "true" role in Brazilian society. By doing so, Brazilian policemen reproduce historically unequal gender relations which place women at subordinate positions or keep them powerless to denounce the violence of which they are victims.

Women's survival in this professional environment tends to be made harder by the lack of a gender policy to protect them from violence of various sorts, ranging from male chauvinist jokes to sexual harassment. This problem is made worse by the small number of police organizations counting on a Code of Conduct to clarify what is gender and what would be appropriate behavior, and to criticize patterns of male chauvinist domination. Further lacking are specific mechanisms for reporting cases of gender violence (such as specialized complaints offices) and a Code of Ethics that would include a discussion on sexual harassment.

Some of the women interviewed stated that there are indeed mechanisms for reporting moral and sexual harassment inside police institutions; nevertheless, these mechanisms are the same available for the general population. Among those most often quoted are bodies such as Internal Affairs—usually staffed by men, incidentally—and the DEAMs, specialized in assisting women, as seen above. Being mostly staffed by female officers, the DEAMs would in principle be endowed with the capacity to better care for women affected by moral and sexual harassment in masculine environments (Mourão 2015).

As an institution, the DEAMs were created to give visibility to gender violence (often hidden inside homes), but their practice indicates that these institutions are also uneven in their gender relations, reproducing and thus potentializing the women's physical and psychological suffering. The policewomen that work at the DEAMs also see the women they assist as responsible for the violence of which they are victims and think that, unfortunately, it is not up to the police to rescue them from a situation they have brought upon themselves (Durão 2013). Thus, when referring to the DEAMs as the main instrument at the disposal of policewomen victimized by violence in their work environment, the interviewees seem to be stressing just how unprepared the police institutions are to deal with gender violence, given that the policewomen are also likely to be blamed for the violence of which they are victims, just like they blame their female peers for displaying behaviors bound to attract chauvinist jokes.

This lack of appropriate mechanisms to tackle the phenomenon inside police organizations serves to multiply situations involving threat, coercion or force and causing physical and sexual suffering to women, at substantially higher rates than to men, given that a sense of assured impunity felt by a superior who harasses his subordinate is the rule rather than the exception. In view of this, there is a pressing need for implementing a program for quality of life in the work environment, one that proves capable of minimizing or extinguishing the occurrence of such violations of rights, which—in addition to debasing women—causes the policewomen to fall prey to the very sort of violence they are expected to prevent, thus sustaining a vicious cycle that could further entail the naturalization of moral and sexual harassment against women beyond the walls of police institutions.

Notes

1. Art. 3 The following are fundamental objectives of the Federative Republic of Brazil: (. . .) IV—promote the welfare of all, irrespective of origin, race, sex, skin color, age or any other forms of discrimination.
2. Source: www.unodc.org/unodc/en/data-and-analysis/statistics/crime/cts-data-collection. html, accessed on 16 October 2015.
3. Per the last IBGE survey on the matter, available at www.ibge.gov.br/home/presidencia/noticias/imprensa/ppts/00000020091812202014183816455337.pdf, accessed on 22 October 2015.
4. The Portuguese term *bandido* would carry similar connotations to *bad guys* for US cops.
5. For an analysis of how this phenomenon occurs historically from the moment women first joined the Military Police in Brazil, see Lima (2002).

References

Abreu, M. A. 2011. Cotas para mulheres no Legislativo e seus fundamentos republicanos [Quotas for women in the Legislative and its republican fondaments]. In *Texto para Discussão (TD) 1645*, ed. IPEA, 1–33. Brasília: Instituto de Pesquisa Econômica Aplicada (IPEA).

Araújo, C., and AlvesAlves, D. 2007. Impactos de Indicadores Sociais e do Sistema Eleitoral sobre as Chances das Mulheres nas Eleições e suas Interações com as Cotas [Impacts of social indicators and the election system on the women chances in elections and their interactions with the quotas]. *Dados* 50: 535–577.

Calazans, M. E. 2005. Polícia e gênero no contexto das reformas policiais [Police and gender in the contexto of police reforms]. *Educação* 10(2): 21–34.

Carvalho, M. P. 2004. O fracasso escolar de meninos e meninas: articulações entre gênero e cor/raça [The school failure of boys and girls: The link between gender and race]. *Cadernos Pagu* 22: 247–290.

Donadio, M. 2009. La mujer en las instituciones armadas y policiales: resolución 1325 y operaciones de paz en América Latina [The woman in armed forces and the police: Resolution 1325]. In *Proyecto GPSF N° 07–184: La mujer en las Fuerzas Armadas y Policía en América Latina: una aproximación de género a las operaciones de paz* [The woman in armed forces and police in Latin America: A gender approach to Peace-keeping operatons], ed. M. Donadio, 1–256. Buenos Aires: Red de Seguridad y Defensa de América Latina.

Durão, S. 2013. Silenciamentos sutis. Atendimento policial, cidadania e justiça em casos de vítimas de violência doméstica [Subtle silencing, police response, citizenship and justice for victims of domestic violence]. *Análise Social* 209: 878–899.

FBSP. 2015. *9°. Anuário do Fórum Brasileiro de Segurança Pública* [9th annual report Brazilian security forum]. São Paulo: Fórum Brasileiro de Segurança Pública.

Freitas, M. E. 2001. Assédio moral e assédio sexual: faces do poder perverso nas organizações [Moral Harassment and sexual harassment: Faces of perverse power in organizations]. *RAE* 41: 9–13.

Freyre, G. 2000. *Casa Grande e Senzala* [Slaves and masters]. 40th edition. Rio de Janeiro: Civilização Brasileira.

Giddens, A. 2001. *A transformação da intimidade sexualidade, amor e erotismo nas sociedades modernas* [The transformation of intimacy: Sexuality, love and eroticism in modern societies]. São Paulo: Unesp.

Hirata, H., Laborie, F., Doré, H., and Senotier, D.2009. *Dicionário crítico do feminismo* [Critical feminist dictionary]. São Paulo: UNESP.

Küchemann, B. A., Bandeira, L. M., and Almeida, T. M. C. 2015. A categoria gênero nas ciências sociais e sua interdisciplinaridade [The gender category in social sciences and its interdisciplinarity]. *Revista do CEAM* 3: 63.

Lima, M. A. 2002. *A major da PM que tirou a farda* [The police woman that took off the uniform]. Belo Horizonte: Qualitymark Editora Ltda.

Lima, M. G. R. 2012. *Um estudo sobre o adiamento da maternidade em mulheres contemporâneas* [An study about the postponement of maternity in contemporary women]. Doctoral dissertation. São Paulo: Universidade de São Paulo.

Mourão, B. 2015. Diálogos sobre Mulheres Policiais [Dialogues about police women]. In *Polícia e democracia: 30 anos de estranhamentos e esperanças* [Police and democracy: 30 years of unfamiliarity and hopes], ed. R. S. Lima and S. Bueno, 212–236. São Paulo: Alameda.

Muniz, J. 2012. O Preto no branco? Mensuração, relevância e concordância classificatória no país da incerteza racial [Black or white? Measurement, relevance, and classificatory concordance in a country of racial uncertainty]. *Dados* 55: 251–282.

Musumeci, L., and Soares, B. M. 2004. Polícia e Gênero: participação e perfil das policiais femininas nas PMs brasileiras [Police and gender: Participation and profile of female police officers in Brazilian gendarmerie]. *Revista Gênero* 5: 183–207.

Sandes, W. F. 2007. Uso não-letal da força na ação policial: formação, tecnologia e intervenção governamental [The use of non-lethal force in police action: Formation, tecnology and governmental intervention]. *Revista Brasileira de Segurança Pública* 1: 24–36.

SENASP. 2013. *Mulheres na Segurança Pública* [Women in public security]. Brasília: Secretaria Nacional de Segurança Pública (SENASP); Ministério da Justiça: 1–103.

Silveira, M. L. 2004. Políticas públicas de gênero: impasses e desafios para fortalecer a agenda política na perspectiva da igualdade [Gender public policies: Deadlocks and challenges to streghten public agenda in equality perspective]. In *Políticas Públicas e igualdade de gênero* [Public policies and gender equality], ed. T. Godinho and M. L. Silveira, 1–11. São Paulo: Coordenadoria Especial da Mulher.

Soares, B. M., and Musumeci, L. 2005. *Mulheres policiais: presença feminina na Polícia Militar do Rio de Janeiro* [Policewomen: Female presence in the military police of Rio de Janeiro]. Rio de Janeiro: Civilização Brasileira: 1–250.

Souza, M. S. 2011. Novos espaços do feminino: Trabalho, gênero e corporações militares no Brasil [New female spaces: Work, gender and military corporations in Brazil]. *Revista Sociais e Humanas* 24: 133–147.

UNDOC. 2014. *Study on Global Homicide 2013*. Vienna: United Nations Office on Drugs and Crime (UNODC): 1–166.

Section II

The Police and Their Problems

Police Action and the Drug Business in Brazil

6

Paulo Fraga and Joyce Keli do Nascimento Silva

Contents

This chapter examines initiatives carried out by the Brazilian Federal Police in recent decades to combat illicit cannabis cultivation. We see these measures as largely a reaction to external criticisms of government drug policies and practices. The actions that were taken in response, in order to diminish illegal cultivation, were fundamentally repressive in character. They focused on the forced eradication of cannabis plants, the elimination of seedlings, and the destruction of processed marijuana. No broader initiatives were envisioned. For example, no consideration was given to programs aimed at replacing illegal plantations with functioning farms that would also employ and feed people, nor to incentives for traditional farming in the area. Such alternative, nonrepressive strategies could have worked in concert with a policy of eradication driven by repressive actions, but they were not considered.

While the initiatives that were fielded (in combination with other public security measures developed by the government of the state of Pernambuco) were judged successful in terms of breaking up drug gangs and reducing homicide rates in the region, the eradication policy did not diminish the most consistent forms of cultivation. Instead, they innovated and persisted by changing their organization and operations and by expanding the number of agents active in the production process.

This chapter draws upon historical, legal, and sociological research on Brazilian drug policy and field research carried out by the authors with financial support from the *Fundação de Amparo à Pesquisa do Estado de Minas Gerais* [Minas Gerais' State Foundation for Research Support] and *Conselho Nacional de Desenvolvimento Científico e Tecnológico* [National Counsel of Scientific and Technological Development].

Drug Laws in Brazil

Brazil has a history of laws dealing with questions related to the use, trafficking, and production of psychoactive substances. They have always been in line with international norms and regulations. Beginning in 2006, the law in Brazil laid out a National System of Public Policy on Drugs (SISNAD) that addresses the prevention of undue drug use and attention to and social reintegration of users and addicts. It established procedures for repression of the unauthorized production of psychoactive substances, including their cultivation and illicit trafficking.

The New Drug Laws, as they came to be known, are a target of both criticism and praise. They both set severe penalties for drug trafficking and introduced innovations in the judicial treatment of those charged with carrying drugs for personal use, backing away from prison sentences in those cases. The latter represented a significant change from previous legal regimes. There are also notable gaps in the legislation, such as the absence of objective criteria for differentiating between drug users and traffickers. Earlier legislation had outlawed the cultivation of narcotic substances and the preparation and production of controlled substances able to create physical or psychological dependency (Pierangeli 2001). In 1971, legislation increased the maximum sentence allowable for drug offenses and introduced the concept of gang-specific drug trafficking, which could involve as few as two people (Karam 2010).

The New Drug Laws were particularly innovative, owing to the mix of legal responses that were allowed for prevention and education for those who acquire, keep, have at their disposal, transport, or carry on their person illicit drugs for personal use. They also recognized a different status for those who sow, cultivate, or harvest plants for the production of small quantities of narcotic substances, including for personal use (Greco Filho 2011). All of these provisions reflected a significant change in drug policies that had been set in the 1940s, when the first systematic modern drug laws were introduced.

The Production of Cannabis in Brazil

In Brazil, cannabis production is concentrated in one of the poorest regions of the country, and the recent expansion of production there is attributed largely to an expanding internal Brazilian market (Fraga 2006). Plants are cultivated in the São Francisco Valley region in the Northeast of Brazil to supply the urban markets of the main northeastern capitals and midsize cities in the region. Pioneering studies of cannabis plantations in Brazil (Bicalho 1995; Bicalho and Hoefle 1999) suggested otherwise, that marijuana produced in the Valley was targeted for the Southeast region, including for cities such as Rio de Janeiro, São Paulo, and Belo Horizonte. There were also suggestions that plantation production was already serving markets outside the country. Other studies, however, did not verify this account (e.g., Fraga 2006, 2015).

To the contrary, information from ex-producers, active dealers, and the Federal Police indicate that production from São Francisco Valley is destined for the consumer markets of the Northeast region, close to the area of production. There are other consolidated and well-organized cannabis distribution networks in the Southeast. They distribute marijuana coming from Paraguay, which is of good commercial value and produced in regions closer to the principal consumer markets of Rio de Janeiro and São Paulo. This competition also directed cannabis production of the São Francisco Valley region toward the main northeastern capitals (Fraga and Iulianelli 2011).

Though the presence of cannabis plantations in the São Francisco Valley is long standing (Pierson 1972; Burton 1869), recent increases in production have been tied to three fundamental drivers: the consolidation of the "industrialized" agricultural industry for producing tropical fruit in the São Francisco Valley region; the crisis in traditional agriculture in the region due to the construction of the Itaparica damn, which dislocated populations; and an increase in the country's consumer market for marijuana, specifically in the Northeast (Fraga 2006; Bicalho 1995).

Fraga (2003) and Fraga and Iulianelli (2011) noted that in Brazil, the centralization of the cultivation and sale of cannabis in the hands of groups who control the stages of production and the distribution process has tied rural workers without land or not connected to family agriculture to the commercial drug business. Those without ties to land see themselves ensnared in an economy of a semi-slave character, tied to living where they work. This process has intensified over time, beginning with a period of rapid growth in production of cannabis in the region in the 1980s and continuing into the 2000s. There was a parallel trend in production that involved some associations of workers who labored collaboratively in cannabis fields, usually on public lands or in areas where land ownership was contested. The distribution of their produce, however, always remained in the hands of organized gangs (Fraga 2011). Currently, there is a tendency for the decentralization of production into smaller farms. This has been in response to federal anti-drug efforts, which became more intense in the 2000s and led to a breaking up of previously large production organizations. Repression has also had the effect of extending plantation areas out of the so-called "Marijuana Polygon" into nearby areas, such as the state of Piauí and south of Bahia, where a great number of plantations have sprung up in recent years.

As noted earlier, campaigns against these illicit plantations have been undertaken without considering the economics of farm work and the often desperate situation of rural agricultural workers. These factors were also involved in the spread of cannabis plantations in recent decades, in order to serve a market avid for the product (Fraga 2012). The increase of production in the São Francisco Valley region in recent decades led to the incorporation of these new actors into the cannabis productive circuit. It is now possible to trace generations of farmers who base themselves in illicit production. The traditional cultivation of tropical fruits, a long-standing feature of agriculture in the area, was mechanized and converted into a factory-like industry by the 1970s, and this contributed significantly to the movement of labor into the cannabis cultivation business (Fraga, Cunha and Carvalho 2015). Driven by their precarious economic situation, workers who did not have land claims make up a significant proportion of all cannabis laborers. Through the 1980s, the expansion of cultivation areas, the fertile soil of the islands of the São Francisco River, and the need for greater numbers of people in the production and distribution of cannabis made work for the first generation of displaced agricultural workers (Fraga 2006). Ironically, the expansion of industrialized agriculture in the region facilitated the growth of cannabis production, since illicit cultivators could make use of the improvements in highways and infrastructure that were established to facilitate the tropical fruit business.

The 1970s and 80s, therefore, can be characterized as a period of the institutionalization of large-scale illicit cultivation in the São Francisco Valley. New economic relations were established and new actors emerged in the drug trade, and these changes transformed the economy of the region, which is hot and faces long dry spells that have a major impact on agriculture. The expansion of criminal networks was made possible by two distinct factors that complemented each other. The first was confrontations between families for control of politics and local power. They fought to dominate cannabis production, which was beginning to generate significant wealth. Their knowledge of the region and their history of involvement in other illegal businesses—including the appropriation of land, political crimes, murder, and corruption of public officials—were important factors in their establishment of criminal networks to successfully spread production. The second factor was the drug control efforts of the state, which struggled to contain the growing commercialization of the drug trade (Fraga 2010).

The structural elements that facilitated the spread of cannabis cultivation in the São Francisco Valley did not differ from factors that led people in other parts of the world to involve themselves in illicit cultivation. As the United Nations Office on Drugs and Crime itself recognizes (2014), around the world, illicit cultivation is driven by vulnerability and opportunity. For poorer rural people, survival can depend on money made in cannabis cultivation. For them, participation in illicit markets is particularly attractive, despite the resulting risks. Cannabis is a relatively durable product, it can be stored for longer periods, and has a good final price and a good market for sale, when compared to other traditional and more perishable agricultural products. It was being grown in areas that lacked public investment in agriculture and had serious water problems. In poor regions where other agricultural products cannot sustain the population, illicit cultivation facilitates the development of an underground economy of considerable magnitude (United Nations Office on Drugs and Crime 2014).

The Repression of Illicit Plantations

The growth of marijuana production, the formation of criminal networks, the violent incursion into the cannabis business of criminals from other illicit activities, and a burgeoning homicide rate led the Brazilian government to act more forcefully in initiatives that promised to tackle the problem. Beyond these domestic concerns, Brazil also felt pressure from multinational organizations to intensify its repression of the drug trade (Fraga 2007, Fraga 2015). Prior to this period, the federal and state governments in the Brazilian Northeast had undertaken some countermeasures. Even while production was still low, the authorities viewed it as a public health problem demanding repressive measures. In 1946, a consortium was formed by the states of Bahia, Sergipe, and Alagoas and named the Interstate Marijuana Agreement. They sought to implement collaborative measures to prevent and restrain practices tied to the use, sale, and cultivation of marijuana (Cardoso 1958). The report of the meeting recognized the southern zone of São Francisco, in the states of Sergipe and Alagoas, as one of the biggest cannabis production regions in Brazil, together with Maranhão and Pará. Representatives from the Civil Police, the secretaries of education and health of each state, as well as representatives from the federal government, participated in the creation of the agreement.

At the end of three meetings of the commission, 19 measures were proposed for adoption by the states. In relation to the repression of the plantations, two points stand out: (1) the destruction of marijuana plantations, except for its production for medical and industrial ends; and (2) small plantations could be placed under watch by the State Commissions of Oversight of Narcotics (SCON), with the aim of studying marijuana from pharmacological, clinical, psychological, and sociological points of view.

This meeting inspired, in the following year, a National Commission of Oversight of Narcotics (NCON) to establish standards that would be followed by all of the states in relation to the eradication of marijuana, or *diamba*, plantations, throughout the whole national territory, that is to say:

a. The marijuana or *diamba* plantations found in the national territory were to be destroyed by police authorities, under the technical supervision of the Agriculture Ministry, requiring these authorities to give immediate notification to the National Commission of Oversight for Narcotics;
b. If there were no representatives from the Agriculture Ministry in the local area where the plantation was encountered, the destruction could be undertaken by police authorities in conjunction with the sanitation authorities or by functionaries from the state agricultural services, with the technical capacity to proceed with the identification of the narcotic plant;
c. Samples of the plantations destroyed or to be destroyed were to be sent to the closest state or federal establishment, where its botanical characteristics could be carried out;
d. The authorities who carry out the destruction of the marijuana were obliged to immediately send to the National Commission for the Oversight of Narcotics a detailed report of their conduct, indicating the place, the report regarding the plant's classification, a sample of the plant appropriately authenticated, as well as other details referent to the case.
(Pernambuco Filho 1958, pp. 178, 179)

Brandão (2014) observes that the creation of the national commission was at the initiative of doctors who dedicated themselves to combating *diambism* (the habit of smoking marijuana) because of the addiction attributed to marijuana use. For these doctors and other members of health agencies and the police, many forms of drug addiction were viewed as acceptable, with the exception of marijuana, which needed to be combated. Marijuana use was understood by the establishment as an addiction of the lower classes, one resulting from their ignorance and in need of being stamped out in order to preserve public health. The creation of the National Commission for the Oversight of Narcotics in 1936 was the first effort to regulate and even seek to legalize transactions involving some with drugs. The Commission, at this first stage, was directly subordinated to the Ministry for Exterior Relations. This connection should be understood as an initiative to bring Brazilian governmental norms and measures into line with those defined in the international sphere.

Police repression during this period was the domain of the state Civil Police and of the Federal District. Despite all the efforts of the NCON, initiatives for eradication of cannabis plantations were sporadic and targeted mostly at small producers. In the 1940s, health and agricultural authorities had a say in the process, and addiction control was dealt with in the public health sphere. The regional police acted under the coordination of the Agriculture Ministry in their eradication initiatives. This does not mean that repression was absent, but what drove the eradication efforts of the time was not so much crime control as the principles of public health.

Only in the 1960s and 70s, when marijuana use spread more widely in society and began to affect the middle classes, did eradication projects become more frequent and under the supervision of the Federal Police (Misse 1999). This increasing criminalization was a feature of the military dictatorship installed in the country in 1964. By the 1980s, it was the Military Police, which are organized at the state level, that took over efforts to repress illicit cultivation. The Federal Police took action when areas of cultivation and marijuana distribution networks spanned more than one state. The modern Federal Police was formed in 1944. At the time, their new powers centered more specifically on public security services, such as policing maritime areas, airports, and the border. With the move of the federal capital to the city of Brasilia, the Federal Police incorporated other police departments from that area, and in 1967 it took its current form.

The Federal Police are under the control of the national Justice Ministry. It has many functions, such as investigating crimes against the political and social order or protecting the goods, services, and interests of the national government or its public enterprises. They also take on crimes whose practice has interstate or international repercussions and demand an orchestrated approach to enforcement. Among its newer functions is responsibility for the prevention and repression of drugs and contraband trafficking that spans state lines. When national and regional governments are concerned about the cultivation and interstate trafficking of marijuana, the Federal Police is their vehicle for action.

The growth beginning in the 1980s of cannabis plantations in the São Francisco River region led to a reaction from the Brazilian government, which in turn intensified its repressive efforts. Through the 1970s, the Federal Police were already involved in drug enforcement, but only in a nonsystematic way. It was only in the 1980s that enforcement would become more organized and methodical.

Henman (1986) describes the serious violations of human rights that characterized the haphazard efforts taken against cannabis plantations during the earlier period. At that time, Brazil was under a military dictatorship, and during the second half of the decade it began to direct more resources toward combating the use and trafficking of drugs in general and illicit cultivation of cannabis in particular. These operations were conducted on a small scale, however, and they were scattered and did not represent an overarching enforcement plan. Rather, they reacted to reports that came in. In one of these initiatives, in the state of Maranhão and on the lands of the Guajajara Indians, police agents tortured an alleged drug kingpin. This led the national Indigenous Missionary Council (IMC) to denounce such acts and to continue to pressure the authorities concerning their activities on native lands during the remainder of the decade.

In the 1980s, enforcement operations were intensified and undertaken with greater frequency. But despite this, plantations continued to expand. The quantity of plants eradicated, processed marijuana destroyed, and seedlings seized grew. It was not uncommon for 50,000 seedlings or cannabis plants to be uncovered in a single plantation (Fraga 2000). Even as the authoritarian regime came to an end during the 1980s, there was no significant change in the strategies of the Federal Police in relation to its eradication operations, and they continued to inflict human rights abuses. In a study of individuals accused of participation in cannabis cultivation in the Valley region between 1974 and 1985, around 20% of cases presented some type of irregularity, including the presentation of dubious confessions signed by illiterates, preventative prison sentences imposed without a legal basis, and allegations of confession under torture (Fraga 2015).

In the 1990s, eradication efforts became more frequent in the São Francisco Valley region, but production again continued to grow. There was a further escalation in drug-related violence during the decade, eventually reaching alarming levels. In 1997, of the ten cities with the highest homicide rates in Brazil, three were in the São Francisco Valley region: Floresta (112.6/100,000), Belém do São Francisco (98.0/100,000), and Terra Talhada (86.4/100,000). The growth of violence was a direct result of crime organized around the plantations and increasing levels of drug trafficking. In this period, the gangs that organized themselves around illegal cultivation continued to have strong family connections, and struggles between the families aggravated the situation. Another feature of the 1990s was an increase in homicides involving heavy weapons; an arms race had come to the Valley.

The police strategy was to hit plantations close to harvest time. This would undercut their revenue after many of their production expenses had been incurred. The high point of operations that took place in the São Francisco Valley region in the 1990s was Operation Mandacaru. This sweep through the Valley lasted 53 days and was the biggest eradication effort undertaken until that point. Table 6.1 summarizes official reports on the successes of the mission. Many vehicles were inspected and some seized; thousands of people were questioned and a few hundred arrested; and many plants and kilos of processed cannabis were destroyed.

However, the operation had its costs as well. Financially, it cost 7.5 million *reais* (around US$3.8 million in the era). This was an unprecedentedly high expense, but a force of almost 1,500 agents had been assembled from various enforcement agencies within the federal government, and it had to be paid for. The operation was coordinated not by the Federal Police, but by the new National Antidrug Secretariat (NADS). This had been created by the Brazilian government during the term of President Fernando Henrique Cardoso, in response from pressure by the Organization of the American States (OAS). This external pressure led Brazil to agree to abide by an OAS directive on the

Table 6.1 Numbers of Operation Mandacaru

eradicated marijuana plants	544,424
plantations located	255
seedbeds destroyed	294
seedlings destroyed	223,598
marijuana seized	612.3 kg
immediate arrests	188
arrest warrant issued	16
inspected vehicles	109,475
seized vehicles	155
repossessed vehicles	9
people taken in	242,054
firearms seized	257
Other weapons seized	105

Source: Institutional Security Office of the Presidency of Republic

reduction of demand for drugs (Garcia, Leal and Abreu 2008). The creation of the NADS and its subsequent highly visible crackdown in the Valley was a political move by the Brazilian government to show to the international community that they were taking action and that reducing drug trafficking would be a government priority.

But shifting control of Operation Mandacaru to the NADS also resulted in pushback by the Federal Police. They argued that, with their more efficient use of resources, in operations costing 85,000 reais (44 thousand dollars), they had eradicated more plants using fewer agents. The NADS alleged in return that the Federal Police had also received funding from the U.S. Drug Enforcement Administration for purchasing equipment and reimbursing other police agencies (Isto é 1999). In Operation Mandacaru, the NADS did not have American support.

The plan had been that following Operation Mandacaru, responsibility for plantation eradication would pass to the state of Pernambuco. The federal government did transfer equipment and money to the state, but the Federal Police continued to take the lead in drug eradication campaigns, and they continue to do so until this day. They claimed that the NADS did not actually have the powers of the police, and that coordination of eradication actions by this "civilian" secretariat would be unconstitutional. The ensuing controversy led to the fall of several Justice Ministers, and it was finally resolved by a decree of the president limiting the powers of NADS. NADS lost its police-like roles and retreated from coordinating and directing direct eradication operations. In 2011, it was folded into the Justice Ministry and given a policy-advising role in support of actions by other agencies in drug use prevention. The Federal Police continues to coordinate significant eradication operations around four times a year, still coinciding with harvest times. Control of operations in the São Francisco Valley have been decentralized to a local branch of the Federal Police in the region, rather than being centralized in Brasilia.

Most recently, it appears that continued enforcement efforts have changed the character of the drug business there. Important gangs have been broken up, and the size of plantations has gone down, with a reduced quantity of cannabis now being grown in many but smaller operations. An officer we interviewed in the area reported that enforcement operations have become more effective when they are guided by satellite photographs, which identify in advance the location of farms. Enforcement has pushed production from the mainland bordering the São Francisco River out onto islands in the river itself, where smaller plantations are to be found. In compensation, producers have been employing more fertilizer in order to enhance their harvests.

Police officer: Today, few plantations are encountered on "the continent" (on the riverbank). And another thing which is also interesting is that the farms have diminished in size. They prefer to plant a small farm here, plant another smaller one there. It is difficult to find a plantation of forty thousand plants, which we had already considered to be a big farm. This year we only managed to find one big farm, of more than forty thousand plants. You asked me how the calculation is made. What happens generally is that in each hole (we call them holes), they plant from 3 to 4 plants of marijuana, right? Previously we made the following calculation, 3 marijuana plants generates about 1 kilo of marijuana at the time. Today each plant will give 700 grams. Now, the size of the plant then increased a lot. So, why did the size of the plant increase so much? Because they are using follicular stimulants, the fertilizers, right? So today each hole manages to produce more or less 3 kilos of marijuana; 2 and-a-half to 3 kilos of marijuana.

Interviewer: That is to say, it increased the productivity, is that it?

Police officer: Exactly. So in this way, they diminished the quantity of plantations, but the productivity is either the same or perhaps greater. So the count is more or less done in this way.

(Police officer, 35 years of age, 2015)

Forming more, if smaller, plantations has also increased the participation of poorer rural workers, also leading new families who planted in smaller quantities in the past to be integrated into the productive process. So, there was success in breaking up the family groups and gangs, which had sparked violence during the 1990s. But a consequence of this success was the decentralization of the production process and the involvement of more people than before, putting at risk vulnerable people who had not previously had contact with criminal life.

Police officer: We observed that, every day more people became involved in the cultivation on the marijuana farms.

Interviewer: Increasingly more?

Police officer: Always more, right? We don't have any more big producers in the region.

Interviewer: Sorry. Big cultivators you would call people who are like what?

Police officer: It would be a clan, a family.

Interviewer: Which were the first to get into this business, is that right?

Police officer: Exactly.

Interviewer: The first to work with the plantations in the region.

Police Officer: So like this, today you will no longer find clans that are directed toward gigantic farms. We have a photo here in the station of a marijuana farm, where there was gunfire on one side of the farm. Those on the other side of the farm could not hear the gunfire. This marijuana plantation was that big, understand? Today you don't encounter this anymore. You just don't see it anymore.

(Police officer, 35 years of age, 2015)

Federal Police Statistics indicate that between 2005 and 2014 there was a general reduction in the quantity of plants eradicated. As Table 6.2 reports,

Table 6.2 Cannabis plants destroyed in forced eradication of the Federal Police operations (2005–2014)

Year	Number of forced eradication operations	cannabis plants (millions)
2005	2	1,822
2006	3	2,095
2007	1	131
2008	3	2,131
2009	4	1,652
2010	4	1,026
2011	3	847
2012	3	537
2013	3	719
2014	2	1,080

Source: Federal Operations

these numbers vary considerably from year to year. However, the success of eradication campaigns appears to have declined, especially after 2010, perhaps in the isolation and decentralization of the new production process.

Discussion

Globally, Brazil is not considered a drug-producing nation. Cannabis is the only drug cultivated on a large scale, and that is to supply the domestic market. Brazilian production, in fact, supplies only around 30% of that market. The repressive measures undertaken to destroy cannabis plantations only became large scale beginning in the 1990s, despite the fact that legislation had been on the books outlawing them since the 1940s. The belated attention given to the problem was owing to international pressure to demonstrate Brazil's involvement in the war against drugs.

Only when the Federal Police became the principal organization for combating cannabis production could significant operations to do so be sustained. They had federal resources and the assistance of the U.S. Drug Enforcement Administration. The result of their two decades of repression was the breaking up of local gangs, significantly reducing the number of large plantations, and helping diminish the homicide rates in regions where the larger plantations were located. However, more recently there are indications of a migration of plantations to other states outside the São Francisco Valley region, to areas such as Piauí and Pará. There also seems to have been an increase in the productivity of new, smaller plantations, including due to the use of chemical fertilizers. Decentralization also has led to greater involvement by poor agricultural workers in these many new, smaller farms.

The Brazilian government did not choose a strategy of offering transitional income support and farming alternatives for these workers. Farming in the São Francisco Valley region is marginal because the area is often beset by extensive drought, so their prospects outside of the drug business were dim. So instead, more farmers are involved in the drug business than in the past, still working at the margins but seeing in the cultivation of cannabis their best option for a better life.

References

Bicalho, A. M. 1995. A Produção de Maconha No Sertão do São Francisco [The production of Marijuana in the Hinterlands of São Francisco]. *Boletim de Geografia Teorética* 25: 289–300.
Bicalho, A.M.D.S.M., & Hoefle, S. W. (1999). From Family Feud to Organised Crime: The Cultural Economy of Cannabis in Northeast Brazil. *Bulletin of Latin American Research*, 18(3): 343–360.
Brandão, M. D. 2014. Ciclos de atenção à maconha no Brasil [Marijuana attention cycles in Brazil]. *Revista de Biologia*, 13(1): 1–10.

Burton, R. F. 1869. *Exploration of the highlands of the Brazil.* London: Tinsley Brothers.

Cardoso, E. 1958. Convênio Interestadual da Maconha [Interstate Marijuana Agreement]. In *Maconha, Coletânea de Trabalhos Brasileiros* [Marijuana, Brazilian Collection of papers], 165–174. Rio de Janeiro: Serviço Nacional de Educação Sanitária, Ministério da Saúde.

Fraga, P.C.P. 2000. Juventude, Narcotráfico e Violência no Brasil [Youth, Drug Trafficking and Violence in Brazil]. In *Narcotráfico e Violência no Campo* [Narcotrafficking and Violence in the Field], ed. A.M.M. Ribeiro and J.A.S. Iulianelli, 81–108. Rio de Janeiro, DP&A.

Fraga. P.C.P. 2003. Da Favela ao Sertão [From the Favela to the Hinterland]. In *Jovens em Tempo Real* [Youngsters in real time], ed. P. C. P. Fraga and J. A. S. Iulianelli, 117–147. Rio de Janeiro: DP&A.

Fraga, P.C.P. 2006. Plantios ilícitos no Brasil: notas sobre a violência e o cultivo de cannabis no polígono da Maconha [Ilegal crops in Brazil: Notes on the violence and cannabis cultivation in the Marijuana Polygon]. *Cadernos de Ciências Humanas-Especiaria* 9: 95–118.

Fraga, P.C.P. 2007. A Geopolítica das Drogas na América Latina [The geopolitics of drugs in Latin America]. *Em Pauta* 10: 83–105.

Fraga, P.C.P. 2010. As ações de erradicação de plantios considerados ilícitos na América Latina e no Brasil [Eradication actions of considered illegal plantations in Latin America and Brazil]. In *Crimes, drogas e políticas* [Crime, drugs and politics], ed. P. C. P. Fraga, 187–225. Ilhéus: Editora da UESC.

Fraga, P.C.P. 2011. Plantar o ilícito e colher renda: alternativas, redefinição de conflitos no entorno do cultivo ilícito de cannabis no Sertão [Planting the illicit and reaping income: Alternatives, redefinition of conflicts surrounding the illicit cultivation of cannabis in the Sertão]. In *Violência e Dilemas Civilizatórios: as práticas de punição e extermínio* [Violence and Civilizational Dilemmas: The practices of punishment and extermination], ed. C. Barreira, L; Sá and J. P. Aquino, 89–108. Campinas: Pontes Editora.

Fraga, P.C.P. 2012. Plantaciones ilícitas como fuente de ingresos alternativa y expresión de desigualdad: el caso del cultivo de cannabis en el nordeste de Brasil [Illicit plantations as alternative source of income inequality expression: The case of cannabis cultivation in northeastern Brazil]. *Estudios Sociológicos* 30: 143–169.

Fraga, P.C.P. 2015a. A participação feminina no plantio de *cannabis* no Vale do São Francisco [Female participation in cannabis plantations in the São Francisco Valley]. In *Mulheres e Criminalidade* [Women and criminality], ed. P.C.P. Fraga. 1st edition, 9–36. Rio de Janeiro: Letra Capital.

Fraga, P.C.P. 2015b. *Vida bandida: histórias de vida, ilegalismos e carreiras criminais. Um estudo com presos do sistema carcerário do Rio de Janeiro* [Thug life: Stories of life, ilegality and criminal careers: A study with inmates of Rio de Janeiro's prison's system]. Lisboa: Ed. Nova.

Fraga, P.C.P., Cunha, S. M., and Carvalho, L.C.D. 2015. Políticas de repressão e erradicações de plantios de cannabis no nordeste brasileiro [Repression and eradication policies of cannabis plantations in northeastern Brazil]. In *Plantios ilícitos na América Latina* [Illegal plantings in Latin America], ed. P.C.P. Fraga, 55–80. Rio de Janeiro: Letra Capital.

Fraga, P.C.P., and Iulianelli, J. A. S. 2011. Plantios ilícitos de cannabis no Brasil: Desigualdades, alternativa de renda e cultivo de compensação [Illicit cannabis plantations in Brazil: Inequalities, alternative income and compensation cultivation]. *Revista Dilemas* 4: 11–40.

Garcia, M.L.T., Leal, F. X., & Abreu, C. C. 2008. A política antidrogas brasileira: velhos dilemas [Brazilian anti-drug policy: old dilemmas]. *Psicologia & Sociedade*, 20(2): 267–276.

Greco Filho, V. 2011. *Tóxicos: prevenção—repressão* [Drugs: Prevention—repression]. 14th edition. São Paulo: Saraiva.

Henman, A. 1986. A guerra às drogas é uma guerra etnocida [The war on drugs is an ethnocide war]. In *Diamba Sarabamba: coletânea de textos brasileiros sobre a maconha* [Diamba Sarabamba: collection of Brazilian texts on marijuana], ed. A. Henman and O. Pessoa Jr., 91–116. São Paulo, Ground.

Isto é. 1999. *A viagem da maconha: operação de R$ 7,5 milhões descobre que Maranhão tomou o lugar de Pernambuco como maior produtor* [The marijuana trip: operation of R $ 7.5 million finds that Maranhão took the place of Pernambuco as the largest producer]. n. 1575, http://istoe.com.br/28905_A+VIAGEM+DA+MACONHA+/ (accessed January 10, 2016).

Karam, M. L. 2010. *Drogas: legislação brasileira e violações a direitos fundamentais* [Drugs: Brazilian legislation and fundamental rights violations]. In *Law Enforcement Against Prohibition—LEAP.* Brasil: Disponível em. www.leapbrasil.com.br/textos (accessed December 15, 2015).

Misse, M. 1999. *Malandros, marginais e vagabundos: a acumulação social da violência no Rio de Janeiro* [Rogues, Punks and Thugs: The social accumulation of violence in Rio de Janeiro]. Ph.D. Dissertation. Instituto Universitário de Pesquisas do Rio de Janeiro, RJ.

Pernambuco Filho, P. 1958. Estudo sôbre as conclusões aprovadas pelo Convênio da Maconha, realizado na Cidade do Salvador, em dezembro de 1946 [Study on the conclusions approved by the Marijuana Convention, held in the City of Salvador in December 1946]. In *Maconha, Coletânea de Trabalhos Brasileiros* [Marijuana, Brazilian Collection of papers], 175–180. Rio de Janeiro: Serviço Nacional de Educação Sanitária, Ministério da Saúde.

Pierangeli, J. H. 2001. *Códigos penais do Brasil: evolução histórica* [Penal codes of Brazil: Historical evolution]. 2nd edition. São Paulo: Editora Revista dos Tribunais.

Pierson, D. 1972. *O Homem no Vale do São Francisco* [The man in São Francisco valley]. Rio de Janeiro: SUVALE.

United Nations Office on Drugs and Crime. 2014. *World Drug Report 2014.* Vienna: Author.

Race, Class and Law Enforcement in Brazil[1]

7

Renato Sérgio de Lima and Jacqueline Sinhoretto

Contents

In March 2015 Brazil reached a landmark: it had been 30 years since the end of military dictatorship in Brazil and the restoration of democracy. This ensuing period is one of the longest democratic cycles the country has enjoyed. However, Brazil's democracy did not advance seamlessly during this period. There was progress in several areas of the country's development agenda, such as the fight against absolute poverty, and the consolidation—albeit inconsistently applied—of such rights as consumer protection. Since the return of democracy a number of protections have been enshrined in the nation's new Civil Code, there has been increased use of alternative criminal penalties, and there has been new investment in police training regarding the principles of human rights.

There have also been steps backward, and new obstacles to the implementation of democratic principles in state institutions have arisen. Above all, there have been roadblocks to the democratization of Brazil's criminal justice system (the police forces, the state prosecutors' offices, the offices of the public defender, the judiciary and the prison system). Examining these, it can be seen that in the field of public safety there is a pendulum movement between—on one hand—measures intended to modernize police forces and the criminal justice system along democratic lines, and—on the other—resistance from contrary forces that are not inclined to challenge the institutional violence, inefficient operations, and poor protection of human rights that characterize the police forces of Brazil. As Costa and Lima (2014) put it, an enormous dispute is currently being waged as to the meaning of law, order and public safety in Brazil.

Countless factors contribute to this state of affairs. The first of these is the historical coincidence between the return of democracy and the upswings in violence, fear and general feelings of insecurity. Violence is ever present in the newspapers, above all taking the form of the fear of violent crimes against property, including robbery and personal theft. Among poor people, violent death is almost commonplace: there are over 58,000 intentional violent deaths each year, and in addition, more than 3,000 deaths are provoked annually by the police forces themselves. The victims of all of this are mainly poor, young black males. Theirs makes up a whole universe of "invisible victims" that need to be dealt with. The enemies of the Brazilian state are not other countries, but portions of its own population that are historically and politically invisible.

Racial Inequalities, Violence and Black Youth

Among issues invisible to the population of Brazil as a whole, racial inequality ranks as one of the major taboos of the political culture. However, data are available that help deconstruct some of the myths that stubbornly maintain an image of Brazil as a nation without racial inequalities, or without a racist ideology, and instead one that needs to tackle economic inequality. The Brazilian Forum on Public Safety edited its "Index of Youth Vulnerability to Violence and Racial Inequality" (*Índice de Vulnerabilidade Juvenil à Violência e Desigualdade Racial*) at the request of the federal government. It shows, for example, that young black males from 12 to 29 years of age are on average 2.6 times more likely to be murdered than young white males, and that in some states of Brazil's Northeast, such as Paraíba and Pernambuco, they are 11 times more likely (Brasil 2015a).

Such facts are increasingly better known, albeit without taking center stage or causing great indignation in mainstream public opinion. The scarcity of analyses of the color or race of victims, offenders and the police is in itself evidence of how invisible the racial issue is when considering how violence is produced in Brazil. Data on color and race are available in reports and on forms stored away by the criminal justice system. Close analyses of the racial component of the crime and justice problems of the country have generally not loomed large in interpretations of violence (Sinhoretto 2014b). In the collective imagination of Brazilians, racism has been subsumed and attenuated by the idea that the inequality affecting young black males is essentially a social class issue. The most commonplace explanations of violence in Brazil tend to focus much more on inequalities of experience between classes. However, the data emphatically prove that race is a core issue.

Although, as we noted, lethal violence is a class experience, class is insufficient to express the extent of inequality in the distribution of violent deaths. Race relations intertwine with it—and occasionally go beyond it. Regarding violent death, blacks are the most vulnerable. Proportionately, black people die unexpectedly 30% more often than do whites in Brazil (FBSP 2015), forcing us to think equally of links between class, race, generation and territory. Put differently, it is common sense to state that the police forces treat the rich and poor unequally, but very little has been invested in research into how the process of construction of unequal treatment comes about in the daily routine of law enforcement personnel on the streets.

Violent death is marked by color, age and territory in Brazil. The flash point in some portion of violent deaths lies in interactions between police and youth. On the one hand, young people—and particularly black youth—do not enjoy policies seemingly intended to assure their right to life and safety. On the other hand, youth—and particularly black youth—are the favored targets of police surveillance, as revealed by data on the prison population and on deaths resulting from police actions.

A survey conducted in Rio de Janeiro, São Paulo and Minas Gerais found that more young blacks die in police operations than do young whites. The more frequently deadly force is applied by the police, the more it is targeted at blacks. Taking 2011 as a benchmark, and calculating death rates at the hands of police among the white and black populations of each state, reveals that in Minas Gerais twice as many blacks as whites were killed by the police. This rate was three times more unfavorable to blacks in São Paulo. While in Rio de Janeiro, police killed almost four times more blacks than whites. Among all the states surveyed, the victims of deadly violence are mainly young, while the average age among black victims is lower than the average age among white victims (Sinhoretto et al. 2014).

In addition to violent deaths caused by law enforcement actions, rates of imprisonment point to young blacks being the main target of policing. Young blacks are not only overwhelmingly the main victims of homicides in Brazil, including those committed by law enforcement agents, but on average they also go to prison 18% more often than do whites. Additionally, the data in the study entitled "Map of Imprisonment: Brazil's Young People" (*Mapa do Encarceramento: os jovens do Brasil*—Brasil 2015b) show that most often young black people are placed in pretrial detention while awaiting a judicial sentence, one that may take years to be handed down. Once sentenced, many are found guilty of crimes that could have been punished by alternative sentencing, as in the cases of crimes against property and crimes linked to the drug trade. In other words, the fact that there are many young people and black people in prison cannot be explained by the supposition that the police are, in their daily activities, watching the most violent criminals—those that commit heinous crimes. Only 12% of Brazil's inmates are serving sentences for murders. The core of criminal policy is driven by punishment of crimes against property or linked to the drug trade, in line with the war on drugs begun by the United States in the 1980s.

Criminal justice policy in this regard differs very little from judicial policy that can be observed in the civil justice system. An overwhelming concern about managing conflict linked to the protection of wealth can be seen in who has access to civil justice—an analysis of which we have described elsewhere (Sinhoretto 2014a; Lima, Sinhoretto and Bueno 2015)—and it is reflected in the profile of inmates. Criminal punishment in Brazil falls mainly upon young black men committing crimes threatening wealth: robbery, theft and drug trafficking.

The main concern of the justice system thus is with the protection (either necessary or undue) of wealth, to the detriment of the treatment of violent conflicts and the protection of life and well-being. Observing this system in operation, it seems clear that the handling of violent conflicts is not a core concern for the institutions of justice. Furthermore, given that the bulk of the work done in the criminal justice system seems to begin with arrests of people caught in the act of perpetrating crimes, it can be seen that the most active role in managing violent conflict falls to Brazil's Military Police. Their routine operations select their targets for enforcement and prioritize the crimes they are actually interested in focusing on.

The Role of Brazil's Military Police

Within the Brazilian criminal justice system, the Military Police (a uniformed, militarized gendarmerie run at the state level) plays a central role, as they carry out daily deterrent policing of the streets and select the types of crimes and of criminals on which to concentrate. Brazil's Military Police are responsible for determining the practical implementation of public order policies and drawing the boundaries of what is legal or illegal on the street. But in the "logic as practiced" of current policing procedures, this boundary is tenuous and hardly ever made explicit, and varies in accordance with the segment of the population that is the target of policing and with the type of crime committed.

The Civil Police have helped produce this state of affairs as well, due to their inability to carry out effective criminal investigations. As a result, the actions of the Military Police determine the outputs of policing generally. The activity of the Civil Police has been studied by generations of researchers, including Paixão (1982), Kant de Lima (1995) and Misse and colleagues (2010). There has been an over-reliance on police investigations known as "inquiries" (*inquéritos policiais*), a process that was formally created in 1871. Inquiries were a bureaucratic feature of the Empire and the Republic, and have been maintained throughout democratic and authoritarian periods alike. The form of an inquiry rather than its content is privileged. There is no coordination of the work of inquiries with other police forces, and investigation is mistaken for what one would think of as a "police inquiry." Little attention is given to the idea that a decent investigation depends on such actions as preserving the crime scene, collecting technical evidence and building trust with the population at large, so that they will provide information or step forward as witnesses to events that have taken place.

As to the Prosecution Office, its responsibility seems to reside in a failure to exercise its constitutional role as an external control on police action. Instead, prosecutors go through the motions of processing inquiries as they receive them from the police precincts, and do not concern themselves with how either the Military or Civil Police is working or with guaranteeing the rights of the population when they are targeted by their actions. Rather, they accept what the police give them, despite alarming figures regarding the incidence of police use of force and deadly force. The actions of the judiciary, in its turn, simply reproduce the existing profile of Brazilian inmates, illustrating how it has given up any oversight of other elements of the criminal justice system.

As in several other South American countries, the criminal justice system finds it acceptable that some 40% of Brazilian inmates are incarcerated in pretrial detention. Detainees can remain in this limbo for an extended period: a CRISP/UFMG/SRJ/MJ (Centro de Estudos da Criminalidade e Segurança Pública–Universidade Federal de Minas Gerais/Secretaria da Reforma do Judiciário–Ministério da Justiça) (2014) survey documented that in the five Brazilian states that were examined, the average time that elapsed before concluding manslaughter cases in the judicial branch was 7.3 years. Given what is known of the working of the criminal justice system and its consequences for the demographic profile of inmates, the high rate of pretrial detention further reinforces the leading role of the Military Police in creating disparities in the system. Arrests of young inhabitants of the violent outlying neighborhoods of Brazil's cities (the "periphery"—*periferia*) and of black men are driven by acknowledgment of the bodily stigma that they bear: that of the "*mala*" (petty drug dealer—Jesus 2014), the "*peba*" (a young person who lives in the periphery—Suassuna 2008) and/or the "*vagabundo*" (slacker, street punk, beggar).

Briefly, the leading role of the Military Police is created by the tacit acceptance of all involved that what is important is to maintain public order, even if this means delegating the definition of what this actually entails to law enforcement officers on the street rather than to the judicial branch. Officers interacting on a daily basis with the inhabitants of the street corners and bars that make up the urban maze (*as quebradas*) and give shape and color to the centers and peripheries of Brazilian cities are empowered to make what essentially are the final decisions regarding what is legal and illegal. The autonomy delegated to the Military Police in Brazil is not the conscious choice of this organization only, however ardently it may promote the cult of its indepen-dence; it is a political and institutional option taken by all the organizations making up the criminal justice system.

As violence is accepted as being a legitimate response by the state, and because many in the population call out for it to be applied in order to guar-antee peace for law-abiding citizens (*cidadãos de bem*) through the repression of "bad guys" ("*bandidos*"), nothing could be taken more for granted than the ideology that "good criminals are dead criminals—*bandido bom é o bandido morto.*" This is according to a study by Bueno (2014), although recent data show that Brazilian society is split down the middle over this issue (FBSP 2015). Many Military Police forces still operate following the logic of military operations: that criminals need—just like an enemy—to be taken down, neu-tralized, killed. This "war on crime" stance is reinforced by the fact that police officers are three times more likely to be killed in confrontations than are aver-age members of the population at large. Instead of using force to defend the democratic rule of law, the militaristic stance that they are fighting the enemy persuades people that killing—and its corollary, being killed—is the calling of law enforcement officers. However, it is essential to draw attention to the fact that this only occurs because it is policy choice regarding how to handle social conflict that was made in Brazil, rather than because it is a necessarily efficient way of reducing crime. The persistence of homicides (which exceed the figures of any other country), studies of police victims (which show how fragile is the right to physical integrity), and the growth in the number of rob-beries and rapes all indicate that the result of this militaristic style of police has not brought crime down.

Police Officers' Origins and Views

Examining the background of law enforcement officers draws further atten-tion to the intersection between race and social class in the makeup of the police forces. By far the majority of law enforcement officers are poorly paid, and yet relatively well educated. They are mostly black, as a result of a race relations model that has built a job market offering slightly enhanced oppor-tunities to blacks in public careers[2] (Jesus 2014; Sansone 2002; Ramalho Neto 2012; Pires 2010). However, there are obstacles to full citizenship in the sworn ranks, because consonant with the militarized structure of the police forces, their members are not entitled to form trade unions or to assemble politically, and they are often subject to anachronistic disciplinary codes.

In a joint survey of more than 21,000 Brazilian law enforcement officers by the Brazilian Forum for Public Safety (FBSP) and the Getulio Vargas Founda-tion (Lima, Bueno and Santos 2014), most officers interviewed said they were favorable to demilitarization, which they understood not as the abandonment of hierarchy and control mechanisms, but rather as a change from an unequal and segregated personnel system and as the end of the arbitrary humiliation and punishment that employees often undergo. In accordance with this, 57% of law enforcement officers favored the end of the military justice code; 76% favored a formal separation of the Military Police from the army; 94% advocated modernization of the disciplinary code in order to bring them into line with the Federal Constitution; 87% wanted the right to join trade unions and to strike to be regulated; and 87% wanted the work of the Military Police forces to be reoriented towards the protection and assurance of citizens' rights.

In this paradoxical situation, what guides the practice of these officers? By all accounts, it seems that there has developed a rudimentary but decidedly nonmilitary set of new ideas concerning how police should deal with young people who express an ethical and aesthetic departure from the norms deemed acceptable for their class, color and territory. In addition, there is resistance to institutional practices and an organization culture that sees police as defenders of the interests of the state rather than of the rights of the citizen. Current strategies to control crime are not seen as based on a legal foundation or professional knowledge, far less on any sophisticated criminological theory. This is in the context of a world of complex crime in which trade in drugs and weapons is multinational, professionalized, hierarchical and well organized. The police are deeply estranged from the community, just as they are from young people, and do not see themselves as effectively organized to counter contemporary crime problems.

As a result, according to a national victimization survey (*Pesquisa Nacional de Vitimização*), the population does not see the Brazilian police as trustworthy. Even Brazil's most positively rated police force, which happens to be the Minas Gerais Military Police, does not enjoy the trust of more than one-third of the population (CRISP and DATAFOLHA 2013). This number is drawn from a 2014 study entitled *Índice de Confiança na Justiça*—ICJ ("Index of Trust in the Justice System") by FGV Direito SP (Cunha 2014), which found that only 33% of respondents called the police to solve problems in which they were victims or participants. Of these, only 37% stated they were "very" or "somewhat" satisfied with the services provided by the police. Only 32% of those interviewed in the ICJ declared that they trust the police, a figure very similar to the 33% who stated they trust the judicial branch and below the 48% who trust the prosecutor's office. However, none of these institutions enjoys the trust of more than half of the population of Brazil.

Brazil's unequal and far from smoothly advancing democracy, which ought to rest on the cornerstone of protecting life and promoting equality above any other value, actually rests upon a subjective quality attributed to the law enforcement officers—a hunter's keen sense of smell. Their approach to controlling what is identified as criminal behavior is confrontation and combat. They pursue a militarized form of combat that assumes and authorizes the elimination of the enemy. This is why the distinction between the use of legal force and police violence is, as we have mentioned, a blurred boundary, one that is deliberately ill defined and held to be undefinable. Brazil's paradoxical democracy coexists with the practice of controlling crime which threatens the establishment, while allowing white-collar crime to flourish everywhere.

Within this setting, the Military Police is the body that has been charged with managing criminal violence and has been given implicit freedom to use their own, supported by their widespread description as "combating the criminal." On the other hand, judges and prosecutors are paid high salaries and have strong guarantees regarding their autonomy, working conditions, control of their own budget, political independence, administrative independence, special social welfare rights and ability to choose the conflicts they wish to manage. It is law enforcement officers who earn the lowest salaries, receive the poorest training in all of Brazil's justice system and must rely on their poor training and instincts. The lives of "bad guys" have no explicit value, while police officers "do what nobody else has the guts to do" in order to impose law and order. They can claim the identity of hero when they "fall in battle," victims to a certain extent of their own confrontational social control model. This further contributes to their routine use of violence on the streets.

Social movements defending the victims of police violence, human rights advocates and black youth have organized politically in order to criticize this state of affairs, raising the banner of the demilitarization of the police. But very little has been achieved in terms of credibly diagnosing the causal links between militarization and the production of carnage among youth and the massive imprisonment of young people. Perhaps the difficulty of making such a diagnosis in a politically effective way explains why proposals of reform have been half-hearted and come all too short of the challenge to build full and universal citizenship in the field of safety. No one knows for certain what demilitarizing the police forces would mean. As a result, the demands for less violent, more rights-oriented police forces are vague in terms of a program of action. This lays them open to criticism from opponents and helps discredit any alternatives that are put forward. Without a feasible proposal for police reform, the denunciation of abuses and fatalities takes center stage as the main strategy in the struggle. This is, however, a reactive strategy with very little power to produce short- or mid-term change.

From another angle, law enforcement officers themselves are organizing to claim union status. They are demanding improved working conditions and pay, but few among them have condemned the institutional architecture of policing itself as being responsible for the current situation in public safety. Their solutions seem to repeat formulas that have failed in the past. They boil down to more and bigger weapons, more officers and more cars. Above all, internal critics of the police demand greater firepower, more modern vehicles and officers better trained for combat. And in the midst of this lack of consensus over reform, Brazil has a national congress that has failed to advance modernization in this area (FBSP 2014).

As has been argued elsewhere (Lima and Sinhoretto 2011; Lima, Sinhoretto and Bueno 2015), the restoration of democracy in Brazil in the 1980s did not resolve conflicts over the police. This is not to deny that there have been changes, but the restoration of democracy created new ambiguities regarding the role of the police and antagonisms between actors in the system. From a sociological point of view, this antagonism is the way in which interest groups contend over ethical views, which they advance in debates that arise every day. The ambiguity is a byproduct of conflicts over the role of the police in defending rights versus the legitimate desire of the population to live in peace and safety. The police are a core institution in any democracy, and therefore ensuring control over them and transparency in their policies and operations is central to advancing the citizenship status of millions of Brazilians.

Brazil is not alone in this situation. Throughout the world, there have been pressures to reduce rights in order to control crime, above all within the context of the "war on drugs" and the fight against terrorism. The increasing militarization of police forces is a present concern for the United States and European activists, who draw attention to (for example) the growing militarization of police weaponry. Racial and ethnic biases and filtering mechanisms have increasingly been addressed as issues in democracies. However, in none of the countries with which Brazil is commonly compared is the homicide rate so high and lethal encounters between law enforcement officers and civilians so common. Empirical evidence gathered in Brazil reveals a completely different scale to the problems facing theories of democracy, social control and public safety. The scale of Brazil's dilemmas is what sets the country apart and makes efforts to modernize the public safety institutions so urgent.

A Discontinuous Democracy

The empirical observations gathered here now will help us examine the working of democracy in Brazil and the stop-start nature of its development. Social scientists have already addressed the disconnect between democracy and the assurance of civil rights in Brazil. It has been a major issue of study for 40 years, since Wanderley Guilherme dos Santos (1979) identified how Brazil constructed a peculiar form of "regulated citizenship" under which the mass public is governed somewhat arbitrarily and often violently, a feature which is quite different from that of other democracies. Twenty years later, José Murilo de Carvalho (2000) returned to the discussion, reaffirming that the lack of guaranteed civil rights (to life, freedom from harm, equality and justice) had affected the quality and intensity of democracy in Brazilian society. Teresa Caldeira (2000) and James Holston (2013) described Brazil as a "disjunctive democracy" that does not secure guaranteed civil rights, and a society that accepts violent punishment, torture and the deadly use of force by the police.

Sérgio Adorno and Camila Dias (2014) have also drawn attention to the violence practiced by the state at rates that that would be unthinkable in secure democracies—in rates of death caused by the police and prison conditions, in the multiple types of selective biases practiced by the criminal justice system and in tangible hurdles to the effective implementation of human rights. Angelina Peralva (2001) contributed to an understanding of the violence/democracy paradox in Brazil by showing how, for young people who grew up under democracy and a period of economic expansion, racism is a barrier to integration in a society where mass individualism advocates the consumption of goods and services, but does not ensure equality in their distribution.

In the tradition of this line of analyses, this chapter seeks to contribute to an understanding of ways in which authoritarianism operates in the daily practices of safety and justice. We have stressed that race, in its complex interactions with issues of class, generation and territory is an important component ordering the practices of the criminal justice system. The more policing involves imposing military practices that define potential offenders as the enemy, the more this tendency is reinforced. This is where authoritarianism in institutional practices—which are directly linked to a political tradition that excludes people, represses them and treats them virtually as slaves—shows most tellingly its effects. It hinders their exercise of civil rights, above all—albeit not exclusively—for black youth, by refusing to guarantee their right to life, liberty, physical safety, equality, fair treatment before the law and access to justice.

The deterioration of civil rights in the face of this repression calls for further consideration here. The state's current responses to crime and criminals are echoes of an older culture infused by "violent sociability," a concept well described in the classics documenting Brazilian social thought, particularly in the work of Sérgio Buarque de Holanda (1958), Gilberto Freyre (1933), Victor Nunes Leal (2012), Maria Sylvia de Carvalho Franco (1997) and Raymundo Faoro (1975). Machado da Silva argued that violence must be understood not as a series of isolated behaviors, but rather as a complex of hierarchically articulated practices; in other words, as the social order itself. In this way, urban violence does not destroy conventional patterns of sociability, but coexists with them; in other words it expresses patterns of sociability that are rooted in the use of force as the organizing principle of social relations (Machado da Silva 2008).

The role of the state as the holder of a legitimate monopoly on the use of violence is questioned by this process. One of the major challenges to the real implementation of democracy in Brazil resides in its failure to actually maintain this monopoly and ensure that it is exercised legitimately through law. Instead, violence is also widely used in the actual control of urban populations through the repressive role of the police. That there are two holders of control over violence dictates that there will be a fine line determining the course of police actions, between how force is employed to maintaining law *and* order, and demarcating the boundary between what is legal and what is illegal (Bueno 2014).

Notwithstanding new explanations of the stop and start nature of Brazil's recent democratic development, if we take a long-term perspective we will be dealing with the effects of the economic and social development model adopted in Brazil. It is based on an ideology of society's subordination to the state, which is still very strong, and which has always had a strong racial component. In other words, a very robust model of political and economic development in Brazil has been produced by conflating safety, order and development. The attractiveness of this package to this day imposes considerable democratic, bureaucratic and structural constraints upon the nation. This model did not leap fully formed into the world, nor is it only the heir to the authoritarian regime of 1964. Rather, it has been the fruit of institutional developments and relationships between the military and civilians, as well as of economic and political trends and a legal culture that attributes an ambiguous role to police institutions, as Kant de Lima (2009) points out.

The backdrop to this, as Lima and Brito (2011) have stated, is the idea that the people are to believe that economic development demands society's subordination and absolute control of the state over it. Costa and Lima (2014) identify the option—as a tactic—of the maintenance of legal and law enforcement thinking based on the concept of the primacy of "internal security." Within this movement, public safety is not an end in itself, but interacts with and depends upon the economy, and the state's capacity to intervene. There are constraints upon social participation, and it is the state that defines who will deserve to interact with the policies in this arena and who is to be fought and neutralized. Safety and development thus have become linked, and the operational standards applying today will therefore flow from a strategy that legitimizes institutions tasked with maintaining public order, particularly police forces, by resorting to violence. It still remains to understand better how racialization constructs the internal "enemy" to be addressed by the police in order to accurately dismantle the subtlety with which racialization camouflages itself so as to become invisible.

The fact remains, however, that in a political culture that has acknowledged violence as the legitimate language of the state's action for centuries, there are—paradoxically—several moral prohibitions, and justifications springing from economics and from development models, that prevent Brazil from recognizing itself as an unequal, racist, violent country. Behind the rhetoric of being a peace-loving democratic nation, Brazil has amassed a tainted record in the area of human rights. The country ranks first on national lists of violent crime, institutional violence, inequality, and a lack of respect for civil and social rights. And as a result, the drive toward the democratic modernization of Brazil's society advances only slowly at best. To be feared is the possibility of a return to the institutionalized practices from Brazil's past, of cronyism and the excessive influence of the propertied classes.

Notes

1. A version of this text has been published in *Contemporânea—Revista de Sociologia da UFS-Car*, v. 5, pp. 119–141, 2015.
2. Data on the racial makeup of police forces vary greatly between states. See Sinhoretto, Silvestre and Schlittler (2014) for more details.

References

Adorno, S., and Dias, C. 2014. Monopólio Estatal da Violência. In *Crime, Polícia e Justiça no Brasil*, ed. R. Lima, J. Ratton, R. Azevdeo and R. Ghiringhelli, 187–197. São Paulo: Editora Contexto.

Brasil, Presidência da República. 2015a. *Índice de vulnerabilidade juvenil à violência e desigualdade racial 2014: Secretaria-Geral da Presidência da República, Secretaria Nacional de Juventude, Ministério da Justiça e Fórum Brasileiro de Segurança Pública* [Youth vulnerability to violence and racial inequality: General Secretariat of Republic's Presidency, National Secretariat of Youth, Ministry of Justice and Brazilian Forum of Public Security]. Brasília: Presidência da República.

Brasil, Presidência da República. 2015b. *Mapa do Encarceramento: os jovens do Brasil: Secretaria-Geral da Presidência da República, Secretaria Nacional de Juventude, Ministério da Justiça*. Brasília: Presidência da República.

Bueno, S. 2014. *Bandido bom é bandido morto: a opção ideológico-institucional da política de segurança pública na manutenção de padrões de atuação violentos da polícia militar paulista*. Dissertação de Mestrado. Administração Pública e Governo, Fundação Getulio Vargas.

Caldeira, T. 2000. *Cidade de Muros: Crime, Segregação e Cidadania em São Paulo*. 1st edition. São Paulo: Editora 34 e Edusp.

Carvalho, J. M. 2000. *Cidadania no Brasil: o longo caminho*. Rio de Janeiro: Civilização Brasileira.

Costa, A., and Lima, R. 2014. Segurança Pública. In *Crime, Polícia e Justiça no Brasil*, ed. R. Lima, J. Ratton, R. Azevedo and R. Ghiringhelli, 482–490. São Paulo: Editora Contexto.

CRISP, Centro de Estudos de Criminalidade e Segurança Pública. 2013. *DATAFOLHA. Instituto de pesquisas. Pesquisa Nacional de Vitimização*. Brasília: SENASP.

CRISP/UFMG/SRJ/MJ (Centro de Estudos da Criminalidade e Segurança Pública–Universidade Federal de Minas Gerais/Secretaria da Reforma do Judiciário–Ministério da Justiça). 2014. *Mensurando o tempo do processo de homicídio doloso em cinco capitais*. Brasília: Ministério da Justiça.

Cunha, L. 2014. *Relatório ICJBrasil*. São Paulo: FGV Direito.

Faoro, R. 1975. *Donos do Poder: Formação do Patronato Político Brasileiro*. Porto Alegre/São Paulo: Editora Globo/Editora da Universidade de São Paulo.

FBSP (Fórum Brasileiro de Segurança Pública). 2014. 8° *Anuário Brasileiro de Segurança Pública*. São Paulo: FBSP. Available at http://www.forumseguranca.org.br/storage/8_anuario_2014_20150309.pdf (accessed June 16, 2017).

FBSP (Fórum Brasileiro de Segurança Pública). 2015. 9° *Anuário Brasileiro de Segurança Pública*. São Paulo: FBSP. Available at http://www.forumseguranca.org.br/storage/9_anuario_2015.retificado_.pdf (accessed June 16, 2017).

Franco, M. 1997. *Homens livres na ordem escravocrata*. São Paulo: Unesp.

Freyre, G. 1933. *Casa Grande & Senzala*. São Paulo: Global Editora.

Holanda, S. 1958. *Visão do paraíso: os motivos edênicos no descobrimento e colonização do Brasil*. São Paulo: Companhia Editora Nacional.

Holston, J. 2013. *Cidadania Insurgente. Disjunções da democracia e da modernidade no Brasil*. 1st edition. São Paulo: Cia das Letras.

Jesus, C. 2014. *A relação estigma-desvio como elemento norteador no uso da força ou da violência na atividade policial*. Dissertation (M.A. in Sociology). Universidade Federal de Alagoas, Maceió, Brazil.

Kant de Lima, R. 1995. *A Polícia da cidade do Rio de Janeiro: seus dilemas e paradoxos*. 2nd edition. Rio de Janeiro: Forense.

Kant de Lima, R. 2009. *Ensaios de Antropologia e de Direito: Acesso à Justiça e Processos Institucionais de Administração de Conflitos e Produção da Verdade Jurídica em uma Perspectiva Comparada*. Rio de Janeiro: Lumen Juris Editora.

Leal, V. N. 2012. *Coronelismo, enxada e voto: o município e o regime representativo no Brasil*. São Paulo: Companhia das Letras.

Lima, R., and Brito, D. 2011. Desenvolvimento: da defesa do Estado à defesa da Cidadania. In *Violência e Dilemas Civilizatórios: as práticas de punição e extermínio*, ed. C. Barreira, L. Sa, and J. P. Aquino, 203–220. Fortaleza: Pontes.

Lima, R., Bueno, S., and Santos, T. 2014. *Opinião dos policiais brasileiros sobre reformas e modernização da segurança pública, Pesquisa opinião dos policiais*. São Paulo: CPJA-FGV/Fórum Brasileiro de Segurança Pública/SENASP.

Lima, R., and Sinhoretto, J. 2011. Qualidade da democracia e polícias no Brasil. In *Entre palavras e números: violência, democracia e segurança pública no Brasil*, ed. R. Lima, 129–152. São Paulo: Alameda.

Lima, R., Sinhoretto, J., and Bueno, S. A. 2015. *Gestão da vida e da segurança pública no Brasil*. Brasília: Soc. estado, v. 30, n. 1, p. 123–144, Apr. 2015. www.scielo.br/scielo.php?script=sci_arttext&pid=S0102-69922015000100123&lng=en&nrm=iso (accessed June 5, 2015). http://dx.doi.org/10.1590/S0102-69922015000100008.

Machado da Silva, L. A. 2008. Violência urbana, sociabilidade violenta e agenda pública. In *Vida sob cerco: violência e rotinas nas favelas do Rio de Janeiro*, ed. L. Machado da Silva, 35–45. Rio de Janeiro: FAPERJ/Nova Fronteira.

Misse, M., Vargas, J. D., Costa, A. T., Ratton, J. L., and Azevedo, R. G. 2010. *O Inquérito Policial no Brasil. Uma pesquisa empírica*. 1st edition. Rio de Janeiro: Booklink, 1: 476.

Paixão, A. L. 1982. A organização policial numa área metropolitana. *Revista de Ciências Sociais* 25: 63–85.

Peralva, A. T. 2001. *Violência e democracia: o paradoxo brasileiro*. São Paulo: Paz e Terra.

Pires, G. L. 2010. *A cor da farda. As relações raciais na Polícia Militar de Sergipe*. Dissertation (M.A. in Sociology). Sergipe: Universidade Federal de Sergipe.

Ramalho Neto, J. P. 2012. Farda & "cor": um estudo racial nas patentes da Polícia Militar da Bahia. *Afro-Ásia* 45: 67–94.

Sansone, L. 2002. Fugindo para a Força: Cultura Corporativista e "Cor" na Polícia Militar do Estado do Rio de Janeiro. *Estudos Afro-Asiáticos* 24: 513–532.

Santos, W. G. 1979. *Cidadania e Justiça*. Rio de Janeiro: Campus.

Sinhoretto, J. 2014a. Reforma da justiça: gerindo conflitos numa sociedade rica e violenta. *Diálogos sobre Justiça* 2: 49–56.

Sinhoretto, J. 2014b. *Violência e relações raciais: problematizando evidências e interpretações sociológicas.* Projeto de Pesquisa CNPq. São Carlos, Mimeo: Universidade Federal de.

Sinhoretto, J., Batitucci, E. C., Mota, F. R., Schlitter, M. C., Silvestre, G., Morais, D. S., Souza, L. G., Souza, R. R., Silva, S. S., Ovalle, L. A., Ramos, P. C., Almedia, F. B., and Maciel, W. C. 2014. A filtragem racial na seleção policial de suspeitos: segurança pública e relações raciais. In *Segurança pública e direitos humanos: temas transversais,* ed. I. S. de Figueiredo, 121–160. Brasília: Ministério da Justiça.

Sinhoretto, J., Silvestre, G., and Schlittler, C. 2014. *Desigualdade racial e segurança pública em São Paulo: letalidade policial e prisões em flagrante. Sumário executivo.* São Paulo: UFSCar-GEVAC. www.ufscar.br/gevac/#sthash.KiXLiLc4.dpuf (acessed May 8, 2014).

Suassuna, R. 2008. *O habitus dos policiais militares do Distrito Federal.* Dissertation (M.A. in Sociology). Brasília: Universidade de Brasília.

Use of Force and Police Reform in Brazil[1]

8

Wesley G. Skogan

Contents

The role of crime and justice policies in solidifying modernizing trends in newly democratic nations is well understood by students of Latin American politics, for therein lies some of the most visible challenges to the success of democratizing forces. Especially by the end of the twentieth century, violence fueled by urbanization, inequality, small arms trafficking, and the drug trade threatens to undermine fledgling democracies that find themselves hard-pressed to reform authoritarian police organizations in the face of demands that something drastic be done about crime and corrupt relationships between politicians and organized criminals (Koonings and Kruijt 2007).

Brazil is not alone in the group of Latin American nations transitioning from authoritarianism to democracy, but its problems in doing so may be among the most noted. There is no shortage of descriptions of the violent and corrupt character of Brazilian police and their allied nonstate actors, which include private militias, paramilitary squads, and shadowy private security operations (e.g., see Perlman 2009). There are frequent reports of torture of police prisoners and extrajudicial killings. None of this has helped the state to protect its citizens, who in urban areas face extremely high rates of violence, and the frequency with which they are killed by them has left the police one of the many problems facing the public, not a solution to them. One close observer of the Brazilian scene judged that, in the years since its democratizing moment in January 1984, the criminal justice sector has made the least progress toward supporting that agenda (Leeds 2007). Although varying from place to place, police violence and corruption are endemic in too many Brazilian states, and at the same time violent crime is among the greatest impediments to social and economic development in its urban regions.

While the difficult nexus between crime, policing, and politics in emerging democracies is frequently remarked upon, much less has been written on the effectiveness of the reform efforts that have been—perhaps too sporadically—mounted.[2] This chapter opens one window into police reform in Brazil, by examining the effects of police officers' experience with the National Program of Public Security with Citizenship (PRONASCI). During its time, this was the nation's most ambitious attempt to democratize the police.

In Brazil, policing at the street level is conducted by the federal states and not the national government. At the state level, policing services are largely provided by two distinct bodies. The Civil Police conduct criminal investigations and make decisions regarding prosecution, and often operate in plain clothes. Visible street policing, traffic enforcement, responses to emergency calls, and riot control are provided by the uniformed Military Police. They are heavily armed and organized in strict hierarchical fashion, with an elaborate military-style rank structure. They are trained and operate using traditional military tactics, and in poor areas their operations often resemble those more appropriate for a war zone.[3] Both branches of the police are characterized by cultures that stoutly resist change and outside oversight of their operations and management. As described in this volume by Marco Ruediger (Chapter 12), PRONASCI represented an intervention into local policing by the national Ministry of Justice. He describes the story of its failure, but during its formative period PRONASCI opened a window for research on policing in Brazil, and this chapter is based on the data that could be collected during that period.

For the police, PRONASCI's reform agenda attempted to address a long list of issues, including poor management and inadequate training, bad living and working conditions for low-level police officers, and an authoritarian legacy that is inattentive to issues of human rights. The program aimed at upgrading the condition of officers' lives and standards for police operations. Federal money supported training programs and better equipment. Emphasis was placed on improving managerial practices, with the goal of improving police planning, program implementation, and local evaluation. One problem with policing in Brazil is that no one believes that the police are very effective when they try to carry out standard police work. Because police are very badly paid, a housing subsidy program was instituted. Finally, a nationwide campaign began to promote community policing efforts at the municipal level. However, it was not just a police reform effort. In addition to police reform, PRONASCI aimed at restructuring the Brazilian prison system and encouraging neighborhood capacity building and community involvement in violence prevention.

This chapter uses the results of a monitoring survey to examine the issue of police use of force. Why examine the views of ordinary police officers? For one, it provides a "bottom-up" view of the use of force, listening to the voices of officers on this issue. This approach sheds some light on the apparent rationality of use of force, in the view of officers on the street. Building a more professional force is a long-term effort, for police agencies are human services organizations. The levers for change in policing are recruitment, training, supervision, and discipline; these constitute most of the tools available to any reform effort aiming to upgrade the effectiveness and professionalism of the police. This makes it a slow process—police officers start young and their careers unfold vertically within the organization, so agencies will change more glacially than reformers would hope under the best of circumstances. But in the end, the public will see the consequences of reform only in the quality of service delivered by officers on the street, so understanding where they stand is an important step in the monitoring process. Surveys of police officers and other security personnel constitute monitoring mechanisms thus can yield a "from the bottom up" portrait of the reform process.

The Survey

The survey was conducted in 2008, using the Internet. Recipients of Ministry of Justice educational grants for security personnel were invited to the survey web page when they logged on to perform routine required administrative tasks. The survey was developed and managed independently by Fundação Getulio Vargas (FGV), a university in Rio de Janeiro, and the responses of the participants remained confidential.

The survey involved a broad spectrum of security personnel in Brazil, including employees in the correctional system, firefighters, and forensic examiners, as PRONASCI involved distinctive programs for each group. However, this analysis examines only the responses of members of the Civil and Military Police, the two state-based groups that patrol the streets and conduct criminal investigations. Only low-level personnel were included in the survey; members of the better-educated and better-paid senior officers' corps enter the higher ranks of these organizations laterally, and they were not involved in the educational or housing grants programs. In total, 17,341 respondents are examined here. The data are national in scope, including respondents from 26 of the country's 27 federal states and 1,938 different municipalities. The absence of systematic national records at the time made it impossible to estimate a response rate for the survey, and there are no data with which to benchmark the personal demographics of respondents. This reflects the fact that policing is a state rather than a federal responsibility in Brazil. National data on many other topics are frequently nonexistent as well. For example, there are no national (and frequently local) sources of crime data to match to the over 1,900 jurisdictions with participating survey respondents, and Brazilian census data were in practice unmatchable with these boundaries.

Use of Force on the Street

The dependent variable, self-reported use of force, was measured by responses to the question "How often is the use of force necessary in your work?" Respondents were divided on this with 9% reporting force was necessary very often and 34% often. On the other hand, 48% reported use of force was necessary only occasionally and 9% rarely. This question was included to gauge the general "style" with which officers perform their duties. Note that almost half of officers reported fairly frequent use of force.

Impact of the Risk Environment

Studies in the Northern Hemisphere of the correlates of police use of force stress the significant role played by the risks that police officers believe they face on the job. Real or not, typing neighborhoods as troublesome leads police officers to stereotype residents as uncooperative, hostile, or crime-prone—resulting in a tendency to approach residents with suspicion, to behave more aggressively, and to act more punitively than they do in other kinds of neighborhoods (Terrill and Reisig 2003). Studies based on police records and field observations indicate that police verbal and physical abuse, unjustified street stops, and corruption are more prevalent in disadvantaged and high-crime areas (Fagan and Davies 2000; Kane 2002; Mastrofski, Reisig and McCluskey 2002; Terrill and Reisig 2003).

In this study, officers' perceptions of the risk environment were measured by responses to two questions: "What is the level of risk in your work?" and "How do you evaluate the public security situation where you work?" They rated their personal risks on a scale ranging from average to very high, and the general security situation in their community from "critical—difficult to keep order" to "within the normal limits and tranquil."

Both measures prove to be independently related to reports of the use of force by Brazilian police. Figure 8.1 presents the percentages of respondents reporting that use of force was necessary often and very often when classified by the extent of perceived risk in the areas where they worked. Reported use of force rose with risk, ranging from an average of 7% in the lowest-rated areas to 54% in more threatening places. As an additional analytic tool, Figure 8.1

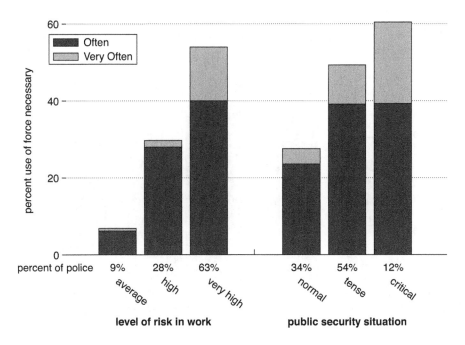

Figure 8.1 Perceived risk and use of force

Source: PRONASCI officer survey

also presents the percentage of officers who fell into each risk category. As it indicates, 63% of officers believed the level of risk in their work to be very high, and among that large group 54% reported that force was necessary in their work. The effect of the sharp risk-force gradient was thus multiplied by the large proportion of officers who saw themselves at high risk.

These officers were somewhat more positive about the general security situation—only 12% rated it as critical, the highest category. But this perception too was strongly linked to the perceived necessity of using force on the job, with more than 60% of officers in the critical category reporting resorting to use of force. In multivariate analyses, both factors were among the most important determinants of assessments of the role of use of force in policing.

Impact of Personal Factors

Because our respondents share a common background—all are working police officers—they are divided by fewer social cleavages than is the general population. However, several social background factors still played a role in shaping reports of the necessity to use force on the street. These included gender, age, education, and seniority, with the last two being more important after other factors are accounted for.

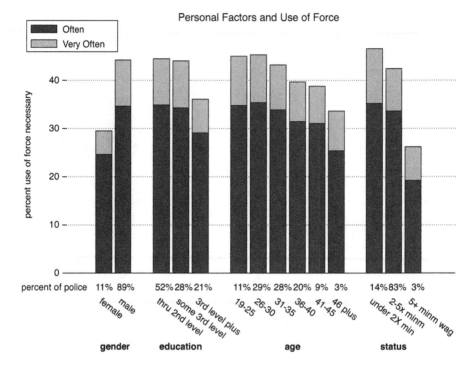

Figure 8.2 Personal factors and use of force

Source: PRONASCI officer survey

The strongest of these personal factors is gender. Studies of police behavior in the Northern Hemisphere typically find few gender differences in the extent to which police are involved in the use of force. For example, Paoline and Terrill (2004) found rates of both verbal and physical use of force did not differ by gender, and that other individual-level correlates of use of force did not vary by gender. Gender differences were very strong in Brazil, on the other hand, as is illustrated in Figure 8.2. Gender was the strongest risk measure in the model. However, because only 11% of police officers are female (this is also reported in Figure 8.2), gender can play only a limited role in shaping police conduct in the aggregate.

Similarly, studies of police behavior in the Northern Hemisphere find that younger officers are more likely to employ use of force as an on-street tactic for controlling risk, perhaps because they lack experience with more indirect but still effective personal risk-management strategies. Harris's (2011) summary of this research in the United States notes that officers get in trouble early in their careers, but involvement in on-street violence declines with experience. In Brazil, many police officers are relatively young—as illustrated in Figure 8.2, and 40% are age 30 or younger—and many of them are thus in their high-risk years. The perceived necessity of force declined with age, but relatively few police officers are found in older categories. In this national study, only 12% of officers were over age 40, and a large majority were under the age of 30.

The other groups that report less necessity in relying on force are the most educated and highly paid police officers in the sample. Both of these factors reflect their standing in the organization. There does not seem to be any North American research on income differentials, but research has consistently demonstrated that more educated officers generally perform better and are less likely to be subjects of citizen complaints. This is, in fact, about the only consistent correlate in research on officer behavior and education (Rydberg and Terrill 2010). In Brazil, the officer corps enters policing via lateral entry, and they were not included in this study. Income, therefore, reflects the rank and seniority of the rank-and-file police officers who were surveyed, and the variation in education is likewise not linked to the higher educational attainment of persons recruited directly into the higher reaches of the organization.

On the other hand, race did not enter into this picture at all. As a result, it is not presented in Figure 8.2. In this survey, about 42% of police officers were white, 46% of multiracial heritage, and 10% self-identified as black. None of these distinctions, however, was related to views of the use of force. Likewise, whether officers lived in the communities in which they worked made no difference in their views. In total, 68% of those interviewed did live and work in the same area, but this was unrelated to reports of the necessity of using force.

Upgrading Police Professionalism

One of the key reasons for conducting this survey was to monitor police reactions to the professionalizing efforts of PRONASCI. As discussed above, the Justice Ministry's police reform agenda involved upgrading the condition of police officers and standards for operations.

Officers' assessments of several of these professionalizing efforts were measured by a single index combining positive responses to a series of questions about training, equipment, and planning. Those who scored highly rated the police academy training that they received as of good or reasonable quality and as reasonably or very useful. Officers also scored more highly if they had attended several in-service training courses in the past year. High scorers also rated the equipment that they were issued as being of good or very good quality. Other components of the professionalism index included if they gave their own computer skills a high rating, and if they thought the planning and evaluation efforts of their agency were good or very good.

Figure 8.3 illustrates that police officers were divided on these points, with almost as many concentrated at the lower end of the scale (the three

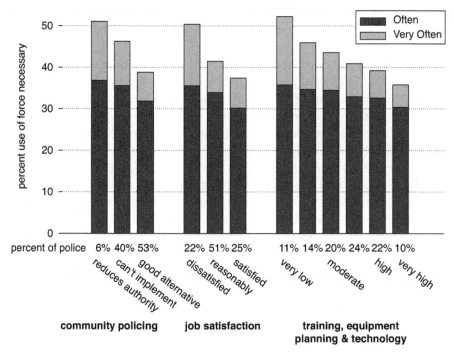

Figure 8.3 Professionalism and use of force

Source: PRONASCI officer survey

left-hand bars) as at the right-hand side, where officers who were more favorably disposed to the program were concentrated. As the figure also indicates, the view that the use of force was necessary in their work declined with reports of improvements in training, equipment, and management. More than 50% of officers in the low-professionalism category ranked high on use of force, while the comparable figure was 36% among those at the upper end of the scale.

A key component of this effort to reform the police was its emphasis on community policing. What this concept meant on the ground was not always clear, and many states were uncertain about how to implement such a project, but few of the police officers interviewed (just 6%) were unfamiliar with the concept. They were asked, "How would you evaluate Community Policing in Brazil?" The response categories were varied, but overall 53% of those interviewed were positive, responding that "it is a very good alternative strategy for police in Brazil since it involves community interaction." About 40% were dubious, responding that "it cannot be implemented everywhere, since some areas, such as favelas, are communities dominated by drug gangs." Another 6% thought that community policing "reduces the authority of the police, but it may have a palliative effect." As Figure 8.3 illustrates, there was about a 10 percentage point difference between the most supportive police officers and those who thought community policing would undermine their authority, when it came to reports of the necessity of using force on the street.

Finally, a measure of the influence of the professionalizing thrust of PRO-NASCI would be increased job satisfaction. These have been shown to be related to features of police work that officers care about, including wages and benefits, quality of equipment, training, and supervision. To measure this, respondents were asked, "How do you evaluate your satisfaction with your professional career?" They rated themselves from satisfied to dissatisfied, with a middle category, reasonably satisfied. As Figure 8.3 documents, the better they felt about their careers as police officers, the less likely they were to feel that use of force was necessary in their work, from top to bottom by about 18 percentage points.

Police views of some components of the program proved to be unrelated to their views of the use of force. In particular, participation in the national housing subsidy program for police officers did not seem to influence their thinking about their work. The program is intended to improve the living condition of poorly paid officers, but based on the survey only 9% of them were participating. They gave the program a high ranking—on a 0–10 rating scale 81% rated it an 8 or above—but too few reported participating for it to have much effect on opinion.

There was also no direct effect of police officers' views of the extent of corruption. Many see police corruption and violence reinforcing one another, for corruption causes them to draw closed "the blue curtain" that shields police operations from public scrutiny. When asked about the extent of police corruption, only 0.4% of those surveyed maintained that it was no problem. Otherwise, the issue was one of how widespread they thought it was. Most police officers maintained that corruption is a problem of individual officers (69%) rather than widespread (24%) or occurring in specific units (7%). Their analyses of the corruption problem, however, were unrelated to their views of the necessity of using force.

Perspectives on Crime and Policing

In addition, several measures of attitudes—the perspectives of these police officers on crime and their role in society—were related to their views of the use of force, albeit more weakly. Officers were more likely to report frequent use of force when they thought that public security issues were the most important agenda item, more important than "other national questions, such as employment, education and health." On the other hand, police who were supportive of PRONASCI's push for sentencing reform were less likely to think that force was necessary in their work; they responded positively to the question, "Are you in favor of swapping of sentences for non-serious crimes for study or community work?"

Other social attitudes proved to be largely unrelated to police officers' views of the use of force. One opinion in particular was whether they thought society trusted the police. Building trust between police and the community was one of the major goals of PRONASCI. On the public side of the equation, FVG is monitoring opinion through surveys they are conducting in poor housing areas (favelas) throughout the country (see Riccio, Ruediger, Ross, & Skogan, Chapter 10, this volume). Those results are at best mixed, and the skepticism of poor Brazilians regarding the police is mirrored on the police side. In this survey, only 8% of officers believed the public thought them trustworthy and effective, a very low number.

Multivariate Analysis

Table 8.1 presents the results of an analysis of the joint influence of all of these variables on officers' assessments of the necessity of using force on the street. The standardized regression coefficients indicate the relative importance of

Table 8.1 Multivariate analysis of perceived necessity of using force

	Use of force necessary		
	B	t	Sig.
risky at work	0.31	42.45	0.00
security situation critical	0.16	21.54	0.00
Female	−0.07	−9.25	0.00
Age	−0.04	−5.25	0.00
Education	−0.05	−6.41	0.00
monthly income category	−0.03	−4.07	0.00
support community policing	−0.04	−4.89	0.00
career satisfaction	−0.03	−3.33	0.00
professionalism index	−0.03	−3.67	0.00
support community service	−0.04	−6.06	0.00
public security most important	0.04	4.99	0.00
Constant		24.25	0.00

$R = .432$; $R^2 = .186$

No. of observations: 16,616

Notes: B = standardized regression coefficients, t = t-statistic, sig = significance level

Source: PRONASCI officer survey

each of the measures. They are ordered in line with the discussion of variables in this chapter.

First, it is clear that officers' assessments of the risks in their environment predominate. Both their own perceived risk on the job and their assessments of security in general in the communities in which they work were strongly and significantly linked to reports of the frequency of use of force. Of the two, the risks they personally face predominate. Any assessment of police behavior must begin with their perceptions of danger, a specter that pervades their lives.

Following risk in importance are three personal factors: gender, age, and education. Controlling for other factors, female officers reported using force less frequently. So too did officers with more experience and those with higher levels of education. Rank-and-file officers from somewhat higher income households (but low-ranking police officers in Brazil most often live in modest circumstances) also were less likely to report using force.

The survey also assessed respondents' involvement in and assessments of the elements of the PRONASCI reform that were likely to affect them. A multi-item professionalism index reflecting their participation in training programs, skill at using technology, and other program-related efforts was among the factors that were significantly related to lower levels of self-reported use of force. Officers who were more satisfied with their careers were similarly inclined. Measures of police views of PRONASCI's reform agenda follow, and remain independently statistically significant. These were support for community policing and support for sentencing reform. In addition, controlling statistically for other factors, officers were more likely to report frequent use of force when they thought that public security issues were the most important national agenda item.

Conclusion

This nationwide study was conducted in the midst of a large-scale police reform effort. It highlights the importance of many components of that effort, which in the survey were linked to reports of less frequent use of force. Consistent with decades of police research, the frequency of self-reported use of force was driven most strongly by perceptions of a risky work environment. Both measures included here proved important, one a self-assessment of respondents' personal risk and the other a general rating of riskiness of the area in which they worked.

Controlling for other factors, personal factors were also linked to self-reports of use of force. In the survey, women, older officers, and those with more education reported using force less frequently. So did those whose households were making a little more money. However, most Brazilian officers were young, male, ill-educated, and poorly paid—when taken together, a recipe for trouble.

Most importantly for the purpose of the survey, which was to help evaluate the reform effort, use of force was reported being used less frequently by officers who had contact with or supported key components of the program. An index of their personal professionalism based on their participation and assessments of training, skill in using equipment, and their views of the planning and evaluation efforts of their agency was independently linked to less frequent self-reported use of force. So was their general career satisfaction. Attitudes were also important. Officers who supported the reform program and community policing, which was also being promoted, were also less often involved in the use of force. On the other hand, officers who thought that crime fighting was the most important issue on the national agenda were more likely to report use of force. Overall, few of those we surveyed were sanguine about their status in society. In the survey, only 8% believed the public thought of them as trustworthy and effective.

The reform of policing in Brazil is, of course, a monumental task. The impediments to reform are legion, but they would be familiar to any police researcher. They include an insular police culture confident of its ability to avoid external scrutiny; organized resistance to change by police unions and associations representing the officer corps; the reform-quashing effect of law-and-order political rhetoric in the face of high levels of violent crime; the close relationship between police and rural oligarchs; frequent turnover among police executives and their overseers; politicians' aversion to seeming to take responsibility for crime rates; tight links between politicians and police; and the corrosive effect of police and political corruption, which creates "dirty secrets" that both must conspire to keep hidden (Leeds 2007). Police in Brazil remain widely mistrusted, in part because they carry the legacy of the country's authoritarian past, both reputationally and in terms of their political conduct. Rank-and-file officers have little education, and their rough and unsophisticated training emphasizes military conduct, discipline, and values. Street-level policing is conducted by the Military Police, which operates best with heavy weaponry. They support a society characterized by one of the most unequal distributions of wealth in the modern world, and they have traditionally done so with disrespect for the rights of the poorer classes.

One vision at its launch was that PRONASCI would strengthen the capacity of criminal justice institutions as part of a larger agenda, that of building trust and confidence between society and the state more generally. But, as the chapters in this volume by Ruediger (Chapter 12) and Riccio, Miranda, and Müeller (Chapter 11) indicate, reform at the national level faltered after several years. Its legacy can still be seen here and there, at the state and local level, but policing in Brazil seemingly proved too daunting a reform project.

Notes

1. A version of this text has been published in *Contemporânea—Revista de Sociologia da UFS-Car*, v. 5, pp. 119–141, 2015.
2. For an exception, see da Silva and Cano (2007).
3. In urban areas, traffic control and other similar functions are also performed by an expanding *Guardas Municipais*, whose officers are sometimes armed but largely conduct "preventive" patrolling operations.

References

da Silva, G. M., and Cano, I. 2007. Between damage reduction and community policing: The case of Pavao-Pavaozinho-Cantagalo in Rio de Janeiro's favelas. In *Legitimacy and criminal justice: A comparative perspective*, ed. T. R. Tyler, 186–214. New York: Russell Sage Foundation.

Fagan, J., and Davies, G. 2000. Street stops and broken windows: Terry, race, and disorder in New York City. *Fordham Urban Law Journal* 28: 457–457.

Harris, C. 2011. Problem behaviors in later portions of officers' careers. *Policing: An International Journal of Police Strategies & Management* 34: 135–152.

Kane, R. 2002. The social ecology of police misconduct. *Criminology* 40: 867–896.

Koonings, K., and Kruijt, D. 2007. Fractured cities, second-class citizenship and urban violence, Urban violence and contested spaces in Latin America. In *Fractured Cities: Social Exclusion*, ed. K. Koonings and D. Kruijt, 7–22. London: Zed Books.

Leeds, E. 2007. Serving states and serving citizens: Halting steps toward police reform in Brazil and implications for donor intervention. *Policing & Society* 17: 21–37.

Mastrofski, S., Reisig, M., and McCluskey, J. 2002. Police disrespect toward the public: An encounter-based analysis. *Criminology* 40: 101–133.

Paoline, E. A., and Terrill, W. 2004. Women police officers and the use of Coercion. *Women and Criminal Justice* 15: 97–119.

Perlman, J. E. 2009. Megacity violence and its consequences in Rio de Janeiro. In *Mega-cities: The politics of urban exclusion and violence in the global south*, ed. K. Koonings and D. Kruijt, 52–68. London: Zed Books.

Riccio, V., Meirelles de Miranda, M. R., and Müller, A. Professionalizing the military police through training. This volume.

Riccio, V., Ruediger, M. A., Ross, S. D., and Skogan, W. Community policing in the favelas of Rio de Janeiro. This volume.

Ruediger, M. A. Police reform in Brazil: The rise and demise of PRONASCI. This volume.

Rydberg, J., and Terrill, W. 2010. The effect of higher education on police behavior. *Police Quarterly* 13: 92–120.

Terrill, W., and Reisig, M. D. 2003. Neighborhood context and police use of force. *Journal of Research in Crime and Delinquency* 40: 291–321.

Gangs, Drugs and Urban Pacification Squads in Rio

9

Vicente Riccio and
Wesley G. Skogan

Contents

The crime problem in Brazil is known worldwide, and its most visible face is Rio de Janeiro. The country's former capital and most visited city is marked by violence, a violence depicted in mass media, academic studies and even films, such as *Elite Squad* and *City of God*. In recent decades, crime in Rio de Janeiro has been linked to drug trafficking, gunfights between criminal gangs, police corruption and violence. Those problems occur mainly in poor neighborhoods, or favelas, where people live in a risky environment.

Crime continues to be a harsh reality in Rio, but it aroused the public especially in the 1980s and 1990s. As a result, rising levels of fear of crime, an economic decline in entire regions of the city and investments losses were a major concern during this period. Criminal events reflected a deeper crime dynamic in Rio, one driven by the territorial dominion exercised by drug gangs in the favelas. In those regions of the city, drug gangs had taken control, imposing their will by violence. They were de facto power holders in those spaces. The extent of the violence problem waxes and wanes. In the last decade, homicide has decreased in Rio de Janeiro. In 2004 the homicide rate was 48 per 100,000 inhabitants, and in 2014 this figure fell to 32 per 100,000 inhabitants. On the other hand, the homicide rate in the state of Alagoas has jumped from 34 per 100,000 inhabitants to 63 per 100,000 inhabitants (Cerqueira et al. 2016). Currently, the poor northeastern states are the most violent in the country.

Despite fluctuating crime and state efforts to attack their hegemony, gang control is still the order of the day in many favelas. Further, there are some

135

regions in Rio in which this kind of oppressive control is performed instead by militias, squads of corrupt police officers with ties to political and economic elites (Zaluar and Conceição 2007; Cano et al. 2012).

The territorial control exerted by those gangs is based on their need to protect the illegal drug trade. This provides the resources gangs need to acquire smuggled heavy weapons, which they deploy to maintain their control. In this context, it is common to observe confrontations between gangs struggling for control of contested territories. Furthermore, gangs also defy the police, and armed conflicts among them are also common in many communities. The intensity of those confrontations can be observed in the kind of weaponry used by gangs and police forces: assault rifles, grenades, machine guns and armored vehicles.

Community residents who are caught in the crossfire between all of these armed bands are the main victims in this process. They face alternating cycles of brutal dominion by gangs, punctuated by the incursion of heavily armed Military Police units undertaking essentially military operations. Their "shock and awe" campaigns then quickly subside, for after such tactical operations the police do not remain in the communities. The main criticisms of this mode of response to crime action are well known: excessive use of violence, many collateral victims and a police force enjoying very little legitimacy among the population. For a long while, the problem of drug-related gang violence in the favelas seemed to be unsolvable.

However, in the 2000s, a series of innovative responses to crime were fielded under the leadership of the state governor at the time, Sérgio Cabral. They were known as the Pacifying Police Units, or "UPPs".[1] The UPPs were created during this administration to bring the state back into communities controlled by drug gangs on a longer-term basis. A key objective was to regain and then hold control of those areas, shifting from the episodic violent incursion staged by the Military Police toward strengthening ties between the public and state institutions. The main objectives of this new strategy were the reduction of crimes, especially homicides, improving police-community relations and further reestablishing state control in these regions by bringing social and economic programs to bear upon them.

The UPPs thus were part of a complex, multi-agency policy that has been implemented for almost eight years. Since its start, there has been an expansion of the UPPs throughout Rio. However, there are at this writing only 38 UPPs functioning among the more than 800 favelas in Rio de Janeiro. There were some overall successes in Rio. Between 2005 and 2013, there were 17,392 homicides registered in Rio de Janeiro, along with 4,707 police killings. The homicide rate for this period was "only" 22 per 100,000, down from the 48 per 100,000 of 2004 (Magaloni, Franco and Melo 2015).

However, most recently the UPPs have faced intense criticism. Armed conflicts have broken out again in areas previously pacified; there has been denunciation of the abuses committed by police officers; and the social programs that were promised have not materialized. This chapter describes the development of UPPs in Rio de Janeiro since their inception. It does so within a larger framework of research on democratic policing in developing countries. Special focus is placed on the relationship of police and community, and the issues facing policies aimed at improving communities marked by high levels of violence and social exclusion. The chapter is organized into three main sections: on police and community relationships in developing democracies, the birth of the UPPs in Rio, and the consolidation of the UPPs.

Police and Community in Developing Democracies

One of the key features of any political transition from an authoritarian regime or a state wracked by civil war to a democratic future is the role of their police in society (Bayley 2005). The police as the state institution responsible for maintaining order and promoting internal peace are central in any constitutional agreement about the kind of political regime that is desired. In a democracy, the police uphold the law, but its power is limited by it. Thus, the police in a democratic society are also bound by legitimacy claims (Tyler et al. 2007). The people need not only the police, but they need a legitimate one.

Since the development of modern policing, the question of the role of state and the legitimacy of its actions is interconnected. In brief, the modern police is based on bureaucratization. The maintenance of order and crime fighting were no longer a task of local militias, powerful landowners or even the armed forces. The police was created to serve as a public institution (Ignatieff 2005). This model, established in London in 1829, spread throughout the world. Recognizably modern policing systems have been established in many different countries and legal cultures. However, the last almost two centuries have been marked by huge changes in the social landscape: urbanization, the rise of industrial capitalism, democratic expansion, decolonization, scientific revolutions, and globalization are some features of this process. Policing was also impacted by those changes in society.

The expansion of democracy during the last century was marked by many contradictions and distinct political cultures. The idea of democracy was accompanied by a huge demand for rights, especially for developing countries. Freedom of speech, to engage in an association, or to run for office were not enough to fulfill the democratic ideal. In many countries there is seen to be a conjunction of political rights with social rights and human rights (Caldeira and Holston 2009). What is the role of the police in this equation? As Bayley (2005) says, one of the central aspects in state building after a conflict or during a period of redemocratization is the role of the police. The rule of the law is central for a democracy, and the police must be the first-line enforcers of democratic norms. The state has the monopoly of violence and the force must be used in a legitimate way (Tyler 2011), meaning with respect to the law, in a transparent and accountable way (Chappuis and Hänggi 2013). This is a matter of rights. So, the police as the first-line enforcers of democratic norms should act in accordance with those guidelines. In short, "good governance of the security sector is achieved within this model by a framework of civilian, democratic control that provides for accountability and transparency in who uses force, when, where, why and how" (Chappuis and Hänggi 2013, p. 169).

However, in actual operation, the police do not act as they should. Their *modus operandi* varies across countries and levels of social economic development. One question arises: are the police working in accordance with society demands? This question has been made since the development of modern policing. The bulk of studies about the police has also tried to grasp this problem. Studies conducted in the United States have settled on a paradigm regarding the evolution of the police in modern societies. The development of police forces in the US was based in the local level of administration. It has allowed a relationship between local political elites and the police, frequently one based on patronage and corruption. This feature was most apparent during Prohibition. In that period, corruption, violence and mistrust in the police skyrocketed.

The answer for this was professionalization and bureaucratization. However, isolating the police forces from many aspects of civil society created problems of its own. One key to modern models of policing is responsiveness. The police must be ready to respond quickly to calls and also to adapt quickly to changes in the character of crime and the needs of particular communities. Insulating the police deepened the gap between them and society. This can be observed in the legitimacy claims being made by residents of poor communities in the US—and Brazil—today. For them, police forces are frequently seen as violent, corrupt and biased. In the 1970s and 1980s, the criticisms of this model gave birth to two alternative models of action: problem-oriented policing and community policing. The first is based on the premises of prevention and action to solve problems that are not so visible or are only about to occur (Goldstein 1979). On the other hand, community policing advocates the decentralization of police and their interaction with the community. Cooperative efforts between communities and the police can provide more security, crime prevention, reduction of fear of crime and the community's strengthening. As a consequence, community policing increases police legitimacy (Skogan 2006).

Those policies that emerged in the United States have proved to be quite influential throughout the world. The spread of community policing programs in the US and the growing academic literature discussing its tenets and results have reached different cultures and realities. Community policing is not only a technique of social control, but it embeds an ideological meaning for developing countries, because it affects a core issue on the state-society relationship: the use of force (Wiesler and Onwudine 2007). This concept has emerged as a hot topic in the public security agenda in places such as Argentina (Glanc 2014), Brazil (Hinton 2005), Mexico (Müller 2010), South Africa (Wiesler and Onwudine 2007) and Nigeria (Hills 2012). However, the adoption of community policing in different cultures and levels of social, economic and political development can raise some questions: what are the conditions to sustain a community policing program in a developing country? How does the extent of development of state institutions provide room for legitimate and sustainable policing in a conflicted area? Are police forces in newly born democracies suitable for those changes? Those questions are important to understand the context in which the UPPs were implemented and the main challenges they face.

In Latin America, for instance, the concept of community policing has been advanced as an important idea underlying police reforms. It resonates by its contrast to the (recent) authoritarian past of many countries there, places in which the mission of the police was to protect the state and not the citizenry. However, any spread of a community policing discourse in the region faces a "wall" of institutional and cultural barriers posed by police forces themselves. As a result, any adoption of the forms of community policing programs does not bring with it broader institutional changes, such as decentralization or more responsive and crime-oriented policies. However, community policing is still seen as a promising instrument to improve police-community relationships (Frühling 2012). Müller (2010) examined the adoption of community policing in Mexico City and found that the influences of clientelism, political interference and police corruption were obstacles for the program. The influence of political context was also stressed by Arias and Ungar (2009) when they summarized research about Latin American policing. They concluded that most studies focused on specific programs, but did not consider contextual and political relationships that also determine a policy's outcomes. There is a tendency to simplify state-society relations when thinking about reform.

Thus, discussion about the inauguration of UPPs in Rio should not narrow its focus to the program itself, but needs instead to consider broader issues raised by the desire to adopt responsive public security policies in developing countries. For the UPPs, these broader issues include the capacity of the state to fulfill its duties in an area controlled by armed gangs; the different demands for security coming from distinct social groups; and the bedrock necessity that the project address the legitimacy component of police-community relations in high-conflict areas. Further concerns have been advanced by Hinton and Newburn (2009) in their discussion of the central issues facing police reform in developing countries: the accountability problem (police forces must be accountable to the law instead of being a government branch); police must protect human rights and not violate them; and police must be accountable to the people and hold that as their top priority. The origins and fate of the UPPs in Rio de Janeiro can be viewed through the lens of these concerns, and thus can be seen not as an isolated program, but rather as a proxy for relating police reform in Brazil to the developing world generally.

The Birth of UPPs in Rio

There has long been criticism of the Rio police, both in the daily conversations of people and in mass media. The depiction of Rio as a city teetering on the edge of violence, with gunfights and territorial gangs everywhere, is well known. Efforts to deal with recurring public security crises often accomplished little. Close to the end of the period of military rule in Brazil, the 1982 election of Leonel Brizola as governor of Rio promised to have a large impact on local crime policy. Brizola was a labor politician. During the military era, he lived in exile in Uruguay, Portugal, Chile and the US. After an amnesty law allowed him to return to Brazil, he settled in Rio. In 1982, he created the Democratic Labor Party and won an unexpected victory in the race for governor of Rio de Janeiro State. He was reelected, ran for president and vice president several times, and was again elected governor of Rio de Janeiro. The question was how a former political exile and progressive social reformer would deal with the state's Military Police. As a critic of the military regime, Brizola issued controversial orders, such as forbidding the police to enter in the favelas in armed units and naming progressive officers to manage the institution. However, despite his efforts to reform the police, he had few practical effects. Crime and police violence continued to grow during the 1980s and 1990s. The inability of even well-meaning and highly placed public officials to accomplish much added to the prevailing perception of Rio as a city out of control, a place where the state could not handle its basic function of maintaining order (Ribeiro 2014).

Violence rose on both sides of the crime-and-policing divide. On the one hand, the gang violence rose and the public demanded tough measures for dealing with crime. On the other hand, police violence was also a big concern of many. Mass killings in Favela Vigário Geral became a widely known example of police violence. To avenge the killing of four corrupt police officers by drug traffickers, a band of Civil Police officers invaded that favela and killed many innocent people, including entire families with no criminal records. This event has shocked the nation, and like similar episodes it deepened an already-existing legitimacy crisis. The continuing inability of the state to provide solutions to complex security issues in Rio could be observed next, during the administration of Rio governor Marcelo Alencar. After another crisis, he appointed a former army general (Nilton Cerqueira) as state secretary of security. He in turn created a "bravery bonus" for Rio officers, something that was criticized at the time by human rights activists, academics and politicians. Officers who engaged in a firefight with a criminal were rewarded for bravery. The not-unexpected result was an increase in police killings, something that was almost unavoidable in a context of extreme violence and little accountability.

However, desperate experimentation continued in Rio. The evident failure of the bravery bonus and high levels of mistrust of the police led to new directions in reform after Alencar was replaced by Anthony Garotinho. He was a former populist radio journalist who supported a new plan for reform that was drawn up with input from the academic community. The plan was drafted by Luiz Eduardo Soares, who later was the national public security secretary during the first Lula administration. He called for more police responsiveness to community concerns and killed the bravery bonus. Community policing was to be the new philosophy behind policing in Rio. But again, the continuing political ambitions of Rio's governors intervened, and Garotinho too left to run unsuccessfully for president. During the term of his replacement, the vice governor, a journalist (Tim Lopes), was murdered while investigating the Complexo do Alemão, a notorious collection of favelas located in the northern region of Rio de Janeiro. This sparked yet another political crisis, as it highlighted the territorial control still being exerted by criminal gangs.

As a consequence, another new program emerged: GPAE (*Grupamento Tático de Policiamento em Áreas Especiais*, or Special Areas Tactical Police Group). Implemented in 2000, this program's main objective was the adoption of a community policing philosophy in the state's toughest favelas. It was inaugurated in two communities, Cantagalo and Pavão-Pavãozinho. GPAE's main objective was to manage tensions between police and poor communities. It was apparent that top-down, occupation tactics were not going to address the legitimacy concerns of members, and that conditions for sustainable traditional policing were no longer present (Silva and Cano 2007).

The incumbent governor's term (again it was Garotinho) then ended, but his wife ran and won her own term as governor of Rio. During her period in office (2003–2007), GPAE was expanded and new initiatives were launched in the communities of Providência, Casa Blanca, Chácara do Céu, Morro do Cavalão (Niterói), Morro do Estado, Vila Cruzeiro and Rio das Pedras. The initial success of the GPAE model was described as a reduction in crime and fear of crime. However, GPAE was not the end point in this reform story; instead, it became the direct precursor of UPP.

The concept of UPPs emerged after the first election of Sérgio Cabral as governor of Rio de Janeiro (2007–2011). He was also reelected for a second term (2011–2015). The strategic plan of the Military Police of Rio noted a need to promote GPAE's expansion to more communities with high levels of crime and fear. The core idea was a "take and hold" one, to use a Battalion of Special Operations (BOPE) to recover territory from the gangs. Then, after the territory was secured, community policing would be implemented there through a GPAE team (Ribeiro 2014). Despite the initial success of the UPP's, Sérgio Cabral has been arrested for corruption charges and condemmed to 14 years in jail. He also faces more 12 lawsuits for the same accusations.

The UPP was launched following an armed takeover of a day care center in the Dona Marta favela, reputedly to use it as a center for drug dealing. The

Military Police decided to expel the gang and forced their way in. But unlike in the past, police did not disappear shortly after this incursion. Rather, they remained, and crime declined. In January 2009, the governor signed an executive order creating the UPPs, and promptly established a bonus of R$500.00 (five hundred reals) for officers working in the unit. The further expansion of the UPPs occurred in March 2009 when the Military Police occupied the communities of Batan, Cidade de Deus and Chapéu Mangueira (Ribeiro 2014). As it evolved, the UPP's intervention plan became a four-step one: intervention, stabilization, community policing and consolidation of state authority (Ganem Misse 2014). They were guided by two goals. The first was to regain control of territories controlled by the gangs and improve security there using more legitimate tactics. The second was to implement a system of incentives for police officers based on sticking to their goals and obtaining good results. Thus, the extra money was for members of battalions that fulfilled the plan (Magaloni, Franco and Melo 2015). Officers who are assigned to these units are trained in community policing, and an evaluation unit monitors their performance. At this writing, there are 38 UPPs in place in Rio.

Decisions regarding where to target the program are thus important. UPPs do not follow a traditional "hottest spots" targeting approach, one of deploying officers in small areas with very high levels of crime. Favelas in general are areas with a great deal of crime, but the first UPPs were implemented in areas with lower levels of violence compared to the worst-off places (Cano et al. 2012; Magaloni, Franco and Melo 2015). In fact, the great majority of UPPs are located in the South Zone of Rio de Janeiro, where businesses are located and more affluent people live. There certainly were criticisms of this model. Cano and colleagues (2012) concluded that UPPs were being sited in more affluent regions because Rio was about to host events such as the World Cup (2014) and the Olympics (2016). There are also strategic considerations. Officers interviewed by Magaloni's team affirmed that the decision to establish a UPP is based on the character and organization of the criminal gang that controls a territory (2015). Thus, a gang known as the *Comando Vermelho* (Red Command) was challenged, because they were tactically violent and willing to challenge police authority. Finally, it has been noted that favelas controlled by the militias (off-duty police officers) tend to be tolerated by the police and politicians (Magaloni, Franco and Melo 2015).

Consolidation of the UPPs

The initial results of the UPPs seemed very successful, with their establishment having reduced levels of crime and encouraging small businesses to emerge in pacified favelas. Another benchmark has been the growth of formal public services in the impacted communities. Where they are in charge, gangs and militias exploit their control of services such as electricity, gas and cable television. Residents pay for these services directly to an illegal provider sponsored by the occupying group (Zaluar and Conceição 2007). After Dona Marta's UPP implementation, there was a large increase in the number of formal contracts with public service companies, and less illegal use of them (Cano et al. 2012). Another interesting aspect has been the emergence of favela tourism. Small restaurants, hostels and bars have opened that attract both tourists and middle-class customers, a sign of economic confidence and the perceived safety of the area. This has drawn attention nationally and internationally to the UPP project.

The concept of an initial takeover by Military Police Special Battalions, followed later by community stabilization efforts by UPP teams, has been maintained. This process can last for months, and when risk declines the UPP officers become responsible for policing the community in a more participatory way. However, the adoption of community policing in Latin America generally has been criticized because the core elements of this strategy are rarely actually present (Frühling 2012). In many places, community policing is a discourse proposed by politicians rather than a real strategy followed by police officers and managers. The UPPs are today one of the largest actual police reform projects in the developing world (Magaloni, Franco and Melo 2015). Considering the structural problems facing nations in these regions, our expectations regarding change should be moderate at most. But how is it possible to make changes in this context? What are the factors that promote the institutionalization of a program like UPP? What are the incentives necessary to foster the adherence of police officers to the program? What are the limits of such programs? Is this sustainable? How can often weak states deal with violent and heavily armed groups?

The questions may be partly answered by the UPP experience in Rio de Janeiro. However, they reflect universal problems in the policing in democratic societies. These include the problems of legitimacy, trust, crime fighting effectiveness and fear of crime. The UPPs may provide a starting point for discussion on how ideas in policing originating in the developed democracies of the Northern Hemisphere can be adopted in different settings and how they can be made to work. The problem of security and crime is relevant for developing democracies, because it is a key element of the quality of their democracy itself (Caldeira and Holston 2009).

Leadership was important. The role of Rio de Janeiro's secretary of security is a relevant part of the story. José Mariano Beltrame was the secretary during the development of the UPPs. He was responsible for coordinating the efforts of distinct police organizations, one to reclaim communities and another for fostering a continuing and effective police presence thereafter. The role Beltrame had as the "top cop" responsible for all of this was apparent, and it is notable that, at this writing, he is still in office. He is the face of the program and has been responsible for the security policy for a decade. After their initially positive results, the UPPs quickly gained broad support among the people of Rio. Beltrame's next step was to jump-start the implementation of UPPs in other communities facing similar problems. The state's "honeymoon" with UPPs could last forever, and reality continues to intervene. Clashes between officers assigned to the UPP and gangsters in the Complexo do Alemão, a group of favelas in the northern area of Rio controlled by Comando Vermelho, did not go well. In 2013, a member of the Rocinha favela was beaten and tortured to death at the police station. The event was caught by a surveillance camera, and the senior BOPE officer and 15 of his subordinate officers were arrested for torture and murder. As is frequently the case when police face failure, José Mariano Beltrame himself declared that police could not be a long-term solution for these communities. He argued for social policies to improve the quality of life in the favelas, to build a sustainable base for resisting crime.

As noted earlier, the UPP strategy includes an evaluation component, and studies of the effectiveness of the program have begun. The bulk of these studies cannot be conclusive about the UPP's results. However, they shed light on the program's development and apparent successes. The studies that have been conducted employed a variety of approaches, but they all focus on how the program is working and what their main positive and negative impacts are. Some track the perceptions of the communities' members regarding the program, police officers working their area, and the main stakeholders responsible for the program (Cano et al. 2012).

A survey conducted at Dona Marta and Cidade de Deus communities in 2009 by Fundação Getulio Vargas (FGV) aimed to assess the perceptions of the people living there regarding fear of crime, trust in police and views of UPPs. The data was gathered in May 2009—almost six months after the initial reoccupation phase—and the perceptions recorded in the survey were quite positive. One of the most interesting results of that survey addressed the question of improvements in the quality of life after the introduction of the UPPs. Fully 81% of interviewees indicated that their life quality had improved a lot, due to the program. Other improvements in the communities were noted: 78% of residents gave a positive evaluation of community policing in their neighborhoods and 73% had observed a reduction in drug trafficking in the area.

In 2010, a phone survey was conducted for *O Globo*, the largest Rio newspaper. It was carried out in seven communities with UPP units. Despite the methodology's limitations, some interesting results were found: 93% of the residents said that their communities were safe or very safe, 79% of the interviewees observed that armed drug traffickers had disappeared from the streets and, for 85% of the interviewees, gunfights had ended in their neighborhoods. Such results would have been unthinkable in the past, and this evidence of apparent success sparked the decision to begin implementing UPPs in other communities (Cano et al. 2012).

A survey with police officers was held in 2010 by *Centro de Estudos de Segurança e Cidadania* (CeSec). Officers working in ten areas were interviewed, including some of those discussed in this chapter. A total of 359 police officers were interviewed in the first survey, and another was carried out in 2012, including in additional favelas. Those surveys generated information about police officers' perceptions of their role in the communities they patrolled. They were asked about the main problems that they observed on a daily basis. The major issues that they noted were related to nuisances and domestic violence. For example, in 2010, 75% of police officers indicated that nuisance disorders were a big issue, and this figure remained stable in the 2012 survey (79%). In relation to domestic violence, 62% of police officers considered it to be an important community problem in 2010, and 65% in 2012. Drug trafficking was ranked as the fifth most important problem for them, at 24% in 2010 and 43% in 2012. The great majority of the issues identified as priorities in the survey were not related directly to drug trafficking at all.

However, when asked about the risks of being assigned to a UPP unit, a great fear among officers in 2012 was that they would be ambushed (32%) or killed or wounded (24%). This is interesting because they recognize the main problems in the community to be nuisance disorders or domestic violence. Those are problems that could be treated in a responsive fashion through the tools of community policing. Nevertheless, the lack of trust by police officers in a different approach is recognized when they affirm that the most suitable weapon to be used in the UPP's patrolling is their assault rifle (94% of respondents in 2010 and 92% in 2012). Rio de Janeiro is the only state in Brazil where the assault rifle is an ordinary weapon used by the Military Police.

In 2012, the Brazilian Forum of Public Security and the Violence Analysis Laboratory from Rio de Janeiro's State University reported on their UPP evaluation. The project aimed at understanding the UPPs' impacts in three areas: crime rates, police/community relations and perceptions about the UPPs. Considering the first dimension, the objective of the evaluation was to understand how the UPPs could reduce homicides and other gun-related crimes. The second impact question was whether the UPPs actually represented a new kind of policing. To examine the last issue, the study evaluated the UPPs' impact on perceived security, levels of association among community members, improvement in the formal economy and integration of the community with the city.[2]

The evaluation found a reduction of homicides in the UPPs' areas, especially in killings related to police actions. After the implementation of the UPPs, the death toll related to confrontations with the police dropped to almost zero in some regions. The fall in the homicide rate across the study areas was about 60 homicides per 100,000 in a year (Cano et al. 2012).

The numbers of police officers deployed at UPP sites is a controversial topic, one of debate between supporters and critics of the program. The evaluation reported that the average number of police officers per inhabitant in the state of Rio de Janeiro is 2.3 per 100,000. In UPP areas, the ratio was 18 police officers per 100,000 inhabitants (Cano et al. 2012). At this rate, it obviously would not be possible to sustain policing for the state of Rio de Janeiro at the UPP level, so that will always be a special feature of this program. When Cano's study was conducted, there were 13 UPPs in Rio. Now the figure is 38, a number that has not grown for some time. Currently, there is a widespread perception that the program has reached its limits. The staffing cost of the program implies that the program has limits on its expansion even to places of need, due to its costs. This limit may have already been reached following the deepening economic crisis that hit Brazil in 2014.

The UPPs' centralization is another critical issue. Despite its rhetoric regarding community policing, in practice community demands are not often considered when the police make action plans. In practice, it appears that the project reproduces a traditional, top-down policing model in which communities do not influence the program (Cano et al. 2012). There is no real decentralization or integration of police and residents that would characterize a real community policing program. If one of the program objectives was the development of a police-community partnership, the actual shape of the project indicates that it is much more a discourse than a reality. This context has not changed until now and reinforces the criticisms held by Frühling (2012) about the structural problems of Latin American police, which do not allow the full implementation of more responsive patterns of action.

On the other hand, Willis and Mota Prado (2014) have argued that that UPPs are a case of "reflexive" planning, in which managers in practice bypass institutional barriers to providing services. This preserves traditional structures, but creates alternative pathways to attaining their objectives in an efficient manner. For those reasons, the UPPs may be more effective than the former GPAE, because there are police managers who take action on their own. UPPs were not located in an independent unit, but were formed inside traditional battalions. By contrast, officers assigned to the UPPs receive orders solely from their UPP commander. This organizational model has allowed for an independent role for UPPs inside the traditional structure of the Military Police of Rio de Janeiro. This may be an important reason why the program has survived.

A study conducted by Beatriz Magaloni, Franco and Malo (2015) at the Center for Democracy, Development and the Rule of Law from Stanford University broadened the focus of UPP evaluations. They conducted an analysis of geocoded violent deaths in Rio from 2005 to 2013. The main objective was to understand the impact of UPPs on homicide. Additionally, the research tried to compare the levels of death on pacified and nonpacified communities within Rio de Janeiro. This research aimed at bypassing a methodological barrier affecting previous studies, the levels at which the data could be aggregated. According to Magaloni, Franco and Melo (2015), the data used for previous UPP evaluations were organized at the police precinct level. Those regions are very heterogeneous and are not policed only by UPPs. Instead, the Stanford group aggregated incidents of lethal violence precisely to the favela level. Then, they compared favelas with UPPs to those being policed in traditional fashion. They manually retrieved and coded the data from more than 22,000 homicides registered in Rio de Janeiro over the period studied. As the UPPs were implemented in different moments, differences in the timing of interventions across Rio helped increase the causal implications of the statistical analysis. They were also able to look at crime displacement along the fringes of targeted favelas. Finally, they also identified "control areas" matching specific UPP targets and "paradigmatic cases" that represent the story of the program, "based on an analysis of Rio's spatial and socioeconomic urban dynamics" (Magaloni, Franco and Melo 2015, p. 6). Those "paradigmatic cases" were the favelas from South Zone in Rio, Cidade de Deus in the West Zone and Rocinha, the largest favela in Brazil.

The study has concluded that the UPPs had no impact on the observed decline of homicides in the favelas of Rio de Janeiro. This trend had been underway since 2000. A similar fall in homicide can also be seen in São Paulo, where the homicide rate dropped to 13 per 100,000 inhabitants in 2015, the lowest registered in years. Homicide rates generally have been rising only in the north and northeast regions of the country (Cerqueira et al. 2016).

The greatest impact of the UPPs in Magaloni's study was on killings by police officers. They concluded that police killings would be 60% higher without the UPPs. The peak was registered in 2007 with 1,330 people killed by the police. After the implementation of the UPPs, the number of deaths occurring from confrontation with police fell to 416 in 2013 (Ramos 2014). So, although it appears that UPPs had little impact on general homicide, it has a good record with regard to reducing police violence. Death rates for black males in Rio dropped "from 25 to less than 7 per 100,000 from 2007 to 2013" (Magaloni, Franco and Melo 2015, p. 42).

The Future of UPPs

Despite positive evaluation findings on a number of dimensions, it appears that there will continue to be a lack of resources to expand the program to other neighborhoods in Rio. Drug gangs have also been reorganizing their operations in response to the program, and there still is widespread lack of trust in the police. It is still a special program, not the regular basis for policing in Rio de Janeiro. In general, it remains more feasible to have an occupation army than a democratic police.

After eight years of implementation, the UPPs have managed to regain some territories from armed gangs and to reestablish the state's presence in those areas. This task was considered unthinkable for many people before the program began. In that sense, the UPPs have sent the message that it is possible for the state to maintain its sovereign power over conflict areas in Rio de Janeiro. However, issues such as sustainability, political interference, institutionalization and legitimacy are critical for the UPPs' future.

As we have seen, political context is an important variable in the shape and sustainability of community-oriented policing in Brazil, as in Latin America generally. The UPPs were an initiative of Sérgio Cabral's administration, and since then his political group has been able to win successive elections. So as yet, the political sustainability of the program has not been tested, and we know little about how a different political coalition would view the program. Another question is how long the UPPs will stick to their vision without José Mariano Beltrame's daily leadership. Since the beginning he has been the face of UPPs, both internally and facing outwardly to the community. It takes exceptional leadership to foster successful new programs, but they must be able to survive leadership transition.

The UPPs' possible expansion is also another problem to be considered. It seems that the program has reached its limits. UPP demands more resources than has traditionally been allocated to policing. The concentration of officers in UPP areas was far larger than for Rio as a whole, and it has many remaining areas in need. There are only 38 UPPs implemented across the 800 recognized favelas of Rio de Janeiro. The resource problem is now aggravated by an economic crisis that has driven Brazil into a major recession. Moreover, the state of Rio de Janeiro is dependent on oil revenues from offshore fields, and the fall of oil prices in international markets has increased the effects of the economic crisis on its finances. The inability of the state to expand and sustain the program in the long run, and to focus more resources on the highest crime areas and in the north of the city, may reinforce the perception that UPPs were designed for the better-off and economically important South Zone favelas.

Legitimacy claims are also relevant to the UPPs' development. One of the remarkable aspects of the UPPs in the beginning was the reduction of fear of crime and their apparent effect on homicide. Their efficacy in reducing killings by the police is also very important. However, the return of gangs and new confrontations between them and the police in areas such as Complexo do Alemão can reduce any legitimacy that has been built up in recent years. Further outbreaks of police torture and abuse could badly hurt their credibility. Moreover, many UPP advocates stress the need to implement social policies in their target favelas, to broaden the scope and effectiveness of the intervention and foster crime prevention. So, the future of the UPPs looks challenging. But—importantly—they provide evidence that the state *can* regain control of areas controlled by armed gangs and foster innovative policies in developing democracies, if they have the will.

Further Reading

For more information, visit: www.upprj.com/index.php/o_que_e_upp

Notes

1. *Unidades de Polícia Pacificadora* in Portuguese.
2. In addition, Oosterbam and Wijk (2015) found in a qualitative analysis that there was a reduction in fear among residents of UPP areas. They also stressed the perception of more integration among favela residents and middle-class citizens after the entry of UPP teams.

References

Arias, E. D., and Ungar, M. 2009. Community policing and Latin America's citizen security crisis. *Comparative Politics*, 41(4): 409–429.

Bayley, D. 2005. *Changing the guard: Developing democratic police abroad*. Oxford: Oxford University Press.

Caldeira, T., and Holston, J. 2009. Democracy and violence in Brazil. *Society for Comparative Studies in Society and History* 41: 691–729.

Cano, I., Trindade, C., Borges, D., Ribeiro, E., and Rocha, L. 2012. *Os Novos donos do morro: uma avaliação exploratória do impacto das Unidades de Polícia Pacificadora (UPPs) no Rio de Janeiro* [The new *Morro* owners: An evaluation of pacifyng police units in Rio de Janeiro]. Fórum Brasileiro de Segurança Pública: Laboratório de Estudos da Violência. www.lav.uerj.br/docs/rel/2012/RelatUPP.pdf (accessed February 12, 2016).

Cerqueira, D., Ferreira, H., Lima, R. S., Bueno, S., Hanashiro, O., Batista, F., and Nicolato, P. 2016. *Atlas da Violência* [Violence atlas 2016]. Working Paper. Instituto de Pesquisa Pura e Aplicada, Brasília.

Chappuis, F., and Hänggi, H. 2013. Statebuilding through security sector reform. In *Routledge handbook of international statebuilding*, ed. D. Chandler and T. D. Sisk, 168–184. London and New York: Routledge.

Frühling, H. 2012. A realistic look at Latin American community policing programmes. *Policing and Society: An International Journal of Research and Policy* 22: 76–88.

Ganem Misse, D. 2014. Cinco anos de UPP: um breve balanço [Five years of the UPP: A brief review]. *Dilemas: Revista de Estudos de Conflito e Controle Social* 7(3): 675–700.

Glanc, L. 2014. Caught between soldiers and police officers: Police violence in contemporary Argentina. *Policing and Society: An International Journal of Research and Policy* 24(4): 479–496.

Goldstein, H. 1979. Improving policing: A problem-oriented approach. *Crime and Delinquency* 25: 236–258.

Hills, A. 2012. Lost in translation: Why Nigeria's police don't implement democratic reforms. *International Affairs* 88(4): 739–755.

Hinton, M. S. 2005. A distant reality: Democratic policing in Argentina and Brazil. *Criminal Justice* 51: 75–100.

Hinton, M. S., and Newburn, T. 2009. *Policing developing democracies.* Abingdon: Routledge.

Ignatieff, M. 2005. Police and people: The birth of Mr. Peel's blue locusts. In *Policing: Key readings*, ed. T. Newburn, 25–30. Devon: Willan Publishing.

Magaloni, B., Franco, E., and Melo, V. 2015. *Killing in the slums: An impact evaluation of police reform in Rio de Janeiro.* Working paper, Center on Democracy, Development and the Rule of Law. http://cddrl.fsi.stanford.edu/publication/killing-slums-impact-evaluation-police-reform-rio-de-janeiro (accessed January 10, 2016).

Müller, M. M. 2010. Community-policing in Latin America: Lessons from Mexico city. *European Review of Latin American and Caribbean Studies* 88, April: 21–37.

Oosterbam, S., and Wijk, J. V. 2015. Pacifying and integrating the favelas of Rio de Janeiro: an evaluation of the impact of the UPP program on favela residents. *International Journal of Comparative and Applied Criminal Justice* 39: 179–198.

Ramos, S. 2014. *Segurança Pública, violência e polícia: o que aconteceu com o Rio de Janeiro?* [Public security, violence and police: what has happened with Rio de Janeiro?]. Working Paper, Centro de Estudos de Segurança e Cidadania: Universidade Cândido Mendes (CESEC).

Ribeiro, L. 2014. O Nascimento da polícia moderna: uma análise dos programas de policiamento comunitário implementados na cidade do Rio de Janeiro [The birth of modern police: Community policing programs in Rio de Janeiro (1983–2012)]. *Análise Social* 211(49): 2182–2999.

Silva, G. M., and Cano, I. 2007. Between damage reduction and community policing: The case of Pavão-Pavãozinho-Cantagalo in Rio de Janeiro's Favelas. In *Legitimacy and criminal justice: International perspectives*, ed. T. Tyler, 186–214. New York, NY: Russel Sage Foundation.

Skogan, W. G. 2006. *Community policing in Chicago: A tale of three cities.* Oxford and New York: Oxford University Press.

Tyler, T. 2011. Trust and legitimacy: Policing in the USA and Europe. *European Journal of Criminology* 8: 254–266.

Tyler, T., Braga, A., Fagan, J., Meares, T., Sampson, R., and Winship, D. 2007. Legitimacy and criminal justice: International perspectives. In *Legitimacy and criminal justice: International perspectives*, ed. T. Tyler, 9–29. New York, NY: Russel Sage Foundation.

Wiesler, D., and Onwudine, I. D. 2007. *Community-policing: A comparative view.* Working paper no. 6, International Police Executive Forum: Geneva Centre for the Democratic Control of Armed Forces.

Willis, G. D., and Mota Prado, M. 2014. Process and pattern in institutional reforms: A case study of the Police Pacifyng Units (UPPs) in Brazil. *World Development* 64: 232–234.

Zaluar, A., and Conceição, I. S. 2007. Favelas sob o controle das milícias no Rio de Janeiro, que paz? [Favelas under militias' control in Rio de Janeiro, what Peace?]. *São Paulo em Perspectiva* 21: 89–101.

Community Policing in the *Favelas* of Rio de Janeiro

10

Vicente Riccio, Marco Aurélio Ruediger, Steven Dutt Ross and Wesley G. Skogan[1]

Contents

In the United States, adoption of community policing became widespread during the 1980s. Although the details varied widely from agency to agency, these programs generally involved decentralizing administration to increase organizational responsiveness, engaging with the community in safety projects, and adopting a problem-solving orientation that extends the police mandate to include quality-of-life issues. Many of its tenets proved popular beyond the boundaries of the US, and community policing has subsequently stimulated new thinking about policing in countries around the world.

This chapter examines the adoption of a version of community policing in two extremely poor communities—favelas—in Rio de Janeiro, the capital city of Rio de Janeiro State and the second largest city in Brazil. They provided a challenging environment. In both areas, large and well-armed criminal groupings challenged the idea that the government held a monopoly over the application of violence to maintain order. Instead, they threatened to install themselves as the de facto state, one that would protect their criminal enterprises, including drug trafficking. Residents of the areas had little voice in this matter. Historically, their relationship with the police was a poor one, marked by widespread experience with police violence and corruption. This had largely extinguished any sense that the state had more legitimacy to exercise violence than did local criminals.

After a review of some of the basic concepts of community policing and how they might apply to the Brazilian context, this chapter discusses Rio de Janeiro's attempt to mount a community policing effort in these two areas. Our initial research question—was Rio's favela initiative "community policing"?—necessarily came first, for skeptics doubted that Rio de Janeiro's State Military Police could do anything of the sort. Then we address the second question: is there evidence that the program they mounted helped reduce crime and rebuild police legitimacy? Using a survey of residents, we examine the impact of the program on those issues.

Community Policing in Rio de Janeiro

In the United States, by the 1980s, initiatives were underway to reshape the relationship between police and the communities they served. There were diverse reasons for doing so but at its heart, community policing was driven by the legitimacy deficit that had grown over the decades in black and brown neighborhoods, and moving in this direction was a political decision (Skogan and Hartnett 1997). Earlier, a "professional" model of policing had spread through the US, and this was also a political matter: it was intended to confer autonomy on the police in relation to politicians, big businesses, and other local power brokers. Police bureaucracies quickly isolated themselves and adopted a performance model based on quick response to calls from the public for police service. Motorized patrolling was the standard police action. One unintended consequence was that police lost contact with many members of the community and mostly dealt with the public as either aggrieved victims or their alleged perpetrators (Moore 1992 [Vol. 15]). Both this gulf between the police and the community and the large legitimacy deficit in poor and minority communities would be familiar to policymakers and politicians in Rio de Janeiro, for they faced the same problems.

Another widely familiar feature of policing is the hierarchical structure of police agencies. In the United States, this probably became more pronounced with the emergence of the professional model for tightening up administrative oversight to deal with the internal corruption and sheer laziness that characterized the even earlier "political" model of policing. The role of hierarchy in organizations is to reduce the autonomy of intermediate-level managers and front-line employees (Jesilow and Parsons 2000). Some have observed that hierarchy impeded the development of a more nimble, locally oriented policing, and thus undermined its preventive effectiveness by getting in the way of the adoption of highly varied community initiatives and responsiveness to different priorities in different neighborhoods (Skogan 2004). In Rio de Janeiro, too, critics of the police could point to hierarchy as one of their problems. In fact, police in Brazil are much more modeled along strict military lines than any North American police department. They are heavily armed and frequently conduct what are essentially military operations. Internally, there is lateral entry into the top officer ranks, cementing large social and educational distinctions between rank-and-file police and their military-ranked top officer corps.

Problem solving, at root, is the idea that police move from exclusively taking care of incidents to developing long-term preventive solutions for community problems (Skolnick and Bayley 1986). The steps involved include problem identification, prioritization, and resolution. The involvement of the community may be part of the solution, but maybe not. The police can take on problems with their considerable resources, perhaps in conjunction with other municipal agencies. Tilley (2004) emphasizes this point when he notes that problem-oriented policing does not redefine the distance between the state and the community. But, adopting a community orientation pushes police to prioritize issues which may not be conventional—or conventionally "serious"—crimes. Community policing presses police to address a wider range of issues (Skogan 2006). Rio's favelas had plenty of those, and it was an open question at the start of this research whether police would recognize them as their problem too.

Visitors from abroad looking into the suitability of community policing might come away confused. Authors like Seagrave (1996) worry that it is difficult to define community policing because of the fluidity of the concept. The difficulty of defining it is seen by some as a major hurdle to deciding, for example, whether "it"—whatever it is—"works." Others like Ratcliffe (2008) celebrate this fluidity, since it can emerge in concrete practice from collaboration between police and particular communities. In this view, community policing adapts itself to context, in response to diverse motives for moving in this direction.

This provides us with an approach to addressing our first research question: was Rio's favela initiative community policing? We first looked for strategic components of community-oriented policing: administrative decentralization, problem solving, and—because of priorities in Brazil—legitimacy building by protecting the public while respecting human rights.

For decentralization, one would look at whether officers have autonomy with regard to acting in response to demands as they arise. This entails risks; for unlike assembly line workers, police officers in practice exercise a great deal of discretion. As state agents who act directly with the public, they have a considerable decision-making autonomy in concrete cases (Lipsky 1983). Their judgments in these situations may be based more on their personal views than on legal rules (Oberweis and Musheno 2001). For this reason, the true acceptance of community policing principles by line officers is very important; alternately, they can ignore, subvert, or sabotage well-meaning policies (Novak, Alarid and Lucas 2003). Research has verified this problem in developed societies with a long tradition of democracy, so there is reason for concern about how police discretion will be exercised in more recently consolidated democracies.

Problem solving promises the preventive aspect of community policing. Because public needs are to play an important role in driving this, we would expect community-oriented policing in Rio to track local priorities and involvement in other public service agencies in tackling a broad spectrum of problems, ranging from health and street cleaning to getting better lighting installed.

While rebuilding legitimacy by effectively policing while respecting citizens' rights was a prime Brazilian priority, the turn toward the community in the United States was also importantly driven by the state's need to recapture enough of it to maintain a politically tolerable level of social peace. Concern for legitimacy is important in societies marked by great social divisions, whether they are economic, cultural, or racial in character. A very large body of important research has documented that the belief in the legitimacy of authorities is crucial to the acceptance of laws and deference to the decisions of the state and its delegates. Democratic nations cannot be built only on coercion involving most of the people almost all of the time (Sunshine and Tyler 2003; Tyler 2008).

Of course, stable states have legitimacy in the eyes of most of the population. It is a deficit that is usually concentrated in selected areas, varying in detail from nation to nation. In reality, community policing is really about legitimating the police in poor, marginalized, sometimes culturally distinct communities. In Northern Ireland, for example, Weitzer (1995) documents how religion dominated the relationship between the police and the community. There, somewhat akin to our Rio de Janeiro communities, autonomous armed bands challenged the legitimacy of the state. In regions under influence of the Irish Republican Army, the population was forbidden to contact the police. From the point of view of many poor Catholics, the police were unresponsive and brutal, and they were called enemies. In societies marked by extreme inequality, recent democratization, and fragile commitment to human rights, legitimacy can be hard to find. This can be observed elsewhere in Latin America (Frühling 2009), as well as in Eastern Europe (Mesko and Klemencic 2007), places with traditions of authoritarian rule which was only recently democratized. In such societies, there is a great distance between the police and the people. In Brazil, favelas are places where police presence has habitually been reactive and violent and police have few links with the community. In these spaces, armed criminal groups predominate and exercise arbitrary and self-serving control over what happens there.[2]

Thus, a central question we address is the extent to which community policing should be established in these locations and successfully build a more legitimate relationship with the public.

But, favelas can be (they vary a great deal) dangerous places. David Thacher (2001, p. 771) therefore raises a relevant question: "how does a police department institutionalize the commitment to justice and respect without weakening crime control?" Can police effectively enforce the law and control crime in this context while avoiding abuse? In the circumstance of the favelas, police face the difficult task of integrating these sometimes competing demands. In the past, they largely had not done a good job at this. The favelas in question had a history of police violence absent of actual long-term strategy for crime prevention. In Rio de Janeiro, their interventions often involved the use of heavy weaponry, armored cars, and helicopters, and they ended up causing a great deal of damage to the people from these communities. However, the state still could not maintain their temporary monopoly of force, and criminal groups in these communities returned to their old ways once they were gone (Costa 2004; Moraes and Cano 2007; Sapori 2007). The criminal groups operating there are mainly connected to the drug trade, which generates a great deal of cash that is used in part to corrupt state authorities. This leads to a dynamic in which the state efforts to impose order are episodic, violently repressive, and widely disrespectful of the rights of residents. On the other side, the control practices of armed criminal groups repress any independent civic articulation of the views of residents. The adoption of community-oriented, legitimacy-building initiatives in these highly conflicted urban spaces certainly was challenging.

Developing the Concept in Rio

As we observed in the previous section, relations between police and the poor communities we studied were marked by mutual distrust and abusive police practices. Like other regions that suffer from these problems, favelas are marked by poverty, receive poor public services, and face high levels of unemployment. The question was, could community-oriented policing be implemented in these areas?

The effort in our study communities, Santa Marta and Cidade de Deus, was not without precedent. In Rio de Janeiro, there had already been an attempt to intervene in other favelas using a similar policing model, by the Police Group for Special Areas (GPAE). Their interventions focused on the Pavão and Pavãozinho favelas, which are located in the Copacabana and Ipanema areas of Rio de Janeiro. That project stemmed from the crisis created by the killing of five young people by the police, who claimed that they were drug dealers. The community reaction to these killings created a local rebellion that spread throughout Copacabana (Moraes and Cano 2007).

The GPAE project involved the participation of other state agencies, civil society, and the area's inhabitants. It was a top-down project and at the beginning, the residents were suspicious of the police. The integration of the police and the community in a context of a high level of conflict, with the presence of several armed groups connected to drug dealing, was one of the objectives of the GPAE. GPAE focused initially on three goals: reduce access to guns and open gun carrying, steer youths away from a life of crime, and halt the violent practices of the Civil and Military Police (Albernaz, Caruso and Patricío 2007). The project did not originally focus particularly on drug dealing. As they began to operate, members of the GPAE unit found themselves receiving many demands from the public that were not immediately connected to crime, such as medical assistance, support for access to public bodies, and educational and work qualification programs. This, of course, has been a standard occurrence when police adopt an open, problem-focused orientation to the community. Being effective troubleshooters will capture the attention of many elements in the area (Skogan 2006). In its first two years, the program was apparently successful, with a significant reduction of homicides in the communities involved.

The GPAE experience was extended to other communities, such as Formiga, Chácara do Céu, Morro do Cavalão in Niterói, and Vila Cruzeiro. In the latter region, GPAE was instituted in response to media pressure, which followed the murder of a journalist. In spite of the initial success of the Pavão and Pavãozinho interventions, problems were identified in the execution of the program. It was too top down, too unorganized to respond effectively to the many social demands that came its way, and did not promise to become institutionalized in a fashion that would sustain the intervention for a long period. The program was vulnerable to political interference.

The GPAE experience in Morro do Cavalão in Niterói (a city in Rio de Janeiro's metropolitan area located at Guanabara Bay and connected to the main city by ferry boats and a bridge) was also considered successful, because it resulted in the reduction in the visible presence of armed groups in the community and reduced the spaces where drug dealers could act. Bonds of trust between the community and police leaders on the scene were established, but this did not solve the issue of the initiative's institutional fragility.

Following the election of Rio de Janeiro State Governor Sérgio Cabral, a secretary of security was appointed who came from the Federal Police (Delegado José Mariano Beltrame). There followed a shift in the state's security policies. New initiatives were mounted against drug dealers and the visible occupation of favelas by armed groups. These efforts could lead to intense armed confrontations, as in the case of favela Complexo do Alemão, where an operation resulted in 19 deaths and involved more than 1,000 police officers. In spite of criticisms regarding possible abuses, the action in Complexo do Alemão was considered successful and had the support of several social sectors.

Importantly, the occupation of Complexo do Alemão clearly defined the state government position of not negotiating with armed groups. An initial emphasis on their containment process was followed by the adoption of a policy that combined territorial reoccupation to repress drug dealing and the adoption of a form of community policing. The units assigned to the job were dubbed Pacifying Police Units (UPPs), and they remain active to this day.

The UPP model mounts interventions in poor communities in order to reduce the space for organized crime. It takes into consideration the particular features of the communities in which the units will operate, including the character of the armed groups exerting territorial control there. The initial occupation has the objective of driving out the most significant criminals and establishing an enduring police presence in public spaces. Police regain control of former drug dealing points and the escape routes used by the criminals. The initial interventions are conducted by special groups of the Military Police, such as the Special Operations Battalion (BOPE).

In a shift, instead of withdrawing after making arrests, police units remain in place. This is to create a security situation in which community policing can be implemented by the UPPs. These officers are especially trained for doing this, and they receive special financial compensation to acknowledge the importance of their pacifying role. The continued occupation of an area and the inauguration of local UPP teams make it possible to work on the provision of other public services demanded by these communities. It was described in a speech by the secretary of security:

> It is necessary to respond to the population's demand. We used to have the old speech: there is no school, there is no doctor because there is no security. Now there is security. Let the services come. Rio de Janeiro's population needs to be more active, demand more from its governors, its politicians. To know from whom they can demand. The police will create the peaceful environment for other people to solve. The more we value citizenship, the less security will be needed.
>
> Available at http://g1.globo.com/notícias/Rio/0,MUL1252476-5606,00.html
> (accessed on December 8, 2009)

Community Policing in Dona Marta and Cidade de Deus

In this section, we address the implementation of the next iteration of community policing in Rio de Janeiro, in the communities of Dona Marta and Cidade de Deus. The operations in Dona Marta began in November 2008 with an intervention by BOPE to drive out the criminal groups that visibly occupied the community. UPP teams were installed one month later, in December 2008. This operation functioned as a "test run" in order to be assessed and reproduced in other areas. All the action was preceded by careful planning and analysis.

New police efforts in Cidade de Deus began in 2009, and UPP took over in February 2009. This project was adapted to local issues in Cidade de Deus, which is a large and populous community. In addition, there are geographic differences, for Santa Marta is located on a hill whereas Cidade de Deus is flat and spread out. For this reason, the Cidade de Deus intervention focused on a specific part of the area, Caratê. By measuring the perceptions of residents of these two communities, we were able to provide some evidence on the impact of community policing in Rio de Janeiro.

Surveys were conducted in both communities during May 2009. A structured questionnaire was administered to 600 residents, 300 from each favela. The field research was carried out in Santa Marta from 22 May to 24 May 2009, while in Cidade de Deus it took place from 25 May to 27 May 2009. Quota sampling was used to select respondents. Rio's sprawling favelas are not laid out on a grid or with official addresses, and dwelling units are piled on top of each other and frequently subdivided to house diverse family units. This made it impractical to sample by listing residential addresses for random selection. Most favelas do not officially exist, so there were also no official population lists from which to draw or evaluate standard survey samples. Instead, interviewers were positioned at points of high population movement. They approached adults asking if they were the head of their household or the spouse of the head of their household. Interviews were conducted to achieve an approximately 55–45% female–male distribution of respondents. For purposes of this evaluation, the dependent variables were measures of various aspects of the perceived security of residents in the areas. We examine these in relation to their views of the implementation of the UPP model in their area, which is the independent variable.

Measures of crime, fear, and police violence were included in the brief questionnaire. They reflected the main security problems that residents of these two areas faced and the issues that were targeted by the UPP teams. Respondents were asked fear of crime questions concerning (in translation) perceived improvements over the last year in "your personal and family security" and "your ease of coming and going safely." They rated these issues as improving "very much," "a little," or "not at all." They were also asked to rate improvements in the presence of "armed drug dealers in the street" and "murders." Finally, the survey monitored the potential for police abuse by responses to questions about perceived improvements (or not) in "violence by the police" and "police respect for human rights."

The analysis reported here examined the relationship between these perceived changes in the community environment and respondents' views of the UPP teams. They were asked, "how do you evaluate the community policing in your area?" They were asked to rate the new police teams using one of four categories, ranging from "poor" to "normal," "good," and "very good." The results are presented in Figures 10.1 and 10.2.

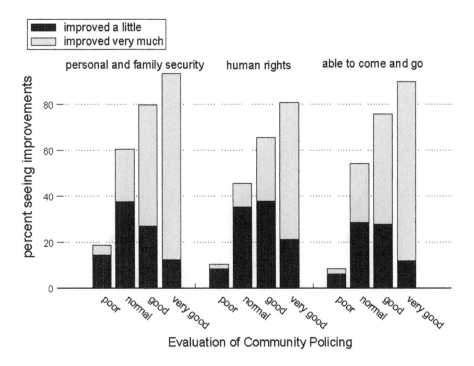

Figure 10.1 Community policing and resident perceptions of personal security, human rights, and freedom of access

Source: Fundação Getulio Vargas survey

Figure 10.1 presents the distribution of responses to the fear of crime items. They first asked about possible improvements in personal and family security. The left-most chart in Figure 10.1 illustrates the percentage of respondents who reported that their security situation had improved a little or very much. These two percentages combine to determine the overall height of each bar. The bars thus represent positive views of varying strength and a bar is presented for each assessment of community policing. As can be noted there, the more positive respondents were regarding community policing, the more they reported that they and their families felt more secure. The difference was most dramatic in the percentage of respondents indicating that their situation had improved "very much." More than 80% of those most favorable toward community policing in their area choose this response, and together with the "improved a little" group, the total percent positive was 94%. Among those who thought the program was implemented poorly, on the other hand, only 4% saw their security was improving a lot and 15% thought it went up "a little." Statistically, the Spearman correlation between the two measures was +.50.

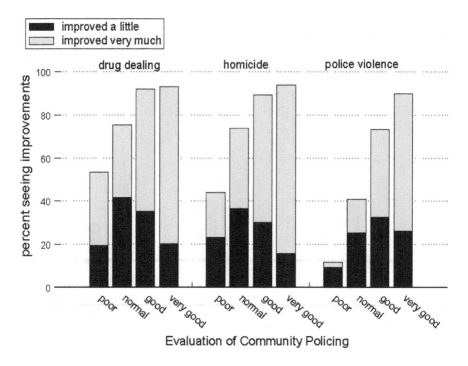

Figure 10.2 Community policing and resident perceptions of drug dealing, homicide, and police violence

Source: Fundação Getulio Vargas survey

The right-most panel of Figure 10.1 examines the second fear of crime question: resident perceptions of their freedom to come and go as they please. This was an important issue in areas previously marked by extreme violence and policing by armed criminal groups. Evaluations of community policing were directly related to their ability to come and go; the Spearman correlation between the two measures was +.49. The percentage of respondents who saw their access rights "much improved" was particularly notable.

The center panel in Figure 10.1 examines residents' perceptions of police respect for human rights in their area. Their evaluations of community policing were also linked to this factor. At 11% positive, those giving the program a poor rating stood far below the 81% in the most positive category seeing improvement in police respect for human rights. The Spearman correlation between the two measures was +.46.

Other factors were linked to our respondents' views of community safety. The strongest correlates of the two fear measures described in Figure 10.1 were education and income. Higher income and more educated residents (relative to the others living in these poor areas) were most critical of the police. For example, among those in the bottom income quartile, 44% thought that the police had improved very much, while the comparable figure for those in the highest income quartile was only 21%. The most educated respondents were the most critical regarding the protection of human rights; 61% of those in the highest education group gave them a rating so low that it was not included on the bars in Figure 10.1, and only 12% thought they had improved very much.

Figure 10.2 presents the distribution of two crime-specific ratings of community change in these favelas. The left-most panel focuses on reports of changes in the extent of visible drug dealing. While the link between this and assessments of the quality of the community policing effort in their area was somewhat weaker than the findings illustrated in Figure 10.1 (the Spearman correlation was +.32), we note that this question was asking for reports of observable conditions in their area. Reducing the extent of visible criminal activity was one of the primary goals of the UPP teams, and we see here that the view that there were improvements in this respect were relatively widespread. Perceived improvements in visible drug dealing were commonly reported even by respondents who were less positive about the program.

The center panel of Figure 10.2 examines perceptions of trends in homicide. Murder is a tremendous problem in Brazil's poorest areas, and our study sites were no exception. However, the higher the satisfaction with community policing, the more residents saw improvements—and especially large improvements—in the homicide count. Again, this was also somewhat more common even among those who were not positive about this new policing effort, so the Spearman correlation was lower, +37.

The right-most panel in Figure 10.2 examines the reports of trends in police violence. As we discussed above, this is an issue of tremendous salience for even common residents of Rio's favelas, for historically the police response to their problem was one deploying "shock and awe" tactics in their community. The Spearman correlation between the two measures was +.49, and it is clear in Figure 10.2 that there was a very strong link between satisfaction with community policing and the view that police violence was much reduced in their community. As in Figure 10.1, these three measures were negatively related to income and education, with more educated and higher income respondents seeing fewer community improvements and more problems with police violence.

Conclusions and Implications for Policy in Brazil

The impact of UPP teams in these two Rio favelas seems to have been positive. The introduction of this new policing model practice was well received. All of the perceived security measures we gathered were positively linked to views of community policing. Those who thought police were doing a good job reported feeling safer and could more easily come and go in their community, they saw improvements in the extent of police violence and disrespect for their rights, they thought there was less homicide, and they saw less drug dealing. All of these features of their lives were targets of the UPP teams. The UPPs have become an important element in the architecture of a new security policy for the city of Rio de Janeiro. This study was carried out shortly after the creation of the two first units in Rio. Their initial success led to the insertion of more new units in various parts of the city, and there was great demand to expand the program, especially in view of the 2014 World Cup competition in Rio and the 2016 Olympics. Two challenges to the UPPs and to the broader community pacification policy that we have described here are their sustainability once Rio leaves the world stage and their possible expansion to other areas of Brazil. Future studies of the UPP program could follow its evolution and the level of support for reform in communities that need their assistance.

Notes

1. This is a revised version of an article by the same title that appeared in *Police Practice and Research: An International Journal* 14: 308–318.
2. Two recent films address the problem of urban violence and the relation between the police and the community—the movies *Cidade de Deus* and *Tropa de Elite*. The first is based on a novel and describes the involvement of youngsters in a peripheral Rio community in drug dealing, whereas the second addresses in a factual manner the routine activities of a special battalion of the Rio de Janeiro Military Police and their use of violent methods to contain the actions of criminal groups in the area.

References

Albernaz, E., Caruso, H., and Patrício, L. 2007. Tensões e Desafios de um policiamento comunitário em favelas do Rio de Janeiro: o caso do grupamento de policiamento em áreas especiais [Tensions and challenges of community policing in favelas in Rio de Janeiro: The special areas policing group case]. *São Paulo em Perspectiva* 21: 39–52.

Costa, A. T. M. 2004. *Entre a lei e a ordem: violência e reforma nas polícias do Rio de Janeiro e Nova Iorque* [Between law and order: Violence and reform in Rio de Janeiro and New York Polices]. Rio de Janeiro: Editora FGV.

Frühling, H. 2009. Research on Latin America police: Where do we go from here? *Police Practice and Research* 10: 465–481.

Jesilow, P., and Parsons, D. 2000. Community policing as peacemaking. *Policing and Society* 10: 163–182.

Lipsky, M. 1983. *Street-level bureaucracy: Dilemmas of the individual in public services.* New York: Russell Sage.

Mesko, G., and Klemencic, G. 2007. Rebuilding legitimacy and police professionalism in an emerging democracy: The Slovenian experience. In *Legitimacy and criminal justice: International perspectives*, ed. T. Tyler, 84–114. New York: Russell Sage Foundation.

Moore, M. H. 1992. Problem-solving and community policing. In *Crime and justice*, ed. M. Tonry and N. Morris, 99–158. Chicago: University of Chicago Press.

Moraes, G., and Cano, I. 2007. Between damage reduction and community policing: The case of Pavão-Pavãozinho-Cantagalo in Rio de Janeiro's Favelas. In *Legitimacy and criminal justice: International perspectives*, ed. T. Tyler, 186–214. New York: Russell Sage Foundation.

Novak, K. L., Alarid, L. F., and Lucas, W. 2003. Exploring officers' acceptance of community policing: Implications for policing implementation. *Journal of Criminal Justice* 31: 57–71.

Oberweis, T., and Musheno, M. 2001. *Knowing rights: State actors' stories of power, identity and morality*. Aldershot: Ashgate.

Ratcliffe, J. 2008. *Intelligence-led policing*. Cullampton: Willan.

Sapori, L. F. 2007. *Segurança pública no Brasil: desafios e perspectivas* [Public security in Brazil: Challenges and perspectives]. Rio de Janeiro: FGV Editora.

Seagrave, J. 1996. Defining community policing. *American Journal of Police* 15: 1–22.

Skogan, W. 2004. Representing the community in community policing. In *Community policing: Can it work?*, ed. W. Skogan, 57–75. Belmont, MA: Thomson Wadsworth.

Skogan, W. 2006. *Police and community in Chicago: A tale of three cities*. New York: Oxford University Press.

Skogan, W. G., and Hartnett, S. M. 1997. *Community policing, Chicago style*. New York: Oxford University Press.

Skolnick, J. H., and Bayley, D. H. 1986. *The new blue line: Police innovation in six American cities*. New York: The Free Press.

Sunshine, J., and Tyler, T. R. 2003. The role of procedural justice and legitimacy in shaping public support for policing. *Law and Society Review* 37: 513–548.

Thacher, D. 2001. Conflicting values in community policing. *Law & Society Review* 35: 765–798.

Tilley, N. 2004. Thinking realistically about crime prevention. In *Handbook of crime prevention and community safety*, ed. N. Tilley, 3–13. Cullampton: Willan.

Tyler, T. 2008. *Legitimacy and criminal justice: International perspectives*. New York: Russell Sage Foundation.

Weitzer, R. 1995. *Policing under fire: Ethnic conflict and police community relations in Northern Ireland*. Albany, NY: State University of New York Press.

Section III
The Police and Public Policy

Professionalizing the Military Police Through Training[1]

11

Vicente Riccio,
Marcio Rys Meirelles de
Miranda and
Angélica Müller

Contents

This chapter examines the role of high-level officer training in the police reform agenda of Brazil, and how in one setting federal guidelines designed to improve training were implemented in actual practice. The first new training class for the Amazonas State Military Police in Brazil was the setting chosen for this study. They were trained under new guidelines developed by the Ministry of Justice, which is attempting to standardize police education across the nation. This training initiative is part of a larger police reform effort in Brazil, one aimed at increasing the professionalism, efficiency, and civility of the police. The ministry's guidelines provide a direction for change, but there is large variation among the Brazilian states in terms of how far they must come.

Police reform is a major issue on the Brazilian political agenda due to the historical positioning of the police forces in the country. They suffer from low legitimacy in the view of society, they are inefficient in the execution of their duties, and they have a reputation for corruption and systematic abuses of power. Professional education for high-level leaders is seen as an important instrument for the improvement of the police in Brazil, one route to making them more efficient and capable of integrating with civil society. These issues are addressed by the new training program, and they are its objective.

In this chapter, we first describe the Brazilian context and the issues it raises for police education, and police reform more broadly. Then we present a few details regarding the new national training plan. A third section describes the actual implementation of the program in Amazonas State. This is followed by the findings of our observations and interviews with participants in the course. In-depth personal interviews were conducted with several members of the first graduating class after they had been serving in the field for three years, in order to understand their experiences and gauge the impact of the program on practice. The chapter concludes with some conclusions regarding the progress of police reform on the ground. The conclusions are critical of the program, due to the flawed execution of this innovative education program for the Amazonas State Military Police.

The Origins of Police Educational Reform

Police and policing policies have been the subject of much discussion around the world, for they are linked to other emergent problems in contemporary society. These include increasing social, economic, and political risks, plus high or fluctuating crime rates, which reduce the legitimacy of the police and impose the need for reform (Ericson and Haggerty 1997; Kelling and Moore 2005). The resulting model that has emerged in many places envisions a results-oriented performance culture in organizations that make use of new information technologies, and at least in poorer areas, operate in closer collaboration with the community, with greater transparency and with more measured use of force (Bayley 2005; Roth, Roehl and Johnson 2004; Skogan 2004, 2006). However, in practice, too often what has actually emerged has been instead more tough traditional policies aimed at deterring crime that has continued to undervalue integrating the police and the community (Hough 2007). Further, even managing traditional policing resources "smartly," through modern practices such as hot spot policing and making better use of information technology, also calls for improving the academic qualifications of police leaders (Jaschke and Neidhardt 2007).

Another general trend is cited by Bayley and Shearing (2005), who noted the "pluralization" of policing. The monopoly enjoyed by the public police has eroded, and we have witnessed the appearance of parallel organizations aimed at crime prevention that are rooted in the community and in business. In parallel, there has been increased acknowledgment of the limits of traditional, reactive "professional" policing and its focus on motorized patrol. These challenges to traditional police practices and culture also call for changes in police education that would inform more nimble and innovative reactions to these shifts in the policing environment.

Finally, democratization processes are at work around the world that also call for more sophisticated policing. In societies marked by recent democratization, one of the changes called for has been the implementation of democratic forms of policing (Bayley 2005; Beato 2005; Frühling 2009; Mesko and Klemencic 2007; Scott, Evans and Verma 2009). The focus of many new democracies has been to reconstruct the legitimacy, efficiency, transparency, and civility of the police, usually in parallel with reform efforts more generally. The police reflect the central characteristics of the state that sponsors them, and how they act is crucial to the maintenance of the basic conditions of democratic life, such as the right to come and go, freedom of speech, the right of association, and the right to vote without intimidation (Bayley 2005). An important point to be highlighted is the fact that police education must reflect this emerging social complexity.

All those themes are connected. The complexity of society and the growing complexity of some forms of crime, the obvious benefits of using information technologies, a growing emphasis on crime prevention, and the expectation that police will reform in parallel with the growth of other aspects of democratization all call for changes in police perspectives. One lever for changing these perspectives is leadership education. The issue of police education has been discussed from several perspectives in the literature. These studies revolve around themes such as the distinction between the training received in the academy and the daily practice of the profession (Bayley and Bittner 1984); the impact of curricular changes (Chapel 2008; Jaschke and Neidhardt 2007; Jaschke 2010); the importance of higher education in the policing practice (Domincy 2010; Farrow et al. 2010; Jones, Jones and Prenzler 2005; Paoline and Terrill 2007; Roberg and Bonn 2004; Vickers 2000); and the process through which training reinforces the obedience of new recruits (Paes-Machado and Albuquerque 2006; Conti 2009).

The question here is, how can police education in a recently democratized country such as Brazil be structured in order to deal with high levels of urban violence, without losing sight of other trends calling for a more innovative policing paradigm? The attempt to redemocratize Brazil's police forces near the end of the twentieth century took place in parallel with an increase in urban violence, as well as mounting criticism of the way in which they operated. The difficulty in reducing violence persists in Brazil, even though progress in alleviating social disparities has been recorded over the last decade. There has been significant improvement in the lives of many Brazilians, especially the poorest. One example is the evolution of the per capita income of the poorest 10%, which increased by 57% between 2001 and 2006 (Neri 2009). But in spite of this, violence remains high, especially in poorer areas.

In the Brazilian case, one of the legacies of the earlier authoritarian regime was the subordination of police forces to the army. The resulting approach to internal security and public order problems was characterized by harsh crime fighting (Costa 2004). The division of police work in Brazil puts most of the responsibility for law enforcement into the hands of the federal states. Two police forces predominate: the Military Police and the Civil Police. The former is responsible for street patrolling, and the second for criminal investigations. In both cases, there are two entry points into the profession. In the Military Police, officers (superiors) and soldiers (privates, corporals, and sergeants) are separately recruited and trained. The same is true in the Civil Police, where the relevant distinctions are between *delegados* (superiors) and detectives. The Military Police have adopted an organizational hierarchy that mimics that of the armed forces, with the highest rank being colonel (Lino 2004).

In this chapter, the term "officers" refers to recruits to the upper level ranks of the Military Police, or the officer class. The different training regimes for various ranks are most striking in the Military Police. In that institution, officer training lasts an average of four years, while soldiers are trained in between six months and two years, depending on the state in question. But the education that they have been receiving is considered inadequate for the complexity of operating in a democratic society (Basílio 2004; Poncioni 2005). Public security in Brazil until recently has been guided more by judicial regulatory criteria than by the adoption of policies aimed at promoting police problem solving, community policing, and other innovative practices (Sapori 2007).

Among the questions raised by crime and criticisms of Brazilian police practices has been about police training. It is widely believed that each new generation receiving inadequate police training essentially reproduces the existing model of policing, one that emphasizes crime fighting, reactive strategies, strict adhesion to the organizational guidelines, and rote decision-making (Poncioni 2005). An Albuquerque and Paes-Machado study (2004) of training in the Bahia Military Police points to the maintenance of traditions of military training and war fighting. There, recruits routinely endured punishment and humiliation, which were deliberately inflicted to set the stage for their socialization as officers. Such practices were an expression of an informal culture that was not adapted to the requirements of a new training curriculum, one based on modern thinking and emphasizing respect for human rights and community-oriented policing practices.

The impact of the global human rights movement on police roles in societies that have democratized can be observed in the inclusion of human rights themes in the training of the Northern Ireland Police Service. Engel and Burrus's study (2004) discussed this change towards a democratic training model. The inclusion of the human rights themes was one of the key aspects of this initiative. The difficulties in doing so had to do with the historic context of that society and the fact that big divisions had been structured due to the conflicts that had occurred there. The inclusion of the human rights theme came with its acceptance, which indicates a focus on a more democratic model of policing. Curricular changes, in turn, require proper institutional support; otherwise, the effects expected from its adoption shall have little or no result. This aspect is relevant in relation to other aspects, such as the adoption of community policing, the use of information technologies, and assessment mechanisms. Education is relevant since its objective is creating a new culture of policing practice.

Brazil's National Curricular Plan

In 2000, the Brazilian Ministry of Justice, through the National Public Security Secretariat (SENASP) released a new police training plan, with the purpose of standardizing police education among the different federal states. The absence of specific police training policies and assessment criteria led the federal government to define the first set of national requirements for police education. These were redefined in 2003 with the incorporation of new elements, as part of an initiative taken in the first term of office of President Luiz Inácio Lula da Silva. In 2005, there was another revision in the training plan, which was once again amended in 2009. This latter change was for the purpose of coordinating training with perspectives created by PRONASCI (the National Program of Public Security with Citizenship). PRONASCI was launched in 2007 by the Ministry of Justice to support actions to reduce violence in accordance with the principles of safety and citizenship. Enhancing the quite low status of public security professionals was one of the goals of PRONASCI, and in the training realm this included education grants (*bolsa-formação*). These were financed by the Ministry of Justice and provided a salary supplement to those who attend training courses. This included Military Police officers (officers and soldiers), Civil Police officers (*delegados* and detectives), firefighters, and other professionals connected with public security, such as prison staff (Riccio and Basílio 2007). The amount of the allowance was R$400.00, and in the first year more than 250,000 security professionals were receiving grants.

As a program, PRONASCI gathered multiple initiatives under one reform umbrella. Some of those actions had begun before the program's launch and other ones were established later. The guidelines for police training in the Brazilian Curricular Plan were among those established before PRONASCI's launch, but all of its policies were continued and state training programs for Brazilian officers and other security professionals were obliged to follow them. Thus, one of PRONASCI's main goals was to enforce the new curricula. For example, an important PRONASCI policy was the creation of national educational grants for police employees (*Bolsa-Formação*) and to qualify their officers for these grants, the states had to follow the guidelines. These kinds of strategies for strengthening training guidelines continue today.

The program envisioned ensuring basic cognitive, operational, and attitudinal competency in the following areas: fast learning, flexibility of thought, objectivity, method of organization, being observant, oral and written expression skills, interpretation ability, responsibility, ability to be cautious and adapt to new situations, coordination spirit, physical fitness, and ability to work in teams, among others. Attention was also given to enhancing professional skills in planning, implementing, and assessing programmatic activities.

The new curriculum also involved an ethical dimension that emphasized respect for human rights as an element underlying all decision-making and action. The idea was to ensure compatibility between human rights and police efficiency. A great deal of stress was placed on valuing different social groups, especially the most vulnerable ones, and stressing how they provide a context in which the police action will be carried out. For example, Amazonas, which is considered here, includes diverse indigenous groups who lead a traditional life and are in turn linked to the region's vast biodiversity. Other important contexts involved racial minorities, disfavored populations, and gender issues.

The model training plan that was instituted allowed for some flexibility in its implementation, so that additional content could be combined in accordance with regional need. Training was understood to be an open process and aimed at the formation of networks among the teachers and security institutions, so as to spread a new pattern of practice among Brazilian security institutions. The knowledge and experience of public security professionals was accordingly respected, and the pedagogic principles for training made space for taking these into account.

The guidelines set forth by this new national training plan were ambitious, aimed at changing fundamental aspects of Brazilian police forces. The research question was, were the police and other security institutions involved able to incorporate its content?

Training Military Police Officers in Amazonas

The region of Amazonas was selected for study because Military Police training there was brand new in all respects and could be responsive to our research findings. Until 2002, all officers of the Amazonas State Military Police were trained in other states, such as São Paulo, Ceará, and Rio Grande do Sul. Due to its geographic isolation and limited economic development, there was no independent training academy there. It could be observed that Military Police officers responsible for street patrolling and managing their department were trained in ways that were distinct from the reality they faced on the ground. There was no special focus on what was going on in their state or on fundamental characteristics of their region and its diverse cultures. Most obviously, this state includes almost 20% of Brazil's land area, but has a population of only 3,590,985 million inhabitants. The population is concentrated in Manaus, the capital, which has 1,861,838 inhabitants. Logistics in the state are complex, and several cities and regions can only be reached by air or by river.

The first locally conducted officer training class in Amazonas was the result of a partnership between the Military Police and the State University of Amazonas (UEA). This bachelor's course in Public and Citizen Security was held between 2002 and 2005, lasting a total of four years. Fifteen students were selected by public entrance examination to be part of the class. They were all unmarried; 40% had attended private rather than public secondary schools; nine were studying at another university when they joined this new career; and four students already had a higher degree. The course of study they pursued was prepared based on federal guidelines, and, taking into account local adaptations to take into account the reality of working in this vast region, the central concepts of the national plan were incorporated into the program.

The course ran for four years. The faculty members were employees of the UEA and the Military Police of Amazonas. Each institution was responsible for the selection of teachers and instructors, all of whom had the equivalent of at least a university degree. The "basic" training subjects were anthropological, sociological, philosophic, psychological, ethical-professional, political, behavioral, and economic in nature. There were also courses on information technology and legal topics. The "professional" training subjects included theories and practices of police techniques, but there were also courses on operations research, statistics, and technology applications in public security. The participants also fulfilled a required number of internship hours with different police units, taking on both operational and administrative duties. Finally, each student was required to submit a thesis paper at the end of the course (Universidade do Estado do Amazonas 2002). Students were awarded a university bachelor's degree upon course completion.

Views of Participants

This research adopted a qualitative methodology for examining students' perceptions of the training process in Amazonas. This approach was chosen in order to understand in an exploratory way the details of implementing federal training guidelines in a particular locale, and how local issues (which in Amazonas are particularly unique) were incorporated into the training regime. Because the training program was new and still small, it offered the possibility of responding to the findings of our study. Those interviewed were among the first class of officer candidates trained in Amazonas. The objective of the research was to understand how the first police officers to be trained under this program formed perceptions about their profession, the meaning of policing in a democratic society, and their role in the specific Amazonian context.

In-depth interviews were conducted rather than employing familiar closed-ended survey questions. Many of the cultural and political issues involved in transitioning from an authoritarian tradition to democratic policing are not reflected in research on policing in the Northern Hemisphere, nor are the dynamics of an officer class that is as socially and economically distant from street-level workers as they are in the Brazilian Military Police. Instead, we opted for an approach that would let us discover and clarify the subtleties involved in these issues, letting the respondents speak in their own words. This chapter thus provides a first step toward developing a research agenda for policing in Brazil. The conclusions presented here are based on a collaborative analysis by the authors, who also conducted the interviews.

The program had 13 original graduates, of which four could be interviewed. Semi-structured interviews were conducted with them in March and April of 2008. All were serving officers in the Amazonas State Military Police. It was difficult to reach other graduates in their class, because they were serving in cities throughout the state of Amazonas in locations that could be reached only by boat or airplane. As a result, only graduates who were serving in Manaus were interviewed during the research. Other class members contacted were agreeable to being interviewed, but could not be reached and could not be in Manaus between March and April 2008. So only graduates serving in Manaus were able to schedule an interview. Despite the small sample, the officers who were interviewed and those not responding to the research shared a common profile.

The interviews were conducted by one of the coauthors and carried out in the battalions in which each of the officers was designed to serve. Complete privacy was provided during the interviews, and they were conducted in a room in which only the interviewer and the interviewee were present. The interviews lasted between one hour and a half and two hours on average. The interview sessions were recorded and then transcribed for analysis. We gave particular credence to the accounts of different respondents who had similar experiences, for these suggested common themes. We paid particular attention to aspects of the major competing views in Brazilian policing, those reflecting tradition and reform. The training guidelines are part of a more general federal project aiming to promote a democratic and plural society. Those values impact directly the visions police officers have of their occupational identity, their relationship with society, and the meaning of their careers in this context.

The first point to be emphasized is that the officers we interviewed chose a Military Police career. The interviewees introduced themselves not only as policemen (they were all male), but also as military officers; they had taken on two identities, in a combination that—as we have seen—is not always compatible. Second, it was striking how much the interviewees were aware that they would be responsible for providing protection to the citizenry. State public security agents have the duty of ensuring the preservation of public order, as well as safety of people and property. A third theme in the interviews centered on the stability of public employment and its opportunities for career development. Lieutenant "A" was certainly interested in job security and career advancement:

> The main reason is linked to the fact that it is a profession in which you deal directly with the society, where the values of discipline and hierarchy are respected; besides the fact that I have always wanted to be a police officer and have always respected this profession, in addition to the security of having a public job which could give me the conditions needed to evolve in this career.
>
> (Lieutenant A)

Lieutenant A also stressed discipline and hierarchy. His construction of his new identity is interesting, since the reproduction of the army military model and its rank hierarchy in the Military Police is required by the Brazilian Constitution.

Another point that arose in the interviews referred to guiding and monitoring the behavior of their subordinates, with the objective of maintaining order, discipline, and efficiency in the ranks. They worried about their subordinates' performance, since their own reputations would depend on that. Again, Lieutenant A:

> The officer has a great responsibility in the deployment of troops, guiding the actions which shall be taken during the service, in addition to inspecting its progress, to lead in those events in which the presence of an officer is requested, to keep constant contact with their immediate superiors who are coordinating the service all over the city, to check if the vehicles are where they are supposed to be, to keep order and discipline, and from there, the contact with the citizen who needs this crucial service for his/her protection.
>
> (Lieutenant A)

The interviewees focused on the quality of the service rendered and on the negative consequences for their image that might result from managerial mistakes they might make. In their view, public order and social peace depend on their competent performance. They very much voiced a conservative, bureaucratic view of police work, rather than the more innovative—and risky—perspective advocated in their training curriculum. Reform meant acknowledging the role of police as members of a bureaucracy and applying its rules.

In addition, they referred to contradictions between democratic values, policing, and the realities of Brazilian society. Differentiating themselves from the past was an important consideration. Among these officers, condemnation of the anti-democratic acts of the old military regime was strong. In today's values, the police stand as the "guardian of democracy." The corporate spirit does not change, but the ways of thinking and acting are altered. One officer noted that police needed to change because in the recent past it had supported authoritarian laws and military dictatorship. However, this justification for change did not translate into a vision of a more contemporary policing model, less structured by bureaucratic hierarchies, and more aimed at prevention and integration with other institutions of the criminal justice system.

We saw evidence of a vision of democracy that is connected with a very important aspect of the country's recent history, which is the precedence of social rights in relation to the political ones. This is an enduring feature of the Brazilian political culture. In the twentieth century, during Vargas's authoritarian period, social rights were granted to the working masses before they achieved any political rights. The idea was that the state had custody of the people, since the people were unable to responsibly exercise their civic freedoms (Werneck 2001). Officer E articulated this view, that more humane policing is required, because society acknowledges the police as their main guardian, and is largely unable to manage its own path:

> For some, democracy is still a word distant from reality, maybe due to a recent past in which the police practiced some acts on behalf of national security, and in order to end this distortion, we have the duty to progress as soon as possible to undo this absurd misunderstanding. Democracy is the exercise of the rights that each one of us has and owns, through the evolution of conquests and constitutional guarantees throughout our republican history. It is a historic legacy in which each one of us has a share, since it is meant to offer equal opportunities to all within a country, even one as big as ours; it means to respect the principles adopted by it and apply them to the benefit of the greatest possible number of citizens, to distribute the revenue and create jobs; it means to provide enough jobs for as many people as possible; it means ensuring the right to ask protection from the state, it means much more than being able to elect their representatives, it means much more than voting and being voted on; all of this represents the base of a democracy that gets more consolidated every day and that progresses in the improvement of quality of life to everyone, everything ensured by a more human police, which begins to appear now, designed to protect a society that considers the police its greatest guardian.
>
> (Officer E)

This view is similar to that revealed in Heyman's (2002) study of the relationship between American police officers of Hispanic origin and Mexican and Central American immigrants. Officers' perceptions of newcomers were marked by moral judgments based on the idea of mercy, superiority due to their position, and paternalism.

Our interviewees also saw an association between the practice of democracy and security. One perspective on the Military Police was that it was the main instrument guaranteeing the order and safety on which democracy depends. Lieutenant A reaffirmed this view:

> Democracy is the power of the people, by the people and for the people. It is a society turned to the achievement of the common well-being and it is through

the police forces that this same society is ensured the feeling of safety it desires, the Military Police being in charge of keeping the public order focused on the citizen. Democracy is extensive; it is for all, based on respect, on the protection and in the fundamental rights provided for in the Federal Constitution.

(Lieutenant A)

Concerning their training, the interviewees stated that the course lived up to their expectations and was of satisfactory quality. The courses objectives, as they understood them, both in terms of the facilities offered and the quality of the instructors:

Yes, definitely, all of them, officers and teachers were always ready to settle any doubts. Our officers are constantly taking courses outside the state to improve techniques and tactics that are needed in the performance of the Military Police Officer in his/her daily service, where all the instructors were chosen through a rigorous selection within the PM, such as the presentation of résumés and qualification internships; as for the teachers, they were recruited among the best ones available, which gave us the chance to be able to count on the best possible qualification in the basic subjects, where all the knowledge acquired made it possible to have a better performance in the service.

(Lieutenant O)

Nevertheless, they highlighted points that could be improved, such as the preparation of the faculty members:

I believe that concerning the Academy instructors, there should be a staff of officers destined exclusively to teaching and instruction, this way there could be a greater dedication and consequently, a higher level of learning, more qualification courses should be open to deal with the teaching, that if it were possible to allow the teachers of UEA to experiment the routine inside the headquarters, make them familiar with the situations that are part of the police officer routine, and even with the language used, then we would have, the way I see it, a better integration among all the people involved in the teaching process.

(Lieutenant E)

According to Marion (1998), instructors should be chosen based on their knowledge, their skills to instruct, and having good personal qualities such as camaraderie, maturity, enthusiasm, confidence, and high self-esteem. In spite of the flexibility in the classroom practice, it has been observed that the instructor's concern is to transmit the syllabus established in the course plan. One of their responsibilities was to adapt the national plan to local conditions and resources. In this, despite their attempts, there was room for improvement. Interviewees were satisfied by the opportunities for participating in community events that were provided. These allowed them to interact with the kinds of communities that they soon would be working in:

Yes, we participated and with positive results, in several activities that were carried out by the Course Coordination throughout the semesters, such as seminars, lectures, visits to institutions such as Gustavo Capanema, which takes care of children, and also escorting several international authorities which came to our state. It is worth mentioning that we took part in great events in which there were lots of people, thousands of people, as was the case of football games, Parintins Folkloric Celebration, among others.

(Lieutenant O)

Class visits, internships, and classroom instruction helped them learn about areas that had previously been unknown, especially places where there were large numbers of destitute people and land invasions by squatters. They allowed students to get in touch, in a fragmented way, with a bit of the social, political, economic, and cultural features of the cities in which they were to perform their new duties:

Once we graduated in our own state, all the subjects were focused on the reality we experience here, and it was not necessary for us to get familiar with these aspects, as it happened in the past when the officers graduated outside Amazonas and a considerable time was required to adapt themselves to the conformities herein existing.

(Lieutenant A)

On the other hand, none of those interviewed reported learning anything about the connection between this new knowledge and innovative policing models. The students also formed the view that society did not know much about them, and were unaware of the "non-coercive" aspects of their work:

We were always invited to integrate work teams and destitute communities and that was very good, since we had a direct contact with the citizens near to us, asking why were those students wearing the Military Police uniform, so we would say: "We are student officers of the Military Police, we are graduating, and soon we will be the newest class of officers" and this was a surprise for almost everyone who heard us, which the way I see it, is due to the fact that the serious projects, the projects which are born with the public spirit, unfortunately are not duly clarified or informed to the community where we are going to work, and that is too bad because we are getting to know the community in which we will work, but the community does not know whom they are working with.

(Lieutenant E)

This discourse indicated a lack of integration between the police and the community. While they acknowledged the distance between the two, they offered no thoughts on ways to establish any relationship with the community. This signaled that they had not internalized important aspects of their training course. Another concern of these officers was the possibility that the course might be discontinued.

> What I'm afraid is that this great project that was the first class will get lost in time, I mean, there should be continuity, or even better, regularity in the provision of this course. I assess that the compliance with these expectations is not from one side only, but from all of us: Authorities, societies and police forces, not only the military, the civil, the federal and all the others comprising our public security system. I believe that we are performing our role and that this activity is the motive power to keep believing that it is possible to provide public security that is citizen-oriented.
>
> (Lieutenant E)

This doubt over the survival of the course reveals the fragile environment in which reform-oriented police training operated in Brazil.

Conclusion

This research aimed at understanding how training of the Brazilian officer class under new guidelines established by the Ministry of Justice was implemented in a local context. Federal policy provided clear guidance to local training academies and was in accord with a new model of policing for the nation. The guidelines emphasized prevention, proactivity in engaging the community, the adoption of modern crime-fighting strategies, and the role of the police in protecting human rights. It provided the regions with flexibility for accommodating local situations and resources, while promulgating clear new national expectations for policing.

In the case of Amazonas State, Military Police officers prior to 2002 had not been locally trained, and clear locally relevant guidelines for their performance had not been created. This was a problem in a Brazilian state with many indigenous inhabitants living in isolation, the widest expanse of rainforest in the world, and distinctive problems with eco-crime and land seizures. A qualitative study was carried on with the graduates. Only a few of them could be interviewed, because others were not reachable. Those who were interviewed agreed to do so voluntarily and did so in a very cooperative way. They participated in semi-structured interviews. They were questioned about their decision to become a police officer, the meaning of this career in contemporary Brazil, the role of police in a democratic society, and their training experience. Those were the core issues of the project.

Among the findings were, first, that despite the training orientation toward a more responsive and less bureaucratic policing model, the officers shared a common identity as military personnel rather than as civilians in uniform. This a feature of Brazilian policing rooted in the military era. This characteristic was accompanied by the view that civil society is weak. In their perspective, the police are the protectors of this "weak" society, from itself. Third, the training was seen as satisfactory, but they did not see it as integrating with society in a sophisticated way. For them, joining in some meetings means community integration. In the end, we can conclude that despite their formal adherence to a modern pattern of policing, they still operate within the framework of the traditional perspective that dominates Brazilian policing. The training had little or no impact in changing this view.

Despite the innovative prescriptions of the Ministry of Justice concerning officer class training, there are many obstacles to its implementation. There is a gap between the local reality and the guidelines from Brasilia. The discrepancies between policy and practice observed in Amazonas were not a question of training efficacy per se, but reflected persisting problems for implementing policies by the federal government to improve Brazilian policing. The local reality must be considered an object of specific policies. The impact of police training on Brazilian police, as we could see from a particular experience, must be considered with other aspects such as organizational and cultural ones. The adoption of new policies is not simple, and a better knowledge of its context is required. Further research is necessary to understand the distinctive dimensions of policing in Brazil.

Note

1. A revised version of Vicente Riccio, Marcio Rys Meirelles de Miranda and Angélica Müller. 2013. Professionalizing the Amazonas Military Police through Training. *Police Practice and Research: An International Journal* 14: 295–307.

References

Albuquerque, C., and Paes-Machado, E. 2004. The hazing machine: The shaping of Brazilian military recruits. *Policing & Society* 14: 175–192.

Basílio, M. P. 2004. *A Formação do policial militar no estado do Rio de Janeiro: utopia ou realidade possível?* [The military police formation in Rio de Janeiro State: Utopia or feasible reality?]. Master's thesis. Brazilian School of Business and Public Administration: Fundação Getulio Vargas, Rio de Janeiro.

Bayley, D. 2005. *Changing the guard: Developing democratic police abroad.* Oxford: Oxford University Press.

Bayley, D., and Bittner, E. 1984. Learning the skills of policing. *Law and Contemporary Problems* 474: 35–59.

Bayley, D., and Shearing, C. 2005. The future of policing. In *Policing: Key readings*, ed. T. Newburn, 715–732. Devon: Willan.

Beato, C. C. 2005. Reinventar la Policía: La experiencia de Belo Horizonte [Reinventing the police: The experience of Belo Horizonte]. In *Calles más Seguras: Estudios de policía comunitaria en America Latina* [Safer streets: Studies of community policing in Latin America], ed. H. E. Fruhling, 139–175. Washington, DC: Banco Interamericano de Desarollo.

Chapel, A. T. 2008. Police academy training: Comparing across curricula. *Policing: An International Journal of Police Strategies and Management* 31: 36–56.

Conti, N. 2009. A visigoth system: Shame, honor and police socialization. *Journal of Contemporary Ethnography* 38: 409–432.

Costa, A. T. M. 2004. *Entre a lei e a ordem: violência e reforma nas polícias do Rio de Janeiro e Nova Iorque* [Between law and order: Violence and reform in Rio de Janeiro polices]. Rio de Janeiro: Editora Fundação Getulio Vargas.

Domincy, J. 2010. The higher education contribution to police and probation training: Essential, desirable or an indulgence. *British Journal of Community Justice* 8: 5–16.

Engel, S. T., and Burrus, G. W. 2004. Human rights in the new training curriculum of the police service in Northern Ireland. *Policing: An International Journal of Police Strategies & Management* 27: 498–511.

Ericson, R., and Haggerty, K. 1997. *Policing the risk society*. Toronto: University of Toronto Press.

Farrow, K., Hughes, N., Paris, A., and Prior, D. 2010. New occupations in community justice: Inventing the professional curriculum for community safety and anti-social behavior officers. *British Journal of Community Justice* 8: 17–30.

Frühling, H. 2009. Research on Latin America police: Where do we go from here? *Police Practice and Research* 10: 465–481.

Heyman, J. 2002. U.S. immigration officers of Mexican ancestry as Mexican American citizens and immigration police. *Current Anthropology* 43: 474–507.

Hough, M. 2007. Policing, new public management, and legitimacy in Britain. In *Legitimacy and criminal justice: A comparative perspective*, ed. T. R. Tyler, 63–83. New York: Russell Sage Foundation.

Jaschke, H. 2010. Knowledge-led policing and security. *Policing: A Journal of Policy and Practice* 4: 302–309.

Jaschke, H. G., and Neidhardt, K. 2007. A modern police science as an integrated academic discipline: A contribution to the debate on its fundamentals. *Policing & Society* 17: 303–320.

Jones, D., Jones, L., and Prenzler, T. 2005. Tertiary education, commitments and turnover in police work. *Police Practice and Research* 6: 49–63.

Kelling, G., and Moore, M. 2005. The evolving strategy of policing. In *Policing: Key readings*, ed. T. Newburn, 88–108. Devon: Willan.

Lino, P. R. 2004. Police education and training in a global society: A Brazilian overview. *Police Practice and Research* 5: 125–136.

Marion, N. 1998. Police academy training: Are we teaching recruits what they need to know? *Policing: An International Journal of Police Strategies & Management* 21: 54–79.

Mesko, G., and Klemencic, G. 2007. Rebuilding legitimacy and police professionalism in an emerging democracy: The Slovenian experience. In *Legitimacy and criminal justice: A comparative perspective*, ed. T. R. Tyler, 84–114. New York: Russell Sage Foundation.

Neri, M. 2009. Income policies, income distribution, and distribution of opportunities. In *Brazil as an economic superpower? Understanding Brazil's changing role in the global economy*, ed. L. Brainard and L. Martinez-Diaz, 221–270. Washington, DC: Brookings Institution Press.

Paes-Machado, E., and Albuquerque, C. L. 2006. The family curriculum, socialization process, family networks and the negotiation of police identities. *The Australian and New Zealand Journal of Criminology* 31: 248–267.

Paoline, E., and Terrill, W. 2007. Police, education, experience and the use of force. *Criminal Justice and Behavior* 34: 179–196.

Poncioni, P. 2005. O Modelo policial profissional e a formação do policial do futuro nas academias de polícia do Estado do Rio de Janeiro [The professional police model and the future officer in Rio de Janeiro police academies]. *Sociedade e Estado* 20: 585–610.

Riccio, V., and Basílio, M. P. 2007. As diretrizes curriculares da Secretaria Nacional de Segurança Pública SENASP para a formação policial: a Polícia Militar do Rio de Janeiro e sua adequação às ações federais [The National Secretary of Public Security SENASP guidelines for police formation: Rio de Janeiro's adhesion to federal guidelines]. In *A Trajetória das políticas públicas no Brasil: uma reflexão multisetorial* [The trajectory of public polices in Brazil: A multi-sector reflexion], ed. R. S. Xavier, M. H. C. Pimenta and L. H. R. Da Silva, 212–241. Porto Alegre: Sagra Luzzatto.

Roberg, R., and Bonn, S. 2004. Higher education and policing: Where are we now? *Policing: An International Journal of Police Strategies and Management* 27: 469–486.

Roth, J. A., Roehl, J., and Johnson, C. C. 2004. Trends in community policing. In *Community policing can it work?*, ed. W. Skogan, 3–29. Belmont, CA: Thomson-Wadsworth.

Sapori, L. F. 2007. *Segurança pública no Brasil: Desafios e perspectivas* [Public security in Brazil: Challenges and perspectives]. Rio de Janeiro: Editora Fundação Getulio Vargas.

Scott, J., Evans, D., and Verma, A. 2009. Does higher education affect perceptions among police personnel?: A response from India. *Journal of Contemporary Criminal Justice* 25: 214–236.

Skogan, W. 2004. Representing the community in community policing. In *Community policing can it work?*, ed. W. Skogan, 57–75. Belmont, CA: Thomson—Wadsworth.

Skogan, W. 2006. *Community and police in Chicago: A tale of three cities*. New York: Oxford University Press.

Universidade do Estado do Amazonas. 2002. *Projeto Político Pedagógico do Curso de Bacharelado em Segurança Pública e do Cidadão Curso de Formação de Oficiais da Polícia Militar do Amazonas—1ª Turma* [Political-pedagogical project of the officers' bachelor course in public and citizen decurity amazonas' military police officers course: 1st class]. Manaus: Universidade do Estado do Amazonas.

Vickers, M. H. 2000. Australian police management education and research: A comment from outside the cave. *Policing: an International Journal of Police Strategies and Management* 23: 506–524.

Werneck, V. L. 2001. O Estado Novo e a ampliação autoritária da república [The new state and the authoritarian widening of republic]. In *República do Catete* [Catete's republic], ed. M. A. Carvalho, 136–174. Rio de Janeiro: Museu da República.

Police Reform in Brazil
The Rise and Demise of PRONASCI[1]

12

Marco Aurélio Ruediger

Contents

Brazil's National Program of Public Security with Citizenship (PRONASCI)—was launched in August 2007 during President Luiz Inácio Lula da Silva's second term, by the then Minister of Justice of Brazil, Tarso Genro. It had a planned budget of US$3 billion, and its objective was to develop a range of new preventative and deterrent strategies for policing, including the expansion of effective citizenship to the lower reaches of society, enhancing the professional status of public security employees, and focusing new resources on areas with high levels of crime and low social cohesion.

Ninety-six specific projects were proposed under the program, which together formed a systematic effort to increase the operational capacity of state police forces, and—at the local level—to combine an increase in community-oriented policing with an expansion of activities focused on the historic low levels of civic participation and social development in poor areas. In particular, it was aimed at insulating socially vulnerable young people from the drug trade. In short, it was intended to move policing closer to the community, build citizenship and participation at that level, and attack and undermine crime networks. As a whole, these approaches would reduce levels of crime by undermining its foundations and co-opting its potential participants.

When it was created, this initiative represented an innovative, even radical new direction for the criminal justice system, and one that was extremely novel for Brazil's federal government. As in many federal systems, public security in Brazil had been largely a prerogative of state governments. The federal government had previously avoided direct intervention in policing in the nation's large metropolitan centers. By participating more actively in this sector, it was seeking to respond to increasing demands of society for action, even though this necessarily—and not by chance—would expand federal influence and the possibility of intervention at the state and municipal levels through controlling the use of new federal funds. This had to be done very carefully, however, given Brazil's federal government structure.

Therefore, it was decided that this involvement in traditionally local functions should follow a "federative" approach, based on cooperation between the two levels of government that respected the tradition of local control of local affairs. This was of fundamental importance in the Brazilian case, because, as in the United States, the political structure assumes a high degree of regional independence, with layers of executive prerogative within subnational units. By developing a program in a policy area that was widely known to be within the scope of the states of the Brazilian federation, the control of significant federal funds threatened to undermine this autonomy, since it restricted the options open to states interested in obtaining funding. It was a mechanism for the national Ministry of Justice to exercise "soft power" at the local level.

Evaluating Reform

In parallel to the program, the Ministry of Justice constructed a web-based system aimed at monitoring and assisting the evaluation of PRONASCI. This was not done only in regard to the use of the funds provided; in addition, qualitative and quantitative empirical research was also conducted to measure perceptions of the program among the social sectors it affected and participation in them. This management and measurement program was developed by Fundação Getulio Vargas, in Rio de Janeiro. The construction of multiple evaluation strategies, despite being complex to implement, allowed us to monitor the development of PRONASCI and its impacts in a comparative and longitudinal manner. This provided an empirical basis for policy adjustments, as well as highlighting their results. This helped to hold the program accountable and facilitated external pressure toward action at the subnational level. The present chapter is largely based on this research.

As it turned out, there were serious flaws in the design of PRONASCI. The complexity of this program was not effectively managed by the technobureaucracy in the Ministry of Justice. Nor, at the same time, was PRONASCI initially designed to accommodate the traditional policy concepts of Brazilian state governments in terms of public security.

The program was designed to represent a change in the paradigm for public security by a sophisticated and daring faction of President Luiz Inácio

Lula da Silva's *Partido dos Trabalhadores* (Workers' Party, or PT). They proposed an experiment in the radical transformation of the Ministry of Justice and tightening a bureaucratic machine not accustomed to programs of such complexity and deep penetration into the affairs of the Brazilian states. Common wisdom in the Ministry of Justice's bureaucracy and in state security agencies was that the ministry would only expand the traditional scope of federal policy, which was to support the acquisition of equipment by the states and repressive actions by the federal police and the federal highway police, especially those directed at drug trafficking and border control.

However, what was new was the idea of a strategy promoting structural changes in the bureaucratic machinery, as well as of the substance of policies in this area, especially those aimed at promoting the welfare of segments of society such as women, young people, former members of the armed forces, and persons recently released from prison. Needless to say, the introduction of the concept of community policing, and new police training to support community-oriented work, also presented a shock to the system.

Although initially successful, PRONASCI faced continuous resistance from segments of the bureaucracy, and it was eventually impacted by a change in the set of actors who supported it and by changes in the policy implementation process. These had devastating effects on the continuity of the program. This drama came to a head in the 2012 Brazilian budget, when funds for the program were reduced practically to zero.

The aim of this chapter is this to examine the development, outcomes, contradictions, and eventual demise of PRONASCI. The first stage was positive, illustrating that under certain conditions, it was possible to develop and implement an innovative federal policy dealing with historically local public security issues in a strongly federal environment. The second stage turned negative. PRONASCI's progress slowed and the program was eventually dismantled due to a confluence of political factors linked to a bureaucratic struggle between those supporting the new model and forces favoring the old regime.

I also intend to call attention to the conditions under which this kind of innovative political design can be threatened, so policymakers and academics will be better attuned to how policy can be strategically insulated and avoid being dismantled. I will highlight the contradictions and conditions that eventually killed PRONASCI, emphasizing the importance of such factors as the ability of the bureaucratic machine to throttle and resist programs that were contrary to its culture and the survival of structures of power consolidated through more formal practices of policy management.

But while it is correct that PRONASCI encountered difficulties and did not survive more than four years, it is important to highlight that it spawned a number of enduring and successful (thus far) spin-off projects, such as the UPPs in Rio de Janeiro State.[2] Those projects, in turn, were successful in placing the concept of community policing on top of the public agenda, and community policing was one of the centerpiece elements of PRONASCI. This not only created important policy results—as in the case of the police in Rio de Janeiro State—but also helped this state and its capital—Rio de Janeiro city—to win international competitions to host such important events as the 2014 World Cup and the 2016 Olympics. These in turn are calling forth significant new federal and international investment in different economic sectors in the region.

In the case of Rio de Janeiro, the concept of community policing, as well as the social actions of the state and city governments, became paradigmatic of a new approach to public security. Although less daring than what was proposed in the failed federal PRONASCI project, the UPPs have been a relatively successful experiment that have gained a high degree of public support.

As a methodological synthesis, I adopt here an approach based on the analysis of key events and pivotal changes in the political process that determine the construction of policy during a brief historical period and, which, at least potentially, provided an opportunity to construct new policy agendas. The analysis of this process involves specifying the context and key actors, identifying the activities that unite them and the events that develop along the way, as well as modeling the decision-making process in a systematic manner. This approach is centered on strategic political actors and pivotal moments for changing policy processes (Barzelay and Gallego 2010).

We examine them in the course of dynamic processes: dealing with one another, with resources that rise and fall, with events, and within the contexts in which they operate. These together create a menu of policy possibilities and potential windows of opportunity, including perhaps fairly dramatic alterations of the status quo. As we will see, PRONASCI was created and then dismantled as a result of the political forces emerging to fill two windows of opportunity produced by the political process and operated by gifted policy entrepreneurs. We thus structure this discussion around those two pivotal moments, within a temporal grid of events and the influence of actors in interaction. Secondarily, we also considered the Toquevillean perspective expressed by Evans, Rueschemeyer and Skocpol (1985), in terms of the intended and unintended effects of public policies, in this case of the spin-off effects of PRONASCI.

What can be seen from this conceptual and empirical policy effort is that a very complex program was necessary to address solutions to problems in contexts that are also complex and involve multiple causalities. Nevertheless, the success of any program is not only found in its design or in the effectiveness of its implementation and funds disposed, but also in its acceptance by the bureaucracy. At this point, there were political errors in PRONASCI. A vision of this program as the solution for public security in Brazil did not come up as a key issue on the agenda contested during the 2006 presidential campaign, which led to President Lula's second term, although public security as an issue was debated. It was designed and implemented only during 2007–2010. It also did not gain enough traction among key members of the bureaucracy who were responsible for its sustainable implementation. Finally, it had no relevance for the next presidential election in 2010.

To the contrary, the program threatened innovation, which the Ministry of Justice and its bureaucratic agents were incapable of absorbing, and as a result they did not want to insert it into the agenda for debate during the presidential campaign and in policy discussions after the election of a new president.

In this chapter, I first look in more detail to the political genesis of PRO-NASCI. Then, I will explain the policy that emerged and then describe its demise, a circumstance that is not frequently discussed by students of policy-making. As a conclusion, I will consider PRONASCI as a case for reference, in both positive and negative ways, for studies of policy implementation.

The Political Genesis of PRONASCI

After resolving to a certain degree historical problems related to economic development and social justice that had been prevalent for many decades, Brazilian society has been undergoing an apparently sustainable process of economic growth and low inflation. It needs to be taken into account that, during its history, Brazil built an effective state apparatus linked to the promotion of development along many dimensions. A basic social welfare system has existed in Brazil since the 1930s, and this had the impact of strengthening state structures and a professional bureaucracy. As noted by Amsden (2001) in her analysis of later-developing nations, countries that rose toward the top achieved this because they were able to articulate development policies in which a strong national state was the central actor. Included on her list of rising nations is Brazil. In addition, Brazil was also (somewhat episodically) a democratic country, aligned with Western nations.

Nevertheless, despite the existence of a state apparatus that strengthened over time and the nation's general path toward development, Brazil underwent repeated cycles of development and stagnation until the middle of the 1990s, with resulting serious social asymmetries, even though some of these have recently been somewhat mitigated.

Following this, most notably during Luiz Inácio Lula da Silva's two administrations (2003–2010), a strategy of encouraging development with greater social inclusion of the poor was pursued. Above all, this was aimed at strengthening low-income groups, with a consequent increase in their well-being and an expansion of the domestic Brazilian market. These policies raised the consumption levels of 30 million Brazilians considered as poor, altering Brazil's political and economic equation and moving a large part of the population into the lower middle class (Neri 2011).

Together, these social and economic advances were converted into votes that elected President Luiz Inácio Lula da Silva twice, but they also created increasing social demands, both in terms of policies of economic progress and increasingly effective citizenship rights among the poor, who were his strongest supporters. Public security issues inserted themselves in this process in a critical manner, due to increases in crime and negative externalities created by crime in the economy during the 1980s and 1990s.

In general terms, public security in Brazil has been especially challenging in its large urban areas. This has had serious repercussions on the credibility of institutional effectiveness in Brazilian states, in addition to their obvious impact on local attractiveness and the questions that they raise about the effectiveness and honesty of public officials. It has thus hindered the federal strategy of promoting the country as an actor with a rising presence in the international political scene, as well as corroding the foundations of the credibility of state institutions. As noted by Santos (2005), Brazil is potentially risking a movement contrary to that of institution building, with the co-option of young people by the drug trade and the weakening of state credibility, since the web linking the drug trade extends dangerously close to the highest levels of the state. This could not be allowed, and the federal government decided to take a further step.

Although this concern was expressed by the country's political elite on various occasions, it was given an unprecedented central role by the Brazilian president in 2007. This was the first pivotal moment in the policy process, a very public recognition by the popular president of the importance of crime and policing issues on the Brazilian political agenda. In his second inaugural speech, President Luiz Inácio Lula da Silva stated,

> During the campaign I stated that my second government would be a government of development, with income distribution and high quality education. . . . Other vital areas for the population—and something that is constantly demanded—are health and public security. . . . I think that in relation to the question of public security—a real national scourge—the conditions for effective cooperation between the Federal Union and the states of the Federation are increasing, without which it will be very difficult to resolve this crucial problem.
> (President Luiz Inácio Lula da Silva,
> Inauguration Speech, 2007; author's translation)

There followed a confluence between this public recognition of the problem, the beginning of a new second presidential term, and a change in ministerial leadership that brought to office a new Minister for Justice, Tarso Genro. He recognized not only the opportunity created by the situation but also the need to implement a vigorous and innovative public security agenda. In an interview with another of the strategic actors involved in the process, Ferreira and Britto (2010) recorded:

> Then, when Tarso went to the Ministry of Justice, this problem already existed. There was the question of Rio de Janeiro, which was getting worse, there was

the crisis of Alagoas, there were the alarming levels of violence in Pernambuco [these are other Brazilian cities]. This meant that the question of public security gained a new centrality in the second mandate of President Lula [Luiz Inácio Lula da Silva], due to the notoriety which this question was acquiring.

(Interview with Vicente Trevas, Assistant Secretary for
Federative Affairs of the Office of the
Presidency of the Republic; author's translation)

The opportunity recognized by Tarso Genro when he was named Minister of Justice to develop a new federal policy concerning this traditionally local issue was taken up quickly. Four aspects of the problem were widely discussed: (a) the need for a reduction in levels of violence through effective security actions linked to social development in poorer areas; (b) the development of a federative pact recognizing the co-responsibility of states and municipalities in the issue; (c) the need to adapt federal state structures so that they could deal with local issues and authorities; and (d) the political conflict related to this question. In another interview by Ferreira and Britto (2010), the minister himself stated,

Insecurity has become a central category in politics, in the crisis of modernity. In other words, what is called post-modernity—a great fragmentation, the destruction of utopias, the hysterical sublimation of the present, the absence of perspectives, totalizing in the last instance what is social desegregation, the insecurity which is transformed into a central question of politics. I argue, thus, that whoever cannot answer these questions, cannot answer anything politically.

(Interview with Tarso Genro, Minister of Justice; author's translation)

This discussion was expanded to encompass local political elites, the media, and the population in general, especially the various targets of the program. A complex process of negotiation was developed within the Ministry of Planning to allocate US$3.35 billion for the program.

The Political Process and PRONASCI

PRONASCI thus became defined as a progressive response to crime. It recognized that crime was strongly linked to economic distress, and traditional policing practices in Brazil were at the same time repressive and ineffective. Casting community safety as among the expanded rights that the Lula administration was promoting could simultaneously respond to the fears of the urban middle classes and to residents of poor areas routinely subject to violent repression by both criminals and the police. PRONASCI aimed at replacing fear with trust between a reformed security apparatus and the population.

This is in line with Bendix (1996), who noted that authority depends on and is rebuilt through cumulative acts of trust, that a fluidity exists between administrative effectiveness and public cooperation. In this case, police reform and the adoption of a community policing model could facilitate the development of trust and cooperation, becoming a central part of a systemic and culturally sophisticated approach to public security.

Another author, Silver (2004), follows a similar line, observing that the penetration of the police in the context of civil society does not only reside in the crime-fighting activities of the police, but also in their central presence in daily life. Nevertheless, presence in itself does not necessarily unleash an effective transformation process in the relationship of the police with the community. For this, PRONASCI had to reform the practices and culture of its various security forces, in order to achieve an effective paradigm for social change. As observed by Janet Chan (2004) in relation to constructs developed by Bourdieu, a change in the habitus of the police, as proposed by PRONASCI, would achieve results if, and only if, it was also dependent on a change in the field in which it was inserted. In this case, field is the historical reality of relations between police and the community, which are structured on relations of power. PRONASCI sought to shift this agenda, understanding the community as a politically legitimate entity demanding greater citizenship rights. These included recognition of the right of the excluded to better living conditions and personal security, as well as a range of expanded opportunities in relation to Marshall's citizenship (1964). But this vision of a reciprocal relationship between communities and the public security apparatus that would together expand citizens' rights could only be effective if it changed the system.

In this way, the perspective of criminality rooted exclusively in socially and economically depressed regions is altered. In part this is true, since the poorest areas—called favelas—have been a locus for gangs notorious for their connection with the drug trade. However, as observed in the case of Rio de Janeiro by Perlman (1976), favelas are mainly composed of workers and their families seeking to be close to work. Many have been there for decades, creating linkages with their more affluent neighbors and extensive networks of solidarity within their communities, despite their developing in a distinct manner, isolated from inclusion in the mainstream city. So taking these favelas to be homogenous worlds situated alongside the mainstream city is an error that extends the stigma of marginality to the entire community. Many different economic activities take place in them, and they are actually included in an agglomeration of social segments and distinct standards of affluence, though with low levels of social development as a whole. These areas have a logic similar to the economic dynamics of American ghettos, as described by Fusfeld and Bates (1984). Their accumulation processes are not sufficiently strong to alter their economic relevance or even their social status, even though their linkages and networks are intense.

In Rio de Janeiro, continuous efforts have been made to address these issues. The general growth of the country has translated into improvements in living standards in the favelas. However, effective, responsive, and professional policing has been critically lacking, contributing to the emergence in these communities of alternative structures under the control of crime cartels with economic linkages that go beyond their own territoriality.

Therefore, reforming the police could only become effective if linked to a change in their cultural and organizational orientation toward providing police services in the favelas, and their efforts to restore order under law in these areas could only be effective if they were combined with a broad range of new opportunities for residents there. Under PRONASACI, police reform focused on stimulating social mobility and the protection of highly vulnerable groups, such as youths lacking social or familial cohesion, individuals leaving the armed forces, the unemployed, and those returning from prison.

In order to achieve these objectives, PRONASCI fielded a number of programs, ranging from re-equipping security forces to providing new officer training, instituting community policing models, and providing assistance and promoting access to justice and social services to the most vulnerable groups. Community policing and the introduction of non-lethal weapons were probably the most visibly successful PRONASCI initiatives. Brazil's version of community policing involved reaching out to the community with the support of integrated services management offices and local community security councils. It attempted to incorporate central elements of the program observed by Skogan and Hartnett (1997) and Skogan (2006), such as community involvement, restructuring of patrol units and the stable assignment of officers to their patrol areas, problem solving, and the provision of services, among other objectives. Finally, outside of poorer urban areas, PRONASCI supported greater professionalism among highway and border control police, following the strategy of maintaining close relations with other federal programs.

This complex construction of policies was created by the federal government not only with the aim of overcoming the pressure arising out of the increasing demands of civil society for more effective action on the part of the state, but also to invert it, so that the states could—or had to—work within a new agenda. This political engineering of state-national relationships mobilized significant actors at the national level around public security issues, and modified the rules of resource allocation through a complex process of political negotiation.

Figure 12.1 summarizes the processes being described here, focusing on the pivotal points in policy formulation. It is a process-based perspective on the interaction of key actors embedded within macroeconomic and political trends, such as decisions that were impending on the location of World Cup and Olympic events (Barzelay, Gaetani, Cortázar and Cejudo 2003; McAdam, Tarrow and Tilly 2001). In this case, however, the development of policy over time did not follow the predicted path, and explaining the demise of PRONASCI becomes the central issue requiring explanation.

| EA1. 2nd Mandate of Lula: Security X Image of Country, Political Coalitions and Developmentalism, Large Events – World Cup and Olympics

EA2. Ministerial Changes

EA3. Growing Political and Social Pressure for a greater presence of the Federal Government in the area of security. Examples: PAN/MJ and Haiti/MD

EA4. Fragilization of power of the state at a sub-national level and of local competitive strategies with impact on political elites | EC1. Nomination of Tarso Genro as Minister of Justice
EC2. New Command takes over, maintaining existing projects and Structure, but seeking a new agenda for the Ministry
EC3. Suspicion/Expectations on the part of the Federal Gonvernment and States
EC4. Tensions in ministerial bureaucracy with an increase in the demand and scope of the policy (Paradigm)
EC5. Creation of Work Group

E1. Definition of Strategic, Technical and Political Areas of Pronasci
    E.1.1 Pronasci Discussion Colloquiums
    E.1.2 First Draft of Pronasci
    E.1.3 Adjustments and Second Draft of Pronasci
    E.1.4 Presidential Approval
E2. Political Construction
    E.2.1 Federative Agreement
    E.2.2 Legal/Normative Agreement
    E.2.3 Intra- Bureaucratic Agreement (Planning and other Ministries)
    EP2.4 Other Strategic Agreements (RENAESP, ONGs, UNESCO etc)
E3. Implementation of Pronasci
E4. Monitoring of Pronasci and States and Municipalities

ER1. Technical Support of FGV in the Diagnostics, Monitoring and Evaluation of the Implementation of Pronasci | EP1. **Insulation from Political Criticism:** *Strategy, Resources and Data Causing Asymmetries between the Government and Opposition*

EP2. Expansion of the influence of Federal Power: Increase of Resources, Territorialization of Pronasci and Creation of New Assistance Networks (training grant and Housing grant)

EP3. Symbolic Growth: Influence of Pronasci in the Winning of the World Cup and the Olympics, reinformcement of the developmentalism discourse, positive evidence of results

EP4. Hegemonization: Conditioning of Sub-National Security Agendas and the Making Explicit of the Responsibility of Sub-National Managers |
| 03/2007 | 04/2008   11/2009 | 12/2009 |

Figure 12.1 The PRONASCI policy process 2007–2009

The foundational moment depicted in Figure 12.1 arose out of the presidential initiative (E1) described above, announced in his second inaugural address. This was followed by ministerial changes common to a new government, changes made to accommodate political forces and to support changes in the upper echelons of state bureaucracy in order to support the strategic direction chosen by the president. Added to this process are pressures arising out of civil society and the political class related to concern about rising crime. All of this resulted in the nomination of a new Minister of Justice (EC1) who reviewed the strategic direction of the ministry (EC2) and announced plans to move in the direction that eventually led to PRONASCI.

To turn this strategic policy direction into a program required two complementary processes. Initially, it was necessary to overcome obstacles arising from the nation's federal structure (E2, in Figure 12.1). The route to doing so was found in the new minister's experience in CDES (*Conselho de Desenvolvimento Econômico e Social*, or Economic and Social Development Council), another agency that negotiated federal agreements relating to policy and interministerial collaboration. Second, a great deal of consensus building had to be done around this new plan. After being conceptually structured, the program was sent to the president for official approval. Following this came the implementation stage (E3).

Notwithstanding approval for PRONASCI at the highest levels within the administration, it was also necessary to negotiate for support within "technocratic" levels of various bureaucracies, with a special focus on those involved in movement and accountability for funds. This also involved repeated negotiations with multiple bureaucratic actors, both horizontally and vertically. One problem was that, when it was created, PRONASCI had not been considered in the preparation of the budget. Furthermore, the volume and decentralized nature of the fund flows, which were of an extraordinary nature, added to the necessity of creating procedures for monitoring and evaluating the various activities that they were intended to support. This required the development of procedures for controlling the project and analytic tools for monitoring and evaluating its implementation, both from an administrative perspective and in the eyes of the target populations of the programs (E4 and ER1 in Figure 12.1).

The key objective of implementation monitoring was, as noted by Wholey (1991), to gather systematic and continuous information about effectiveness of the various elements of PRONASCI, in order to improve its performance. In addition, surveys were conducted among two targets of the program: residents of the "territories of peace" (as targeted favelas were dubbed) and police, fire service, and other public security employees. These enabled adjustments to be made in the program "on the fly." Shadish, Cook and Leviton's (1991) observation about evaluation was especially useful in understanding that public programs can change from incremental changes to large alterations in their scope and sets of rules. We sought an evaluation monitoring that allowed complex changes to be monitored. This proved particularly important early in the life of the program, when the relevant ministries were unexpectedly slow to implement the program. The Justice Minister was able to challenge the ministry, and he used the media to create pressure on the national government to press the program forward.

Figure 12.2 illustrates the progress of the program, once funds started to flow. It charts the progress of federal transfers to the Brazilian states of training grants to prepare police officers for community policing. Training funds were supplemented with salary money for officers while they were being trained, to encourage states to adopt PRONASCI and promptly spend the money. It can be seen that through 2009, there was great success in budgeting and moving the money that was required; problems were to come later.

Figure 12.3 illustrates the results of monitoring public satisfaction with PRONASCI projects among various targeted populations. These included citizen reservists (*reservista cidadão*), former soldiers looking for employment in the formal economy; PROTEJO (*Proteção a Jovens em Vulnerabilidade Social*, or Protection of Socially Vulnerable Youths), which aimed at assisting young people at risk of entering the drug trade to instead stay in school; and preparatory courses for ENEM (the university entrance exam), which provided preparatory assistance for low-income youth to ready them for their university exams (this project was carried out in partnership with the Ministry of Education). All of these are programs were concerned with stimulating upward

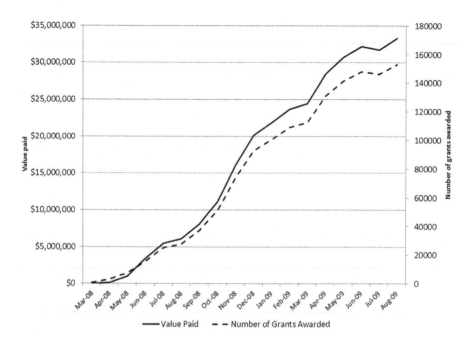

Figure 12.2 Training grants awarded and expended 2008–2009

Source: PRONASCI evaluation

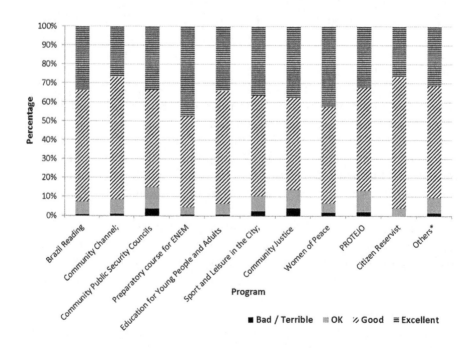

Figure 12.3 Participant evaluation of PRONASCI programs

Source: PRONASCI evaluation

social mobility among residents of poor communities. Figure 12.3 briefly summarizes the findings of a host of target-population surveys conducted as part of monitoring the implementation of PRONASCI, and illustrates the high levels of approval registered by those targeted by the program. Typically, about 30% of program participants gave the highest rating, and almost all the remainder gave ratings that were in the very positive range.

Together, Figures 12.2 and 12.3 highlight the success of PRONASCI as a program and its implementation in the adopting states. PRONASCI linked support for a new policing paradigm to the development of opportunities of social inclusion, combined with implementation monitoring and control of policy feedback (Pierson 1993). A great deal of money was successfully delivered to support key programs, and there was a high degree of satisfaction among program participants. And then it died.

Dismantling PRONASCI

After a great deal of progress following its creation by an October 2007 statute, beginning in 2011 the actual budget for PRONASCI was reduced practically to zero. This concluding section considers the political and policy processes that shifted, leading to this unforeseen and pivotal change.

Figure 12.4 charts the progress of PRONASCI's budgeted and actual expenditures. We first can see a very close match between authorized funds and those actually allocated in 2008 and 2009; the federal ministries transferred over 90% of allocated funds to the states during this period. But in 2010, that figure slipped to 77%, and in 2011 to 38%. Further, this shortfall was largely confined to PRONASCI; it did not reflect some larger bureaucratic failure. Figure 12.5 contrasts comparable figures for the implementation of PRONASCI and for other programs supported by the Ministry of Justice. For each year, it presents the percentage of planned program funds that were actually dispersed. This chart extends only through 2011, the last year for which full-year data is available. As the chart illustrates, the ministry's success at funding its other programs matched the PRONASCI rate during 2008–2010, but then police reform fell off the implementation agenda.

What led to the collapse in fiscal support for such an energetic program? PRONASCI had been created to transform not only operational policies, but also to promote social development and, indirectly, the institutional cultural of the Ministry of Justice and federal-state relationships in this policy domain. In the analytic approach presented by Skocpol (1985), states matter not just in terms of their policies, but because their policies affect governmental processes and standards, alter the political culture, strengthen different political groups, and create opportunities and changes (or externalities) that are sometimes unforeseen. The discussion of the contextual and political origins of the

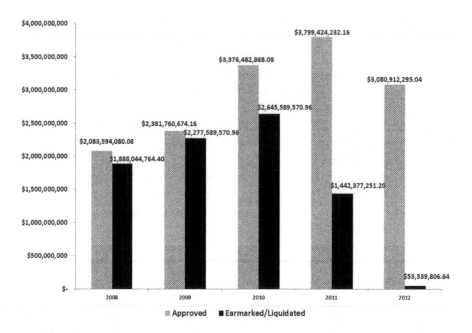

Figure 12.4 Funds authorized and earmarked or expended 2008–2009 (US dollars)

Source: PRONASCI evaluation.

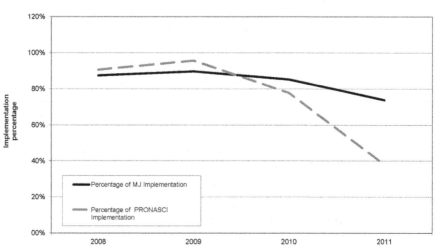

Figure 12.5 Implementation of PRONASCI and other justice ministry programs

Source: PRONASCI evaluation

program, which were summarized in Figure 12.1, predicted a much more successful life course for the policy. This leads us to consider the multiple possible causes of the program's demise, all of which took place contemporaneously and converged to seal the fate of PRONASCI.

First, resistance by bureaucratic structures to the paradigmatic change called for by PRONASCI contributed to weakening support for the program in the budgeting process. Further, the program received a mixed reaction at the state level. The states were anxious to secure federal funds, but they resisted the new state-federal relationship imposed by the program, with its rules for local spending and persistent monitoring of program implementation. However, it was the juxtaposition of this resistance and the next pivotal moment in Brazilian politics, the 2010 presidential election, that explains the program's disappearance.

In 2010, the minister responsible for the original design of PRONASCI left office to run for office in one of the Brazilian states. He was elected governor of Rio do Sul state and left the national stage. At the same time, the party of outgoing president Luiz Inácio Lula da Silva chose as its presidential candidate his chief of staff, Dilma Roussef, who was also victorious. During the presidential campaign, the question of security in large cities was a subject of debate. Roussef's campaign reiterated the importance of PRONASCI's conceptual framework. She spoke of the importance of raising the status of police officers, who needed proper training and higher salaries. The candidate also spoke in favor of new policies and expenditures for modernizing prisons and dealing with highly dangerous prisoners. And in her view, the new UPPs inaugurated in Rio de Janeiro had the potential to be an important element in defeating crime.[3] However, she barely referred to PRONASCI directly. This was in response to mixed views of the program among her campaign managers, who reflected some of the bureaucratic resistance and state-federal tension that the program generated. As a result, there was little public emphasis on PRONASCI as such, which would have committed her politically to the program.

Instead, what happened was in line with Weir and Skocpol's (1985) concept of "policy results." In the case of Brazil, state structures, which are home to bureaucratic careers and have some autonomy of action, do not necessarily bend to the influence of elected administrators, who are more permeable to political forces or ideological agendas. Elite bureaucrats also are not insulated from pressure groups or from the chain of command that begins with elected representatives, but in practice they can postpone, distort, or provide counter advice about the direction of a policy and its administration. Habitus and their own survival instinct lead them toward their zones of comfort and arrangements more optimal for their career and their network of alliances, even though this can be suboptimal for political decision makers faced with contrary interests or legacies of polices in which they participated. PRONASCI's budget disappeared into this maze of state and federal bureaucracies, not having won an explicit seal of approval from the new president during her campaign and no longer protected by its inaugural Minister of Justice.

Conclusion

Policy processes and public administration are continually interconnected. In addition, they increasingly are in dialogue with civil and development possibilities, whether individual or collective, in the public sphere. PRONASCI aimed at promoting both security and social development. It originated out of the capacity of a few high-placed actors to perceive social and political changes that could support this two-pronged definition of the problem, and it was a policy formula that reflected the political stance of the president of the moment. It spoke to social problems on the citizen side of the program, and it promoted police reforms that could rebound to further support progressive social developments. Further, it spoke to one of the most notable shortcomings of Brazilian democracy, the traditions and practices of its police. The program was positive in terms of its results, in spite of its short life. Most especially, its spin-offs included the UPP policing teams that remain effective in Rio de Janeiro.

As a lesson in public administration, policymakers must be careful to take into account the distinct interests of the bureaucracy, the key role played by the media in defining the situation, and the political opportunities that open and close as elite actors come and go. Elites across generations—which can be short in modern political life—need to buy into policies in order to guarantee their sustainability. Finally, in its short life, PRONASCI did not generate enough mass support demanding its continuation. It was from the beginning a top-down program. In the face of all of this, the modern monitoring and evaluation systems designed to promote program implementation did not play a significant role in protecting PRONASCI, despite the many positive signals they gathered.

Notes

1. A revised version of Marco Aurélio Ruediger. 2013. The Rise and Fall of Brazil's Public Security Program: PRONASCI. *Police Practice and Research: An International Journal* 14: 280–294.
2. UPP means *Unidade de Polícia Pacificadora* (Pacifying Police Unit). These units seem to be responsible for an increase in trust in police and declining fear of crime in Rio de Janeiro city. The UPPs operate in a manner that is distinct from traditional, repressive policing, employing a community policing style instead.

3. Source: blog of Dilma (Dilma 13) during the presidential campaign (www.dilma13.com.br/entry/dilma-discute-propostas-para-segurança-publica/).

References

Amsden, A. H. 2001. *The rise of "the rest": Challenges to the west from late-industrializing economies*. Oxford: Oxford University Press.

Barzelay, M., Gaetani, F., Cortázar, J. C., and Cejudo, G. 2003. Research on public management policy change in the Latin America region: A conceptual framework and methodological guide. *International Public Management Review* 4: 20–41.

Barzelay, M., and Gallego, R. 2010, April. The comparative historical analysis of public management policy cycles in France, Italy and Spain, symposium introduction. *Governance* 23: 209–223.

Bendix, R. 1996. *Construção nacional e cidadania* [National construction and citizenship]. São Paulo: EDUSP.

Chan, J. 2004. Changing police culture. In *Policing: Key readings*, ed. T. Newburn, 338–363. Cullompton: Willan.

Evans, P., Rueschemeyer, D., and Skocpol, T. 1985. *Bringing the state back in*. Cambridge, MA: Cambridge University Press.

Ferreira, M., and Britto, A. 2010. *Segurança e cidadania: Memórias do Pronasci* [Security and citizenship: Memories of Pronasci]. 1st edition. Rio de Janeiro: Editora Fundação Getulio Vargas.

Fusfeld, D. R., and Bates, T. 1984. *The political economy of the urban ghetto*. Carbondale, IL: Southern Illinois University Press.

Marshall, T. H. 1964. Citizenship and social class. In *Class citizenship and social development*, ed. T. H. Marshall, 65–122. Chicago, IL: The University of Chicago Press.

McAdam, D., Tarrow, S., and Tilly, C. 2001. *Dynamics of contention*. Cambridge: Cambridge University Press.

Neri, M. 2011. *A nova classe média: o Lado brilhante dos pobres* [The new middle class: The brilliant side of the poor]. Rio de Janeiro: FGV/CPS.

Perlman, J. 1976. *The myth of marginality: Urban politics and poverty in Rio de Janeiro*. Berkeley: University of California Press.

Pierson, P. 1993. When effect becomes cause: Policy Feedback and political change. *World Politics* 45: 595–628.

Santos, W. G. 2005. O Conservadorismo Obsoleto do status quo [The obsolete conservatism of the status quo]. In *Desenvolvimento e Construção Nacional: políticas públicas* [Development and national construction: Public policies], ed. B. S. Cavalcanti, M. A. Ruediger and R. Sobreira, 17–28. Rio de Janeiro: Editora Fundação Getulio Vargas.

Shadish, W. R. Jr., Cook, T. D., and Leviton, L. C. 1991. Good theory for social program evaluation. In *Foundations of program evaluation: Theories of practice*, ed. W. R. Shadish Jr., T. D. Cook and L. C. Leviton, 36–67. Newbury Park, CA: Sage.

Silver, A. 2004. The demand for order in civil society. In *Policing: Key readings*, ed. T. Newburn, 7–24. Cullompton: Willan.

Skocpol, T. 1985. Bringing the state back in: Strategies of analysis in current research. In *Bringing the state back in*, ed. P. Evans, D. Rueschemeyer and T. Skocpol, 3–37. Cambridge: Cambridge University Press.

Skogan, W. 2006. *Police and community in Chicago: A tale of three cities*. New York, NY, and Oxford: Oxford University Press.

Skogan, W., and Hartnett, S. 1997. *Community policing, Chicago style*. New York, NY: Oxford University Press.

Weir, M., and Skocpol, T. 1985. State structures and the possibilities for "keynesian" responses to the great depression in Sweden, Britain, and the United States. In *Bringing the state back*, ed. P. Evans, D. Rueschemeyer and T. Skocpol, 169–191. Cambridge: Cambridge University Press.

Wholey, J. S. 1991. Evaluation for program improvement. In *Foundations of program evaluation: Theories of practice*, ed. W. R. Shadish Jr., T. D. Cook and L. C. Leviton, 225–269. Newbury Park, CA: Sage.

Index

Note: Italicized page numbers indicate a figure on the corresponding page. Bold page numbers indicate a table on the corresponding page.